CONGRESSIONAL COMMITTEE POLITICS

CONGRESSIONAL COMMITTEE POLITICS

Continuity and Change

by
Joseph K. Unekis
and
Leroy N. Rieselbach

PRAEGER SPECIAL STUDIES • PRAEGER SCIENTIFIC

New York • Philadelphia • Eastbourne, UK
Toronto • Hong Kong • Tokyo • Sydney

Library of Congress Cataloging in Publication Data

Unekis, Joseph K.
    Congressional committee politics.

    Bibliography: p.
    Includes index.
    1. United States. Congress—Committees.
I. Rieselbach, Leroy N. II. Title.
JK1029.U53   1984   328.73′0765   84-2141
ISBN 0-03-059539-8

Published in 1984 by Praeger Publishers
CBS Educational and Professional Publishing
a Division of CBS Inc.
521 Fifth Avenue, New York, NY 10175   USA

456789 052 987654321

Printed in the United States of America
on acid-free paper

Preface

Congressional committees are much discussed but seldom studied systematically. There is much anecdote but little detailed data about them. The conventional wisdom assigns committees a critical place in congressional politics, but for a variety of reasons scholars have not devoted as much empirical attention to committees as the centrality they assign to the panels seems to demand. With some notable exceptions--in particular, that of Price and of Fenno--most work on congressional committees has focused on single units (case studies) or relies on some more or less random observations of committees in action. The result has been sweeping generalizations about the "committee system in Congress" that rest on rather flimsy evidence.

One reason for this lack of detailed analysis has been the unavailability of the necessary data. Traditionally, congressional committees met in executive session, beyond the view of the most interested observers. Moreover, they kept, at best, imperfect records of their deliberations; in particular, they seldom kept and made accessible the votes their members cast on amendments or bills. These circumstances required scholars to rely on interviews of varying quality with members and staff to discover what had actually occurred in committee. Alternatively, they used action on the chamber floor as the basis to infer what had taken place in committee.

The Legislative Reorganization Act of 1970 changed all this, requiring committees to record and make public their roll call votes. In this book we use these newly available data to investigate systematically some features of ten committees of the House of Representatives. Specifically, we examine the nature of committee voting cleavage, the place of committee leaders in that pattern of cleavage, and the effects of change and reform on both factional alignments and leadership positions across the full decade of the 1970s. These analyses enable us to advance some generalizations about intracommittee conflict, committee leadership, and the stability (or lack thereof) of these configurations over time.

v

Our investigations employ quantitative techniques, but we use these methods in full awareness that they entail trade-offs with more conventional observational and interview procedures. What we may gain in rigor and replicability requires some sacrifice of the ability to catch the subtlety and nuance of committee politics that flow from personal exchanges among committee members. We make no claim that our approach is in any way "better" than the alternatives; we do suggest, however, that what we have undertaken is "different" and constitutes a valuable complement to the more common approaches. Indeed, we are gratified to discover, at several points in our study, that our "hard" data and the "soft" information of other observers are entirely consistent. This encourages us in the belief that committees can be best understood if viewed from varying vantage points. When assessed in combination, multiple perspectives should produce fuller comprehension of congressional committee politics. This, of course, is what scholarship is all about.

Acknowledgments

It is impossible to carry out a project of this sort without the aid and comfort of other people. We are pleased to note here our gratitude to several institutions and individuals whose help has meant much to us, and at the same time, to absolve them of any responsibility for what appears in the pages that follow.

Kansas State and Indiana Universities provided financial support that facilitated the collection and analysis of the House committee roll call data. Glenn Parker of Florida State University, the pioneer in the use of these data, generously shared his insights with us at an important early stage of our work. Edward G. Carmines, Lawrence C. Dodd, and James H. Kuklinski offered valuable advice as our study progressed. Bruce Ray graciously allowed us to use the fruits of his research on House committee prestige. Marcia Pickett and Jeralee May made manuscript out of our notes and tables, and Praeger Publishers, especially Dotty Breitbart, converted those pages into a book. We applaud their efforts on our behalf.

We have drawn on materials presented elsewhere. Chapter 2 is a vastly revised version of our paper, "The Structure of Congressional Committee Decision Making," read at the 1979 Annual Meeting of the American Political Science Association. Chapter 3 incorporates material from our paper "Congressional Committee Leadership: Stability and Change, 1971–1978," presented to the Everett McKinley Dirksen Congressional Leadership Research Center – Sam Rayburn Library Conference, Understanding Congressional Leadership: The State of the Art, Washington, D.C., June 10–11, 1980, and subsequently published as "Congressional Committee Leadership, 1971–1978," Legislative Studies Quarterly 8 (1983): 251–70. Chapter 4 extends our analysis of legislative change, "Ousting the Oligarchs: Assessing the Consequences of Reform and Change on Four House Committees," Congress & the Presidency 9 (1981–82): 83–117.

More personally, our families sustained our efforts in many ways, direct and indirect, over the years. Shirly,

Keith, David, Brian, Scott, and Kelly Unekis provided constant encouragement as did Richard and Elaine Unekis. Similarly, Erik, Kurt, Alice, and especially Helen Rieselbach created conditions conducive to working and writing. Finally, special thanks go to Karen Rieselbach, without whose cheery "Won't you please finish that book so I can see my name in print?" this volume might still be "forthcoming."

Contents

List of Tables

1
Committee Politics:
Theory and Method

If there is a single generalization about Congress that has gained, and retained, status as "true," it is probably Woodrow Wilson's oft-quoted aphorism that "Congress in its committee-rooms is Congress at work." More broadly, the current conventional wisdom maintains that congressional committees are "at the heart of all congressional activities," in particular offering "Congress its principal opportunity to shape national policy in detail" (Ripley 1978, p. 153). Yet only in the past decade have observers been permitted to glimpse what actually occurs in the committee rooms. The Legislative Reorganization Act of 1970 and various "sunshine" reforms have opened the committees to public scrutiny; meetings are now routinely open sessions and, most important for present purposes, committee members' roll call votes are recorded. Although members tend to act on the floor consistently with their behavior in committee (Unekis 1978), we can now look directly at what they do during committee deliberation and decision making.

Despite the clear centrality of congressional committees in legislative decision making, relatively little is known about them.[1] This follows, of course, from the fact that committees operated for years outside public purview. Not only were scholars uninterested in the legislative process generally, and in committee activity more specifically, but also the panels themselves conducted most of their business

1

in closed sessions. Even when research on Congress revived, beginning in the late 1950s, the focus was on individual committees (see Fenno 1966; Green and Rosenthal 1963; Robinson 1963; Farnsworth 1961; Horn 1970; Manley 1970; Goodman 1968). The findings from such studies were often extended, without a firm foundation in empirical reality, to generalizations about the so-called congressional committee system. Expanded investigation, particularly publication of genuine comparative and empirical work (especially Price 1972; Fenno 1973), suggested, however, that such sweeping generalizations probably concealed more than they revealed. Committees differed, often substantially, and the committee system was less a unified whole than a congeries of discrete, more or less autonomous units. Finally, as noted, Congress itself in 1970 decreed that committee room doors be open to interested observers.

Thus the stage has been set for rigorous, systematic, and comparative empirical research on congressional committees; panel processes are presently as accessible to scholars as they are ever likely to be. In this book we attempt to take advantage of this "window of opportunity" to examine, carefully and critically, the processes of committee politics in Congress. For a representative set of 10 of the 22 committees in the House of Representatives, we seek to describe, explain, and contrast patterns of cleavage and leadership within the committees. We also look at the impact of these forces on committee performance: the decisions the panels make and their success in carrying the day for their legislation on the House floor. Finally, we assess the impact of external change—the remarkable array of reforms Congress adopted during the 1970s—on committee politics. These analyses, we hope, will shed some light on a significant, but still largely unexplored, part of the congressional process.

AN APPROACH TO CONGRESSIONAL
COMMITTEE POLITICS

Our primary focus—our unit of analysis—is the individual committee. We conceive of each panel as a distinct, relatively self-contained unit, with its own characteristic structures, modes of operation, and patterns of decision making.

Each, in other words, is institutionalized (Polsby 1968).
Each is autonomous to some considerable extent; each is free,
within broad limits, to organize its work in congenial ways.
This is not to say, of course, that committees have nothing
in common; they obviously share certain attributes, for example, the use of subcommittees and adoption of similar "leadership" arrangements.[2] Rather, we accept as beyond argument
Fenno's assertion that "committees differ from one another.
And . . . they differ systematically" (1973, p. xv). Our
task is to describe and explain the nature of these differences and to explore the ways that the variations affect committee decisions and the full House's reactions to committee
choices.

Fenno (1973, pp. xiv-xv and chaps. 3 and 4) posits two
central features of congressional committees: "strategic
premises" and "decision-making processes." The former refers
to norms, or decision rules, or consensual understandings that
govern the ways the committee ought to proceed. For example,
the House Ways and Means Committee, in its heyday under Chairman Wilbur Mills (D.-Ark.), aimed to write tax legislation
"that will pass the House" and thus "regardless of the substance of their decisions" enable the committee members to retain their influence while at the same time demonstrating
their responsiveness to the House" (Fenno 1973, p. 55; see
also Manley 1970). These fundamental agreements prescribe to
a considerable degree the committee's strategy for achieving
its collective purposes.

These purposes, embodied in committee decisions, are
also shaped substantially by a second set of considerations:
the panels' decision-making process--"a structure that will
help them implement their decision rules" (Fenno 1973, p. 81).
This structure entails "participation-specialization" and, of
particular concern to us, "partisanship" and "leadership."
The first refers to the degree to which a committee encourages
an internal division of labor that both stimulates individual
member participation in committee activity and operates
through a clearly defined subcommittee structure. Thus, in
the 1960s, the House Education and Labor Committee decision-
making processes provided ample opportunity for members to
participate in all parts of the committee's agenda; despite
an elaborate set of subcommittees, members of Education and
Labor, given this freedom to participate, tended to be gener-

alists rather than narrow specialists in matters within the
committee's jurisdiction. By contrast, the House Post Office Committee in 1965 adopted new rules, including a fully
articulated subcommittee structure, intended specifically to
increase participation and specialization (Fenno 1973,
chap. 4).

Partisanship constitutes another dimension of committee
decision-making processes. Committee choices will most certainly reflect the degree to which the respective partisan
contingents on the panel contest or cooperate with respect
to major policy concerns within the committee. In the House,
the Committee on Rules and the Education and Labor Committee
have traditionally been partisan battlegrounds where Democrats and Republicans commonly faced each other across hostile lines; Ways and Means has pursued a path of more restrained partisan conflict; and the Armed Services Committee
has often put aside acrimony in favor of a bipartisan-consensual alliance that crosses party lines. The relationship of
the parties to one another, then, is likely to be a major influence on committee decision making and on the success committee legislation attains on the House floor.

Finally, leadership--the behavior of important committee members, particularly the chairperson and the ranking
minority member, with respect to the rank-and-file members--
certainly shapes what committees do and the results they obtain. Leadership poses complex questions of causality. Although it is customary to assume that leaders, in fact, lead,
the flow of influence may actually run in the reverse direction. That is, a chairperson may literally steer committee
members in some particular direction; another may hew to a
given course because the rank-and-file adhere to it; a third
may simply share the majority's views and move with it accordingly. For instance, Fenno (1973, p. 144) asserts that
Wilbur Mills dominated Ways and Means decision making in the
1960s; Tom Murray (D.-Tenn.), chairman of the Post Office
panel during this period, was constantly at war with the committee members, who finally adopted new committee rules in
an effort to promote some effectiveness (Fenno 1973, pp. 135-
36). In any case, we will want to explore the ways in which
ostensible committee leaders relate to the ordinary members
and to assess the consequences of these leadership patterns.

    If it is incontrovertible that strategic premises and
decision-making processes contribute substantially to committee politics, it is equally clear that committees do not operate in a vacuum. We treat the congressional committee as
an intermediary institution (Eulau and McCluggage [1982]
call it interstitial). That is, its structures and processes
reflect the intentions, motivations, and goals of those who
serve on the panel, as well as the contacts and communications that members have with political participants in the
environment beyond the committee itself. Following Fenno
(1973), there are three basic goals that motivate members:
reelection, policy, and power (or authority or influence).[3]
Representatives seek positions in Congress, and particularly
in committee, that enable them to pursue these goals; once
suitably located, they act to structure the committee, or to
maintain an appropriate committee organization, so that they
can achieve these purposes. The House Agriculture Committee,
for example, attracts farmbelt lawmakers, eager to provide
for the needs of their rural constituents as a means to promote their own electoral security;[4] the committee employs an
extensive, commodity-based subcommittee structure that enables the members to "deliver the goods" to district resi-
dents (see, inter alia, Jones 1961; Barton 1976; Ornstein
and Rohde 1977).

    Other committees appeal to policy-oriented legislators.
For instance, the Education and Labor (Fenno 1973) and the
Interstate and Foreign Commerce Committees (Ornstein and
Rohde 1977) draw members whose primary interest is in the
content of the programs that fall within their particular
panel's jurisdiction. Presumably, these committees adopt
norms and establish procedures that accommodate their members' desires. Similarly, other lawmakers seek power and influence within the legislature and seek assignment to committees where they can pursue these ends. In the House, the
Ways and Means (Fenno 1973; Manley 1970) and the Rules (Oppenheimer 1981; Matsunaga and Chen 1976) Committees have broad
jurisdictions. The former claims all revenue matters, whereas the latter not only manages the flow of legislation to
the floor but also considers an increasingly important set
of substantive matters. Each, then, has a broad reach, with
a considerable effect on a wide-ranging array of important
questions. Power-motivated members find these panels attrac-

tive, compete for places on them, and adopt appropriate strategic premises and decision-making processes.[5]

Committees also act in an environmental setting. Other parties, inside Congress and without, are interested in the ways that a committee treats items on its agenda. These environmental actors care about committee decisions and attempt to influence them. The panel, in turn, must respond in some fashion to the desires of these policy participants, and its premises and processes will in some degree reflect this need. Environments constrain committees, but in different ways because they impinge differently on individual committees. For example, a committee's environment may be more or less homogeneous (or monolithic). The House Armed Services Committee, given its central role in issues involving military preparedness, is a prime focus of the executive branch in general and the military establishment--the Pentagon and its allied private sector defense contractors--more particularly (Dexter 1969; Ray 1980). By contrast, the environment of Education and Labor is heterogeneous (or pluralistic): Committee members must contend with executive pressures, the desires of clientele groups (outside interests concerned with social and economic policy), political party preferences, and the views of their policy-oriented House colleagues (Fenno 1973, pp. 30-35). Overall committees' internal organization will bear the imprint of both its members' goals and its relations to significant outside influences.

Congressional committees are intermediary bodies in another sense as well. As agents of the full chamber, they process legislation, making policy choices on the many matters within their respective jurisdictions. The content of their decisions should reflect the committees' strategic premises and decision-making structures; these, in turn, flow from members' motivations and environmental constraints. The committee products, then, constitute the work load of the full House. When reported, committee bills may be accepted, amended (in major or minor fashion), or rejected. The extent to which committees "win," have their recommendations adopted on the floor, may vary from committee to committee according to members' goals, environmental forces, and internal panel attributes. Thus, for instance, in the 1960s, Armed Services, Ways and Means, and Commerce were among the most successful House committees, whereas Agriculture, Rules, and Education and Labor saw more of their proposals defeated on the floor (Dyson and Soule 1970, p. 638).

In sum, as Fenno has demonstrated, committees differ fundamentally but with respect to identifiable features. Their members' behavior reflects individual goals (reelection, power, policy influence) and the particular environmental constraints (the chamber, the political party, the adminis-tration, clientele groups) within which the panel operates. These various predisposing conditions, in turn, shape dis-tinctive committee strategic premises (or norms or decision rules) and, of more immediate concern here, specific commit-tee decision-making processes (participation-specialization and particularly partisanship and leadership). Panel deci-sions—the specific results of committee deliberations—and the treatment these recommendations receive on the floor re-flect all these prior conditions. Our intent is to untangle these forces, to provide some insight, on a comparative basis, into congressional committee politics.

Such an undertaking is no simple task. Fenno's scheme highlights intercommittee comparisons, but it does not obvi-ate the need to consider intracommittee contrasts. In a period of increasing importance of the subcommittee (David-son 1981), a single panel may develop separate "committee politics" that govern individual subcommittees. That is, the full committee, our central focus, may treat its various subcommittees differently.[6] Likewise, committee politics may vary with respect to particular issues that constitute distinct parts of a committee's policy domain. For example, Price (1979) shows that the House Commerce Committee treats different items on its agenda in varying fashions: Members find matters of high salience and low conflict attractive and avoid no-win topics of high visibility and pronounced conflict potential. Subject matter like subcommittee struc-ture, then, may create divergent patterns of intracommittee performance.

Finally, the 1970s was a rare and remarkable period of legislative change and reform. Turnover was high, as retire-ment rates rose (Cooper and West 1981), and large numbers of new members, elected in the wake of Watergate and Vietnam, took seats in Congress. New issues (for example, energy and abortion) assumed prominent places in congressional delibera-

tions. The national legislature moved to reassert its authority relative to the executive branch, passing the War
Powers Resolution (1973) and the Budget and Impoundment Control Act (1974). Congress sought to shore up its sagging
popular standing and opened most of its proceedings to public
scrutiny. It also took steps to promote internal efficiency
through enhancing somewhat the powers of the Speaker of the
House and the majority party to control the chamber. In addition, and perhaps decisively, the House adopted a set of
"democratizing" reforms, most notably a "subcommittee bill
of rights," that seemingly distributed influence more widely
within the membership than in previous periods.[7] These
changes affected different committees differently: In some
panels politics altered dramatically over the decade; in
others, persistence seems to be the prominent feature of
their behavior.

Overall, we view congressional committee politics from
the perspective of individual panels. The ways in which
they operate--the lines of cleavage they display and the
styles their leaders evince--reflect their members' goals
and the specific environments within which they act. Their
decisions flow from the intersection of these forces. We
seek to compare and contrast committee performance in an effort to provide some insight into committee politics. We
recognize, however, that committee activity may vary within
as well as between committees, reflecting differences in internal structure, in aspects of committee agendas, and in
the impact of change and reform. We will treat these matters, particularly the effects of change, in the pages that
follow.

TEN HOUSE COMMITTEES: PRELIMINARY PROFILES

We undertake these investigations of congressional committee politics with a comparative analysis of ten committees of the House of Representatives. Although the initial
selection of these panels was on utilitarian grounds--those
that took a sufficient number of roll call votes in each of
the five (Ninety-second through Ninety-sixth) Congresses we
examined to permit meaningful statistical treatment (see Appendix 1)--nonetheless, an interesting set of committees was

produced. The ten committees vary across the full range of
factors that our approach identifies as central to committee
politics. Our "sample" contains committees whose members
seem to pursue each of the three primary goal orientations—
reelection, policy, and power—that motivate representatives.
It consists, also, of committees that act in widely differing—from homogeneous to heterogeneous—political environments. Furthermore, the sample includes panels that endured
varying degrees of change—in personnel, in rules, in subcommittee structure—during the 1970s; and it encompasses bodies
of high and low influence, prestige, and official status.

To the nine committees that our criteria identified, we
added the Budget panel, which came into existence only in the
Ninety-fourth Congress (1975), because of the obvious importance that fiscal matters assumed in the period after its
creation.[8]

In short, this set of ten committees, although not random, nonetheless provides broad and significant variation on
the basic dimensions that underlie analysis of committees;
in consequence, we are quite confident that the generalizations we advance should command serious attention. Following are capsule commentaries on each of the committees to
set the stage for our specific analyses.

Agriculture

The House Agriculture Committee has traditionally operated as a reelection (pork-barrel, constituency-oriented)
panel. Its members, drawn disproportionately from farm districts, promote the crops that their constituents grow. Subcommittees with jurisdiction over particular commodities
(cotton, livestock and grains, tobacco) are a central feature of committee structure; the same set of subcommittees
survived, without substantial change, through the 1970s. In
effect, these units have written the basic farm laws for
their products; the full committee has customarily assembled
the subcommittees' provisions in an omnibus farm package.
In this way, the committee has sought to satisfy the policy
preferences of those in its environment: agricultural clientele interests with specific concerns about particular products. The panel has remained a moderately attractive home

for farm bloc House members; it ranks ninth (of 21) in prestige among the chamber panels (see Table 1.1).[10]

TABLE 1.1

House Committee Attractiveness (Prestige), 1963–81

Committee	93rd–97th Congresses (Rank)	88th–92nd Congresses (Rank)	Change (Ranks)
Ways and Means	2	1	−1
Rules	3	2	−1
Armed Services	5	9	+4
Commerce	6	6	--
Government Operations	8	8	--
Agriculture	9	9	--
Post Office	11.5	20	+8.5
Education and Labor	15	10	−5
Banking	17	12	−7

Source: Bruce A. Ray, "Committee Attractiveness in the
U.S. House, 1963–1981." American Journal of Political Science
26 (August 1982):609–13. Reprinted with permission.

Agriculture has worked in this fashion, moreover, despite undergoing substantial change during the decade. For
one thing, turnover was extraordinarily high (see Table 1.2);
a full 52 percent of the panel were new in the Ninety-fourth
Congress, making the two-Congress (Ninety-third and Ninety-
fourth) rate a remarkable 80 percent. In addition, reform
hit the committee hard. Most dramatically, the Democratic
Caucus, in a stunning repudiation of the seniority principle,
ousted the aging (74) chair, W. R. Poage (D.-Tex.), and replaced him with Thomas Foley (D.-Wash.). Under Foley, the
committee implemented the full range of reforms that the subcommittee bill of rights required, altering the composition
of Agriculture: Southern representation declined, and the
committee became more regionally balanced and more moderate

ideologically. Also, the new chair was more liberal than his predecessor, was more accommodating and flexible in managing the committee, and was generally a more loyal Democratic partisan.[11] Overall, however, the committee continued to pursue constituency concerns within a relatively homogeneous, agriculturally oriented, clientele-dominated environment.

TABLE 1.2

Percentage of Committee Turnover (New Members)

Committee	Congress				
	92nd	93rd	94th	95th	96th
Agriculture	27	30	52	23	17
Armed Services	19	31	22	19	23
Banking	21	22	54	35	18
Budget	--	--	--	52	44
Education and Labor	28	16	35	30	37
Government Operations	29	26	37	30	23
Interstate Commerce	30	18	38	24	23
Post Office	31	31	46	31	44
Rules	00	27	19	24	29
Ways and Means	19	8	51	24	19
House*	13	17	21	13	18

Note: New members include both freshmen and those who transferred from another committee.

*New House members are those who did not serve in the previous Congress (some of whom may have been former representatives).

Source: Congressional Directory (annual volume).

Armed Services

Like Agriculture, the House Armed Services Committee is, in reality, a reelection-oriented committee. Though its jurisdiction covers military matters of great policy significance, particularly the Pentagon's basic defense programs, Armed Services has not often challenged the professional military's expertise. It has consistently supported the services' call for larger budgets, more hardware, and in general a more powerful armed forces. It has done so, moreover, without subjecting defense programs to substantial scrutiny; indeed, Dexter (1969) describes the panel as a "real estate" committee, more concerned with siting military installations throughout the nation than with military strategy and tactics. Thus traditionally Armed Services has been a hawkish committee, where consensus in support of a strong military satisfies the defense establishment component of the committee's environment and a concern for the construction and sustenance of military installations assuages the panel's constituency clienteles.

Change and reform had a decided impact on Armed Services during the 1970s. Most dramatically, as it had with Agriculture, the Democratic Caucus removed the elderly southern chair, Edward Hebert (Louisiana), and replaced him with a northern, presumably more "mainstream" national Democrat, Melvin Price (Illinois), at the opening of the Ninety-fourth Congress (1975). At the same time the committee revised and elaborated its subcommittee structure. General subcommittees, identified only by number, gave way to those with specified jurisdiction (Research and Development, Military Installations, Military Personnel).[12] The chairpersons of these newly established subcommittees assumed a larger role in committee affairs, with an increased responsibility for managing bills on the House floor (Deering 1982). The reforms of 1970-75 were largely in place by mid-decade. On the other hand, turnover was relatively low, exceeding 30 percent only in the Ninety-third Congress (Table 1.2). Given the opportunity the committee provides to serve the reelection goal, without undue pressure from the environment, it is not surprising that Armed Services maintained its position of prestige (fifth) throughout the period.

Banking, Finance, and Urban Affairs

The House Banking Committee[13] appears to be a policy committee; representatives are attracted to it because they

seek to shape the content of public programs that deal with
the nation's financial institutions--both commercial banking
and the savings and loan industry--and a variety of urban
policy matters--mass transit, public housing and housing
subsidies, and urban renewal programs (Salamon 1975). These
issues do not convert so readily as do the services that
members of the Agriculture or Armed Services panels provide
their constituents into reelection advantages. Moreover,
the rather broad and diffuse jurisdiction of Banking presents it with a heterogeneous environment, one without a
single dominant interest (like farmers or the Pentagon) to
galvanize its members.

The reform movement of the 1970s had a clear but, on
balance, moderate impact on Banking. Most dramatically, the
Democratic Caucus removed the committee's irascible, elderly (81), and autocratic chair, Wright Patman of Texas; Henry
Reuss (Wisconsin), a somewhat more liberal, nationally oriented Democrat, fourth in seniority on the committee, took
the chair in 1975. At the same time, turnover was high in
Banking: more than half the membership (54 percent) was new
in the Ninety-fourth Congress, and another third (35 percent)
arrived two years later (Table 1.2). Also, in 1975, the
committee, in implementing the subcommittee bill of rights,
redefined its subcommittee structure, with additional authority devolving to the subcommittee chairs (Deering 1982).
Perhaps because of the difficulty of satisfying so diverse
an environment, on a host of controversial policy matters,
and in a time of diminishing economic resources, Banking,
never a particularly popular or prestigious assignment, declined in attractiveness, to seventeenth, during the 1970s
(Table 1.1).

Budget

The House Budget Committee constitutes a special case;
created under special circumstances, it operates under particular and peculiar structural constraints. Recognizing
the chaotic character of its budgetary process and goaded
into action by Richard Nixon's confrontational challenge--
featuring vetoes and excessive impoundment of appropriated
funds--to its financial autonomy, Congress enacted the Budget

and Impoundment Control Act (1974).[14] The law established new budget committees and charged them to impose fiscal discipline on a budgetary system widely perceived by both parties and members at all points on the ideological spectrum to be out of control. A focus on process, to respond to institutional needs, papered over deep divisions about policy: Conservatives hoped the new procedures would limit federal spending and lead to a balanced budget; liberals desired to reallocate funds from defense to social programs.

Once established, Budget, especially its Republican members, soon shed much of its process orientation and became a budgetary battleground. Thus we categorize the committee as a policy panel, whose members increasingly sought to shape the content of programs while continuing to espouse the cause of a more rational process. Budget members are selected for ideological reasons; they operate on strategic premises—first, to write budget resolutions that will pass the House, and second, to provide economic stimulus that will promote economic growth—that emphasize politics and policy (LeLoup 1979). They pore over the budget proposals line by line, which inevitably leads to decisions about the content of policy. They act within a homogeneous environment, where the parent chamber, and especially the party leaders, dominate and dictate a focus on program. Finally, the emergence of the reconciliation procedure, by which Budget can ask other committees to alter existing laws when it appears that budget targets will be breached, clearly indicates a major potential policy impact.[15]

This emerging policy focus developed during the Budget Committee's "shakedown" period. Though a product rather than the object of congressional reform, the panel has experienced considerable change as it has sought to establish its place in the House budgetary process. Its adaptation reflects a singular feature: Unlike all other committees, Budget members have limited tenure (originally four, presently six, years). Fixed service has undercut members' commitment to the committee as well as their incentive to develop specialization and expertise (Ippolito 1981; Schick 1980). Thus turnover has been high (see Table 1.2) as members have been forced or have chosen to leave the panel. Budget has not developed autonomous, expert subcommittees. It created "task forces" in the Ninety-fourth Congress, but these have no legislative authority (Schick 1980); though "moderately active" (Schick 1980, p. 119), they "do not play a significant role" in the panel's decisions (LeLoup 1979, p. 246).

These conditions, particularly the reduced attractive-ness of the assignment that limited tenure engenders, have made Budget a committee of moderate stature. As Schick (1980, pp. 129-30) suggests, interest in the committee will rise and fall with the ups and downs of budgetary politics: The panel will have greater appeal in periods when financial policy assumes political primacy, such as during the Ninety-sixth Congress (1979-80). But without the esprit de corps and ex-pertise that permanent membership stimulates, the Budget Committee is unlikely to emerge as a truly prestigious panel.

Education and Labor

The House Committee on Education and Labor is probably the epitome of the policy-oriented panel. A multitude of societal interests cares, often passionately, about the many items on the committee's broad and controversial agenda, which includes welfare matters as well as issues of labor and education policy. Major political interests, ranging from the most conservative to the extreme liberal, contest, often clamorously, the major matters within Education and Labor's jurisdiction. The panel's members, regularly con-servative Republicans and liberal Democrats, pursue a policy individualism in response to their own convictions and to the importunings of external participants from the full House, the executive branch, and a vast variety of clientele groups. The committee, in short, focuses on the substance of programs in a heterogeneous, and emotion-laden, environ-ment (Fenno 1973).

Change and reform during the 1970s affected directly if not excessively Education and Labor. Turnover was low: The committee's membership evolved; it was not rocked by revolution (Table 1.2). The panel did, following the com-mittee reforms of 1974, adopt a new, more carefully articu-lated subcommittee system, replacing general bodies (Select Education, Special Labor) with more specific units (Post-secondary Education, Labor-Management Relations, for instance).

Moreover, much authority, for example, the management of committee legislation on the floor, devolved to these increasingly autonomous subcommittees (Deering 1982). The growing
controversy surrounding the items within the committee's
jurisdiction, which economic dislocations no doubt exacerbated, apparently reduced the attractiveness of assignment
to Education and Labor. The committee fell from tenth to
fifteenth on the prestige ladder after 1972, though its
status remained in the moderate range (Table 1.1). Overall,
the committee continued to wrestle with increasingly intractable policy problems in a highly charged political atmosphere.

Government Operations

The fortunes of the House Committee on Government Operations rose appreciably during the 1970s. In 1970, it was
widely considered a "duty" committee, an undesirable assignment (Bullock 1976; Cook and Ragsdale 1982). Representatives reluctantly agreed to serve in order to accommodate
party leaders or because no other suitable posts were available, and they scrambled to escape when more promising vistas
opened up. Despite its broad mandate as the oversight com-
miteee, with responsibility to police the entire executive establishment, the panel did not prosper, ranking in the middle range of attractiveness. Government Operations did not
achieve its potential as an aggressive watchdog because
oversight in general is not seen as productive activity
(Ogul 1976; Harris 1964), because it lacked the opportunity
to write legislation to remedy administrative failings that
its investigations might uncover, and because its members
feared to tread on the toes of the appropriations and authorizing committees of the full House (Dodd and Schott 1979).
Thus the committee's environment, the parent chamber, imposed major constraints on the panel.

These circumstances changed during the 1970s, with Vietnam, Watergate, and reform more generally combining to improve the climate for oversight. Government Operations was
enlarged somewhat, reaching a membership of 43 in the Ninety-
fourth and Ninety-fifth Congresses. More important than
overall turnover, which remained relatively low (see Table

1.2), however, was the arrival on the panel of a group of
more active liberal Democrats, for example, Benjamin Rosenthal (D.-N.Y.). At the start of the Ninety-fourth Congress
(1975), under the aegis of a new chair, Jack Brooks (D.-Tex.),
the committee substantially restructured its subcommittee
system, which, following the dictates of the subcommittee
bill of rights, fell increasingly into the hands of the more
activist members. Several subcommittees became considerably
more forceful overseers as a consequence of this decentralization (Ornstein and Rohde 1977).[16] Overall, the panel's
prestige has remained constant, in the moderate range, and
despite its new assertiveness, it remains beholden to the
full chamber. Nonetheless, in the late 1970s, the committee
achieved a prominence it lacked only a few years previously.

Interstate and Foreign Commerce

The extensive jurisdiction of the House Committee on
Interstate and Foreign Commerce, which includes regulation
of commerce and communications, transmission of power, and
railroads, securities and exchanges, energy, health and bio-
medical research, and consumer affairs and protection, makes
the panel particularly attractive to representatives with a
wide range of policy concerns. Interested legislators can
find a niche on Commerce from which to pursue these important policy issues.

The committee's environment reflects the sweep of its
agenda; numerous external groups have a stake in some of the
subjects that the panel treats. The relationships of these
extrinsic participants to committee activity vary from item
to item within the committee's domain. Some areas generate
client-centered politics; others create more publicly salient
patterns. But, in general, a broad array of clientele groups
dominates Commerce's environment, from which "high-intensity
executive branch and party involvement" is relatively absent
(Price 1979, p. 11).

Given the policymaking opportunities the committee of-
fers, it has remained a coveted assignment (Table 1.1; see
also Ornstein and Rohde 1977).

The attractiveness of the Commerce Committee seems to
have contributed to the substantial impact that reform, in

somewhat delayed fashion, had from the Ninety-fifth Congress (1975-76) onward. To accommodate the increased demand from the enlarged cadre of Democrats (a result of the 1974 elections) for seats on Commerce, the panel added six members, for a total of 43, in 1975. Still, the committee's prestige, especially among the Democrats, kept turnover relatively low (Table 1.2). In 1975, more importantly, Commerce Democrats staged a "palace coup," in which they altered the character of the committee fundamentally. Led by John Moss, of California, they adopted new committee rules that substantially circumscribed the authority of the full committee chair, Harley Staggers (West Virginia), and that gave "virtual autonomy" to the panel's six subcommittees (Ornstein and Rohde 1977; see also Price 1978). At the same time, the committee caucus restructured the subcommittees, to reflect the jurisdictional changes that the full House had made the previous year, and gave Moss the chair of the influential Oversight and Investigations subcommittee that Staggers had formerly held. Increasing subcommittee influence, however, did not alter the basic contours of the committee, which continued to be a prestigious panel that focused on policy matters in a heterogeneous environment.

Post Office and Civil Service

The House Post Office Committee during the 1970s was a committee in flux, a panel in search of a mission. The Postal Reorganization Act of 1970 fundamentally altered the committee's environment when it created an independent U.S. Postal Service, largely beyond the power of the panel. Where Post Office had been a reelection-oriented body, whose members promoted their electoral fortunes through service to constituents and clients (postal unions and mail users), it became a duty or undesirable assignment (Fenno 1973). Its members retain oversight responsibilities and general influence over legislation concerning federal employees' working conditions, but its jurisdiction has narrowed and its environment constricted; the committee responds to employee unions predominantly.

Post Office has evolved over the past decade. Turnover has been high, particularly more recently (Table 1.2), as members who originally accepted the assignment as a second (or third) post moved on to more desirable positions. The panel has adjusted its subcommittee structure regularly, creating at least one new panel in the Ninety-fourth and each subsequent Congress, as part of its effort to find a viable role in congressional politics.[17] Moreover, Post Office subcommittees seem to be gaining in significance; at least, in the Ninety-second Congress and thereafter, the subcommittee chairs managed a high proportion of committee bills on the floor (Deering 1982). Anomalously, despite its travails, the committee's prestige has risen from low to moderate in recent years. Apparently, although for most members the assignment remains obligatory, to be escaped as soon as possible, for a minority, other concerns--policy or reelection--make the committee desirable, and they transfer to Post Office. In general, however, the panel's narrow jurisdiction and homogeneous environment make it of little interest to most House members.

Rules

The House Committee on Rules in many respects is the mirror image of duty committees like Post Office. With its classic "traffic cop" role as the gatekeeper to the House floor (Robinson 1963), which permits the panel to pass in some fashion on most legislation that the authorizing committees report, and now augmented with increased activity in areas of its original, substantive jurisdiction (for example, broadcasting House floor sessions), Rules provides its members with a significant influence base (Oppenheimer 1981). Although the committee has increasingly cooperated with the House leadership--the Speaker has acquired the power to appoint members to Rules--it nonetheless retains substantial independence in managing the House, and though it may use its power "to expedite, not to obstruct" (Oppenheimer 1981, p. 224), it remains a prestige assignment that attracts members interested in House influence.[18] Because its actions structure full chamber deliberation and decision, the parent body constitutes the major environmental constraint on the panel. Nonmembers want their legislation handled satisfactorily and expeditiously; members seek to enhance their influence and to accommodate the party leaders without alienating the House itself.

Continually controversial (see Robinson 1963; Matsunaga and Chen 1976), nevertheless, Rules remains a powerful panel. Turnover has been low, generally less than that on other committees (Table 1.2), and prestige has continued high (Rules ranks third, behind Appropriations and Ways and Means, in the most recent period; see Table 1.1). In the Ninety-sixth Congress, the committee created standing subcommittees for the first time; the two units, Legislative Process and Rules of the House, reflect the increasing concern with matters of legislative jurisdiction. The full committee continues to control Rules's bill management role, however, and this endures as the committee's major function. Within the general changes and reform of the 1970s, then, Rules reveals substantial continuity. It remains a power-oriented, high-prestige panel, whose members seek influence in an environment that the House itself dominates.

Ways and Means

For years the Committee on Ways and Means epitomized the power-oriented congressional committee. The classic studies of Manley (1970) and Fenno (1973) of the committee during the 1960s, under the chairmanship of Wilbur Mills (D-Ark.), picture it as a panel whose members sought to maximize their influence inside the House. Its broad jurisdiction over major matters—taxation, social security, tariff and trade agreements—gave Ways and Means entree to authority; the committee used its position to write finance legislation that the full House, the chief element in the committee's environment, would accept.[19] This strategy succeeded admirably: Ways and Means seemingly satisfied the parent body, it was both responsible and expert, and it was rewarded with high prestige, ranking first among all House Committees (Table 1.2).

The price of this esteem—moderate to conservative revenue policies—proved high as the 1970s unfolded. As the general reform movement gathered momentum, House liberals, long dissatisfied with the committee's fiscal policies, managed to impose some potentially significant limits on House committees. They mandated that all committee markups be conducted in public. They empowered the Democratic Caucus to instruct the Rules Committee to permit certain amendments to be offered on the floor, thus undercutting, in principle, the protection that the closed rule had afforded Ways and Means. At the same time, Mills was experiencing personal difficulties that reduced his attention to and concentration on committee business. When these problems became public knowledge, at the start of the Ninety-fourth Congress (1975), he declined to seek a renewed mandate as committee chair.

The liberal Democrats were not content merely to select a new Ways and Means chairperson. Buoyed by the rising tide of reform as well as by the election of 75 freshmen in 1974, the Democratic Caucus seized the opportunity to capture the committee's helm. It enlarged the committee by half, from 25 to 37 members, and filled the vacancies with legislators more liberal than those traditionally appointed. It adopted a rule that required most committees to establish subcommittees (Mills had employed his leadership skills in full committee, avoiding subcommittees that might undermine his authority or committee unity). After 1975, Ways and Means had six subcommittees (including Health, Social Security, and Trade) that "spread the action" of the panel (Rudder 1977); moreover, the subcommittee chairs took on a somewhat greater responsibility for managing legislation on the floor (Deering 1982). In short, high turnover (reflecting enlargement--see Table 1.2) and new rules drastically altered the circumstances of Ways and Means.[20] While the full House remained the central feature of the committee environment, external interests, concerned about revenue matters, gained greater access to, and thus the opportunity to bring more pressure to bear on, the committee. Yet Ways and Means has retained its "turf," and, given the centrality of the items on its agenda, it has remained an attractive assignment, a high prestige panel (Table 1.1).

Summary

These brief profiles amply demonstrate the rich variety of forms that the panels assume. Table 1.3 summarizes our

TABLE 1.3

Ten House Committees: Basic Characteristics

Committee	Member Goal	Environment	Turnover	Subcommittee Significance	Prestige	Official Classification
Agriculture	Reelection	Homogeneous (farm clientele)	High	High	Moderate	Semiexclusive
Armed Services	Reelection (policy)	Homogeneous (military clientele)	Low	High (increasing)	High	Semiexclusive
Banking	Policy	Heterogeneous	High	High (increasing)	Low	Semiexclusive
Budget	Policy (power)	Homogeneous (House)	High	Low	Moderate	Semiexclusive
Education and Labor	Policy	Heterogeneous	Low	High (increasing)	Low	Semiexclusive
Government Operations	Duty (policy)	Homogeneous (House)	Low	High (increasing)	High	Nonexclusive
Commerce	Policy	Heterogeneous	Low	Low (increasing)	Moderate	Semiexclusive
Post Office	Duty	Homogeneous (unions)	High	High	High	Nonexclusive
Rules	Power	Homogeneous (House)	Low	Low	High	Exclusive
Ways and Means	Power	Homogeneous (House)	High	Low (increasing)	High	Exclusive

Note: We have indicated a secondary, but visible, member goal in parentheses in three cases where such a goal exists.

assessment of these committees' basic characteristics.[21] The
sample committees include two whose members seek reelection
(for example, Agriculture), two where power goals predominate (for example, Ways and Means), four in which policy concerns seem most central (including Education and Labor), and
two that are duty or undesirable assignments (Post Office,
for instance). The committees act in a variety of environments: Seven (like Budget) operate in relatively homogeneous or monolithic environments, whereas three confront
more heterogeneous contexts (for example, Commerce). Some
committees experienced substantial change in turnover (Banking) and subcommittee structure and significance (Armed Services); others retained many of their members (Government
Operations) and sustained a fairly fixed subcommittee organization (Agriculture). We classify five committees as high
in personnel turnover and the remaining five as low. We
find six committees with a relatively significant role for
subcommittees and four that seem to use subcommittees in
less important ways; we note, however, that subcommittees
seem to have become increasingly central on six of the panels.
Finally, four committees (such as Rules) command high prestige, four (including Government Operations) are moderately
attractive, and two (like Banking) provide their members
with lesser status.

We ask, in the chapters that follow, whether these attributes contribute to an understanding of committee factionalism, leadership, and response to change and reform.

A BRIEF NOTE ON METHOD

The Legislative Reorganization Act of 1970, which mandated that congressional committees record and make available their roll call votes, permits identification of committee patterns of behavior. These votes provide a glimpse
into the inner workings of individual committees: They permit definition of the factional structure of each committee;
they enable us to locate the place of the committee leaders
in that structure; and, when assessed separately for each
Congress, they allow observation of change that external
events, personnel turnover, or specific reforms may generate.[22] We describe our methods in detail in Appendix 1.

Briefly, we use cluster-bloc procedures to identify voting factions (or blocs) in each committee in five Congresses, the Ninety-second through the Ninety-sixth; we describe each bloc in terms of its members' party and regional affiliations (Republicans, northern Democrats, and southern Democrats) and ideological propensities (liberals, conservatives, and the conservative coalition). These measures permit us to specify the lines of committee cleavage. Subsequently, using Pearsonian correlation coefficients (r) and interagreement (IA) scores, we attempt to place the committee leaders--the chair and the ranking minority member--in the panel's factional structure. We want to know whether they vote with the major faction or with the major partisan, regional, or ideological grouping in the committee.

We also want to discover whether change and reform alter committee performance. A comparison of committee factionalism and leadership over successive Congresses, for instance, should reveal whether external changes (in the committee's environment, for example) or internal shifts (a revamped subcommittee structure) contribute to changes in committee behavior. Does reform affect panel factionalism? Does a new chairperson act in the same ways his or her predecessor behaved? Does change influence committee integration or committee floor success? These methods, applied to the ten House committees, allow us to answer these questions on a comparative basis.

CONCLUSION: COMPARING CONGRESSIONAL COMMITTEES

Broadly speaking, then, we consider individual House committees as separate, relatively autonomous units. Their members differ in the goals they seek from committee service and in the environments within which they try to attain these purposes. In response, individual panels develop and sustain differing internal structures and processes; partisanship and leadership are of particular concern to us. Committee behavior and committee floor success, in consequence, may vary systematically with these predisposing motivational, environmental, and organizational committee attributes. Although we recognize that there may well be intracommittee variation among subcommittees or across issues, we focus here

on intercommittee comparisons. We want to know whether, and
to what extent, committees differ on these basic dimensions.
The availability of recorded committee roll call votes and
of more impressionistic data on other panel attributes enables us to undertake some appropriate analyses.

Accordingly, in Chapter 2 we turn to committee cleavage. We seek, first, to identify the lines of division that
describe committee conflict. Is partisanship central to
panel decision making? Is such partisan struggle as exists
in any individual committee intense, moderate, or low? Do
specific committee conditions--members' goals or the sort of
environment they confront--seem to engender or retard party
conflict? We also seek to assess the impact of particular
patterns of cleavage on committee performance. Do the sorts
of divisions committees display help to define the decisions
they make or the degree to which the full House accepts those
choices? Given the high visibility of and importance at-
tached to partisanship, this seems an obvious starting point
for investigation of committee politics.

In Chapter 3 we address a similar set of questions in
regard to leadership. First, we define the place of the
nominal leader, the chairperson, in the factional structure
of the committee. Where do the chairs fall along the major
lines of committee cleavage? Do they vote regularly with
one particular partisan bloc, or do they cast their lot more
broadly, seeking support across the full spectrum of their
party or even across party lines? We ask a comparable set
of questions about the behavior of the ranking minority member. We next turn to the effects of leadership patterns on
committee performance. Do particular styles of leadership--
the relationships of leaders to other committee elements--
affect the extent to which the panel is integrated?   Does
the place of a leader in a committee's voting structure contribute to an understanding of whether his or her position
prevails in committee or on the House floor? Again, the
answers to such questions should be enlightening, in view
of the great weight frequently assigned to committee leaders'
influence in panel decision making.

If committees vary in terms of conflict and leadership,
they may also vary in the ways change of all sorts, planned
or inadvertent, affects them. Because we examine five individual Congresses, we can make a conscious effort to chart

change. Do personnel shifts--high turnover or new leaders--
alter either the factional alignments or patterns of leadership on a committee? What, if any, effects do new rules, a
new subcommittee structure, or other reforms have on committee members' behavior or overall panel performance? Do committees, in short, look and act at the end of the 1970s as
they did at the start of the decade? The answers to these
queries will help to clarify the ability of congressional
committees, as the central feature of legislative policymaking, to respond to social, economic, and political change,
in the society at large and in Congress itself. We seek the
answers to these questions in Chapter 4.

These three sets of analyses--of cleavage, of leadership, and of change and reform--constitute the chief concerns of our investigation. In Chapter 5 we weave our findings together, and indeed they produce a rich tapestry: Congressional committees do vary, and vary widely; they do,
however, also vary systematically, in identifiable patterns.
Pulling the threads of our argument together suggests the
need to speak cautiously, if we speak at all, about the congressional committee system. Rather, we must consider individual committees, coping with specific problems, with particular personnel and operating practices, and in a constant
state of flux. This reality makes difficult broad generalization; the propositions we can advance are often subject to
qualification. Such is the price we pay for a fuller and
more precise picture of congressional committee politics.

NOTES

1. A few years after Wilson's (1885) landmark study,
McConachie (1898) published an empirical work, one that has
remained largely neglected, on congressional committees.
More than a half century elapsed before Lees (1967), Morrow
(1969), and Goodwin (1970) offered equivalently comprehen-
sive, though largely descriptive, treatments. See also
Cooper (1970) and Lees (1979).
2. It is these commonalities that justify use of the
phrase "the committee system," so widely employed in the
legislative politics literature. The committees of Congress
do comprise a set of bodies with similar structures, with

similar roles in the larger institution, and with some contacts with one another. Yet we believe the differences among
the committees outweigh the similarities, that their individual autonomy exceeds their interdependence. Eulau and
McCluggage (1982) discuss these and other definitional issues carefully and critically; when published, this analysis
should be the definitive review of the committee literature.
See also Price (1981). Congressional committees do not, we
contend, constitute an interconnected system of action and,
in consequence, we treat them as independent, discrete units.

  3. Power is a nettlesome concept that social scientists
have not treated adequately. It is accurate, but not alto-
gether helpful, to note that some members get others to accommodate their wishes. Power is both reciprocal and implicit and thus difficult to unravel. We recognize these problems, but for present purposes limit our concern to the suggestion that some locations in Congress yield more power
possibilities than do others. For purposes of expository
convenience, we use the terms power, influence, and authority interchangeably.

  4. We need not here enter into the controversy about
whether it is appropriate to view members of Congress as if
they were "single-minded seekers of reelection" (Mayhew 1974,
p. 5). It should suffice to remember that, in one sense, reelection does precede other goals: Without a seat in Congress, a representative can neither shape policy nor exercise influence. Election requisites will probably retain a
central, if not exclusive, motive force, particularly in the
early phases of members' congressional careers (Fenno 1978).
Again, the important point is that some committees are more
congenial than others to reelection concerns.

  5. The relationship between member motivations and committee characteristics raises the question of causality again.
The link is surely reciprocal. Members want congenial committee settings, but because they win seats on established
bodies, they are not entirely free to reshape committee processes as they see fit. That is, new appointees must often
conform to extant practices. Still, to some extent committee rules and procedures will reflect member goals; knowing
something about the latter will surely inform us about the
former.

6. Indeed, there is no reason not to examine individual subcommittees in terms of Fenno's five factors. Doing so should certainly provide insight concerning the degree to which intracommittee variation exists.

7. For useful summaries of these developments, see, inter alia, Ornstein (1975), Rieselbach (1977, 1982), Welch and Peters (1977), Dodd and Oppenheimer (1981), and Mann and Ornstein (1981).

8. Budget did meet our selection standards for the three Congresses after it was established.

9. Our assessment of committee members' goal orientations relies heavily on Bullock (1976), who interviewed freshman legislators about their committee assignment preferences. Scicchitano (1981) and Cook and Ragsdale (1982) reexamined Bullock's typology in light of subsequent developments. Unless otherwise noted, we accept the consensus among these three studies. The category--reelection, policy, power--of course, is a committee tendency that need not apply to each and every member.

10. In evaluating committee attractiveness (prestige), we adopt Ray's (1982) update of Jewell and Chu (1974): The measure of attractiveness is an index of "drawing power," the ability of one committee to attract members who previously served on other panels. The greater a committee's drawing power, the greater its prestige.

11. On these developments, see Hinckley (1976), Parker (1979), Ornstein and Rohde (1977), Barton (1976), Peters (1978), and Berg (1978).

12. During the Ninety-second and Ninety-third Congresses, Armed Services used designated special or ad hoc subcommittees to treat particular issues (for example, Intelligence).

13. The Banking Committee was known as Banking and Currency during the Ninety-second and Ninety-third Congresses. In the Ninety-fourth it was Banking, Currency, and Housing; in the Ninety-fifth it assumed its current name: Banking, Finance, and Urban Affairs. For convenience, we refer to this and other committees that changed names by their most recent designation.

14. For a full explication of the background, enactment, and consequences of the act, see Havemann (1978), Ellwood and Thurber (1977), Schick (1980), and Ippolito (1981).

15. The reconciliation procedure was first used, in a modest fashion, in the Ninety-sixth Congress, the last we consider here. The tactic took on a far greater significance in the Ninety-seventh Congress (1981-82) and became the central strategic device in the Reagan administration's budgetary successes.

16. Subcommittee autonomy seems largely limited to oversight activity; the few bills that Government Operations reports (it has limited legislative authority) are increasingly managed on the House floor by the full committee chair (Deering 1982).

17. In fact, the 1974 House Select (Bolling) Committee on Committees proposed to abolish Post Office; only the unremitting efforts of its clientele--the federal postal and civil service unions--enabled the panel to survive (see Davidson and Oleszek 1977, especially pp. 164-68).

18. During the 1970s, the Democratic Caucus granted the Speaker, at first de facto, later de jure, authority to name the members of the Rules Committee. This appointment power has made the committee, in effect, "an arm of the leadership" (Oppenheimer 1977). Because the Speaker selects the members, few freshmen actually apply for the assignment, and Bullock (1976) thus finds Rules an "undesired" committee. Once on, however, few leave, and the committee retains high attractiveness. Moreover, Rules retains its influence potential, even as an adjunct of the leadership. In consequence, we concur with Cook and Ragsdale (1982) in classifying the committee as a panel whose members serve in pursuit of power (or influence) goals.

19. The influence of committee Democrats was enhanced, of course, because they served as their party's committee on committees; their ability to make committee assignments obviously gave them additional leverage over the party rank-and-file.

20. The Democratic Caucus further diminished Ways and Means Democrats' potential influence when it stripped them of their committee assignment prerogatives, which were transferred to the party's Steering and Policy Committee.

21. These classifications, admittedly, are often judgment calls that reflect our reading of the often sparse literature on the various House committees.

22. For a pioneering effort using these data, see Parker and Parker (1979). Our method of analysis differs from the Parkers'; we look at each Congress separately, enabling us to include more members and to chart change more carefully.

2
Congressional
Committee Cleavage

When members of the House of Representatives cast
their votes on the floor, they tend to stand with their political party. As Jewell and Patterson note: ". . . roll
call votes in Congress follow party lines more often than
they follow any other alignment" (1977, p. 389).[1] Moreover,
party has retained its primacy as a predictor of the vote,
even though on an absolute scale the impact of partisanship
has declined somewhat in recent years (Brady, Cooper, and
Hurley 1979; Clubb and Traugott 1977). Indeed, in assessing
the place of party in congressional politics, we encounter a
paradox: Party is simultaneously a powerful influence on
its members but so weak structurally that it cannot command
the loyalty of its rank-and-file, even when the party position is at issue. The explanation of this paradox seems to
rest on a distinction between the psychological pull of partisanship and the institutional debility of party organiza-
tions.

On the positive side, members are inclined, other
things being equal, to support their parties; that is, when
they can, representatives want to back their leaders (Kingdon 1981). After all, members of Congress, like ordinary
citizens, identify with one or the other of the two great
parties. Not only do they think of themselves as Democrats
or Republicans but they also tend to win elections in districts where "their own kind" constitutes the majority. That
is, the constituency bases of the party are distinct.

Once in office, legislators tend to associate with, to take cues from (Matthews and Stimson 1975), and to communicate generally with others on their own side of the aisle; these contacts generate what Kingdon (1981, p. 122) calls a "compatriot feeling," a sense of commitment to party. This attachment seems most meaningful to those who must defend a president of their own party. Finally, formal party leaders—the Speaker and the majority and minority leaders—do possess some political plums with which to pressure (or persuade) members to vote the party line: influence over committee assignments, the ability to schedule legislative business in an accommodating way, control over congressional communications, and a less tangible "psychological preferment" (Ripley 1978, pp. 215-18).

To whatever extent House members want to demonstrate loyalty, they often encounter forces that pull them away from pure partisanship. Their personal policy preferences may lead them to bolt; electoral pressures from the constituency back home may require them to defect; so, too, may state or regional influences. In addition, committee decisions, executive branch communications and contacts, or interest group inducements may lead away from party loyalty. In the last analysis, party can claim and cajole but cannot compel that loyalty. Members' fate at the polls rests almost exclusively in their own hands. The party lacks the ultimate sanction: the ability to deprive members of their House seats. So long as this is the case, representatives may give or withhold loyalty to party as they, rather than the party leaders, see fit (Mayhew 1974; Hinckley 1981).

When they do choose to stray from the party camp, members may follow ideological paths. The conservative coalition, the alliance of conservative southern Democrats and Republicans,[2] is the most common alternative to party cleavage in Congress (Manley 1973; Brady and Bullock 1981). Over the years, the coalition has been particularly visible on civil liberties and social welfare matters. Writing more recently, some scholars (especially Schneider 1979; Shaffer 1980) have concluded that ideology not party is the basic underlying "fault line" of House voting across the full range of issues that engage the national legislature. Congressional conflict, they suggest, most often pits liberals against conservatives. Finally, some research (Clausen 1973;

Clausen and Van Horn 1977) indicates that partisanship varies according to subject matter. Domestic issues, particularly farm and government management matters, evoke partisan conflict; civil liberties and foreign policy topics, by contrast, mute partisanship.

Overall, then, during the 1970s, party remained the strongest predictor of floor voting, though its primacy was somewhat reduced. Moreover, partisanship varied by issue, and when it declined in potency, ideological cleavage seems enhanced. (As we note below, it is often extraordinarily difficult to disentangle party and ideological influences on the vote.) Given these findings concerning decision making on the House floor, it seems reasonable to ask whether similar results obtain in committee, and we undertake to answer the question in this chapter. Specifically, we describe patterns of committee cleavage, attempt to ascertain their antecedents (in terms of the attributes identified in Chapter 1), and specify the behavioral consequences associated with particular patterns of committee factionalism.

DEFINING COMMITTEE CLEAVAGE

Our point of departure is the approach to committee decision making set forth in Chapter 1. There we argue that, at a minimum, a full, theoretically satisfying treatment of committees would need to account for two sets of linkages. The first connects "prior conditions"--members' goals, environmental constraints, and a committee's strategic premises (decision rules)--with committee decision-making structures--partisanship, leadership, and specialization. The second links these structures to subsequent committee performance, especially "floor success," the ability of the panel to win full House approval for the legislation it reports.[3] Our specific focus is on partisanship, and its alternatives, as the central feature of committee cleavage. What patterns of conflict characterize which committees? Having described and explained the extant committee alignments, we turn to the results that seem to flow from them. Do different patterns of committee conflict engender varying forms of committee behavior?

Several possible patterns of cleavage may appear within congressional committees; three command our attention:

1. Partisanship: If party conflict is common on the House floor, it should also appear in individual committees. In pursuit of policy partisanship, Democrats and Republicans should line up on opposite sides of major issues. This seems to have been the case during the 1960s in Ways and Means (Manley 1970), Education and Labor (Fenno 1973), and Public Works (Murphy 1974), and there is every reason to expect partisan cleavages in many panels in the subsequent decade.

We must acknowledge that partisan alignments are almost impossible to distinguish from ideological conflicts that pit liberals against conservatives. Most commonly, party cleavage finds Democratic liberals opposing Republican conservatives. Although we note the ideological characteristics, using Americans for Constitutional Action (ACA) ratings (see Appendix 1), we do not treat ideological divisions separately. When we discuss party cleavage, we are actually talking about partisan-ideological lines of conflict.

2. Bipartisanship: In direct contrast to the partisan pattern, committees may be "integrated," that is, they may develop consensual, non- (or minimally) partisan decision-making modes. If so, we should find majorities of each party, presumably motivated by shared policy concerns, voting together across the partisan divide. In the 1960s, House Appropriations (Fenno 1973), Foreign Affairs (Fenno 1973), and Armed Services (Dexter 1969) displayed bipartisan-consensual voting patterns, and, again, we should expect to uncover similar alignments in the ensuing period.

The widely noted conservative coalition poses special problems here. Found frequently on the floor, the Republican-southern Democratic alliance is at once both an ideological and a bipartisan phenomenon. Presumably united in support of conservative causes, the coalition draws from both parties. The voting patterns that characterize a conservative coalitional alignment should find the Republicans and southern Democrats uniting in opposition to the liberal wing of the Democratic party. Thus the coalition is, in factional terms, a special case of bipartisanship, one where a particular set of Democrats—those from the South—join the

Republicans across party lines. In consequence, we look at committee alignments to see whether bipartisanship, when it appears, is general, without regional roots, or limited to the conservative coalition.

3. Unstructured committees: Some panels may display no consistent set of voting alignments; their roll calls may be unstructured, or fluid, perhaps reflecting lack of a common approach to issues on the committee's agenda, variation in voting across different portions of that agenda, or divergent treatment of bills within the jurisdictions of different subcommittees. In any case, neither partisan nor bipartisan patterns may adequately describe voting in a given committee in a given Congress.

Our methods (described in Appendix 1) permit a systematic search for these hypothesized patterns of voting cleavage. First, we classify individual roll calls as partisan, ideological, conservative coalition, or bipartisan; this provides an overall sense of the lines of conflict that divide a committee and of the frequency with which each type of cleavage appears. We also calculate committee integration measures to specify the general level of committee cohesion. Needless to say, the greater the proportion of partisan votes on a panel, the lower committee integration will be. Second, we use cluster-bloc techniques to identify voting factions (clusters, blocs) in each committee in each Congress, and we describe each bloc in terms of its members' party and regional affiliations (Republicans, northern Democrats, and southern Democrats) and ideological propensities (liberal, conservative, and conservative coalition). In addition, we compute intercluster correlations to indicate the degree of similarity among the factions that characterize a committee in any Congress.[4] These measures enable us to picture the lines of committee cleavage at any point in time and to chart changes in those cleavages across the 1971–80 period.

Each of the patterns we hypothesize has a set of distinctive attributes. Partisan factionalism, for example, predictably features relatively large numbers of partisan roll calls, pitting majorities of the parties against one another, and ideological votes, on which liberals (most commonly Democrats) oppose conservatives (usually Republicans).

Sixty percent or more of the roll calls should fall into one (or both) of these categories. By contrast, bipartisan alignments, with majorities of both parties in agreement, should be relatively rare on partisan panels. Similarly, committee integration is likely to be low on such committees, usually less than .35. In terms of voting clusters, there should be relatively large (with a half dozen or more members), partisan (exclusively from a single party) factions on these committees. In addition, we expect high (.25 or greater) intercluster correlations between correlations between blocs of the same party and low (-.25 or lower) correlations between opposing party blocs. Collectively, these indicators should suggest a pattern of clear partisan cleavage.

The Rules Committee in the Ninety-fifth Congress presents a typical picture of a partisan panel. Most of its votes (85 percent) were partisan and ideological; committee integration was a modest .27 (see Table 2.1). Few Rules roll calls were bipartisan or activated the conservative coalition. The factional patterns of the committee (Table 2.2) reinforce the sense of partisan polarization. Two Democratic clusters (1 and 2) appeared, encompassing eight of the eleven majority members of Rules. The two blocs were strongly liberal in outlook (ACA scores average 11 and 22, respectively) and agreed with one another regularly (intercluster correlation = .35). Across the aisle was a Republican faction, including three of the four minority members with sufficient participation to be part of our analysis. This strongly conservative bloc (ACA = 85) opposed the Democratic clusters constantly (intercluster correlations = -.35 and -.24, respectively). In short, Democratic liberals confronted Republican conservatives on Rules during the Ninety-fifth Congress.

The bipartisan factional pattern stands in sharp contrast to this picture of partisan conflict. The number of bipartisan roll calls should be higher, often exceeding 50 percent of the total votes; committee integration should be stronger, often above .40. The factions that appear should contain members of both parties and, as inclusive groupings, be relatively large ($\underline{N}$ = 7 or 8). The clusters, moreover, in the absence of party divisions, should be strongly intercorrelated (frequently at .25 or higher). This set of

TABLE 2.1

Committee Roll Call Voting, 92nd–96th Congresses

Committee and Congress	Roll Calls (N)	Committee Integration	Roll Call Type			
			Bipartisan (%)	Partisan (%)	Conservative Coalition (%)	Ideological (%)
Agriculture						
92	11	.38	36	55	9	27
93	48	.35	38	52	21	48
94	75	.25	27	68	44	73
95	61	.30	30	70	25	54
96	36	.33	33	56	14	56
Armed Services						
92	34	.57	85	12	6	18
93	25	.55	84	16	24	24
94	22	.39	64	23	41	59
95	28	.43	61	32	46	43
96	23	.36	65	30	26	52
Banking						
92	149	.31	32	61	34	62
93	117	.38	46	44	14	41
94	80	.31	19	77	15	77
95	103	.37	44	50	20	54
96	53	.34	28	70	13	62

(continued)

Table 2.1, continued

Committee and Congress	Roll Calls (N)	Committee Integration	Roll Call Type			
			Bipartisan (%)	Partisan (%)	Conservative Coalition (%)	Ideological (%)
Budget						
94	20	.18	15	85	50	90
95	67	.25	18	78	16	78
96	73	.25	23	77	30	74
Education and Labor						
92	99	.30	17	80	9	76
93	64	.34	27	69	16	69
94	44	.39	14	84	2	75
95	79	.37	22	75	16	75
96	36	.30	3	94	11	97
Government Operations						
92	13	.27	15	77	23	62
93	18	.42	22	72	22	56
94	16	.24	00	100	38	94
95	38	.30	11	89	26	79
96	31	.26	16	81	26	74

Commerce						
92	25	.21	12	84	4	88
93	51	.21	14	78	16	80
94	105	.25	8	85	17	40
95	65	.20	14	83	31	88
96	99	.24	25	69	30	75
Post Office						
92	23	.49	48	43	17	43
93	19	.34	21	74	11	63
94	16	.23	13	75	13	81
95	59	.34	25	66	14	58
96	12	.23	0	100	0	100
Rules						
92	21	.28	29	48	24	67
93	86	.27	20	71	9	67
94	99	.28	16	76	4	76
95	65	.27	12	85	12	85
96	70	.34	11	77	7	77
Ways and Means						
92	32	.40	64	34	38	44
93	75	.32	36	55	32	63
94	235	.22	21	74	48	75
95	161	.25	34	62	32	68
96	112	.23	18	75	21	74

Note: The percentages total more than 100 percent because these categories are mutually exclusive. The operational definitions of the categories are presented in Appendix 1.

TABLE 2.2

Partisan Factional Pattern: House Rules Committee, 95th Congress

Representatives	Party	State	Clusters		
			1	2	3
Bolling, R.	D	Missouri	.43		
Long, G.	D	Louisiana	.38		
Delaney, J.	D	New York	.44		
Meeds, L.	D	Washington	.55		
Moakley, J.	D	Massachusetts	.52		
Murphy, M.	D	Illinois		.57	
Pepper, C.	D	Florida		.41	
Young, J.	D	Texas		.47	
Quillen, J.	R	Tennessee			.50
Latta, D.	R	Ohio			.52
Lott, T.	R.	Mississippi			.40
Clawson, D.	R	California			
Anderson, J.	R	Illinois			
Dodd, C.	D	Connecticut			
Chisholm, S.	D	New York			
Sisk, B.	D	California			
Bauman, R.	R	Maryland*			

Roll Call = 65

*Member participated in less than 60 percent of the votes.

Mean Cluster Scores:	1	2	3
ACA	11	22	85
Party identification (percent Democrat)	100	100	00
Conservative coalition	22	32	87

Intercluster Correlations:	1	2
2	.35	
3	−.34	−.24

measures, in sum, should make clear the lack of partisan antagonism.

The Armed Services Committee in the Ninety-Third Congress nicely illustrates the bipartisan factional pattern. As Table 2.1 reveals, 84 percent of the committee's roll calls were bipartisan; only 16 percent were partisan and 24 percent were ideological. Committee integration was strong, .55, indicating high agreement among the membership. The factional structure of Armed Services was entirely consistent with this view (see Table 2.3). The two largest clusters (1 and 2) were bipartisan; one thirteen-member bloc consisted of eight Democrats and five Republicans, and the smaller of the two had one Democrat associated with three members of the GOP. All the factions were moderate to conservative ideologically (ACA scores ranged between 61 and 83) and all involved members sympathetic to the conservative coalition (coalition support averages were between 76 and 82). Finally, the intercluster correlations among the four factions were positive, and most were modest to strong (between .20 and .38). Overall, our measures make clear that Armed Services voting in the Ninety-third Congress trancended partisanship; the committee was united by bipartisan consensus.

The unstructured voting pattern, the third possibility, provides a still different portrait of committee factionalism. In contrast to the other alignment structures, this pattern features a mix of roll call types--roughly equal proportions of partisan and bipartisan votes--and moderate (.35 to .40) committee integration. In terms of cleavage, the unstructured pattern should display a large number (usually six) of small ($\underline{N}$ = 5 or fewer) clusters. Moreover, there should be low intercluster correlations among these blocs, given that there is no overriding base of division in the committee. Finally, in light of this lack of focus, we expect large numbers of members to be unaligned, outside the committee's factional structure.

The House Banking, Finance, and Urban Affairs Committee in the Ninety-fifth Congress illustrates this fluid, unstructured pattern. The panel's roll calls were more or less equally distributed among partisan (50 percent), ideological (54 percent), and bipartisan (44 percent) categories; in addition, one fifth of the votes (20 percent)

TABLE 2.3

Bipartisan Factional Pattern: House Armed
Services Committee, 93rd Congress

Representative	Party	State	Clusters			
			1	2	3	4
Bray, W.	R	Indiana	.66			
Hebert, E.	D	Louisiana	.72			
Fisher, O. C.	D	Texas	.69			
Price, M.	D	Illinois	.69			
Nichols, B.	D	Alabama	.72			
Spence, F.	R	South Carolina	.53			
Whitehurst, G.	R	Virginia	.56			
Bennett, C.	D	Florida	.69			
Davis, M.	D	South Carolina	.66			
Holt, M.	R	Maryland	.48			
Montgomery, G.	D	Mississippi	.60			
Daniel, W.	D	Virginia	.53			
Beard, R.	R	Tennessee	.51			
Brinkley, J.	D	Georgia		.39		
Armstrong, W.	R	Colorado		.54		
King, C.	R	New York		.51		
Treen, D.	R	Louisiana		.53		
Price, R.	R	Texas			.47	
Gubser, C.	R	California			.58	
Hunt, J.	R	New Jersey			.51	
Arends, L.	R	Illinois				.46
Wilson, B.	R	California				.49
Daniel, R.	R	Virginia				.42
Aspin, L.	D	Wisconsin				
Schroeder, P.	D	Colorado				
Mollohan, R.	D	West Virginia				
Mitchell, D.	R	New York				
Ichord, R.	D	Missouri				
Dickinson, W.	R	Alabama				
Pike, O.	D	New York				
Stratton, S.	D	New York				

			Clusters			
Representative	Party	State	1	2	3	4
Hicks, F.	D	Washington				
Wilson, C.	D	California				
Leggett, R.	D	California				
Powell, W.	R	Ohio*				
Young, B.	R	Florida*				
Randall, W.	D	Missouri*				
Nedzi, L.	D	Michigan*				
Murtha, J.	D	Pennsylvania*				
Hillis, E.	R	Indiana*				
Jones, J.	D	Oklahoma*				
Dellums, R.	D	California*				
Runnels, H.	D	New York*				
O'Brien, G.	R	Illinois*				
White, R.	D	Texas*				

Roll Calls = 25

*Members participated in less than 60 percent of the votes.

Mean Cluster Scores:	1	2	3	4
ACA	71	61	79	83
Party identification (percent Democrat)	61	25	00	00
Conservative coalition	76	78	76	82

Intercluster Correlation	1	2	3
2	.20		
3	.38	.03	
4	.31	.04	.20

TABLE 2.4

Unstructured Factional Pattern: House Banking
Committee, 95th Congress

Representative	Party	State	Clusters					
			1	2	3	4	5	6
Kelly, R.	R	Florida	.51					
Hansen, G.	R	Indiana	.40					
Rousselot, J.	R.	California	.45					
Ashley, T.	D	Ohio		.49				
Spellman, G.	D	Maryland		.49				
Watkins, W.	D	Oklahoma			.41			
Barnard, D.	D	Georgia			.45			
Oakar, M.	D	Ohio			.38			
Fauntroy, W.	D	District of Columbia				.42		
Mitchell, P.	D	Maryland				.37		
Reuss, H.	D	Wisconsin				.36		
St. Germain, F.	D	Rhode Island					.43	
Hanley, J.	D	New York					.43	
Stanton, W.	R	Ohio						.37
Wylie, C.	R	Ohio						.38
Brown, G.	R	Michigan						.41
McKinney, S.	R	Connecticut						
Hyde, H.	R	Illinois						
Grassley, C.	R	Iowa						
Vento, B.	D	Minnesota						
Mattox, J.	D	Texas						
Cavanaugh, J.	D	Nebraska						
Pattison, E.	D	New York						
Hollenbeck, H.	R	New Jersey						
Caputo, B.	R	New York						
Evans, T.	R	Delaware						
Steers, N.	R	Maryland						
Leach, J.	R	Iowa						
Fenwick, M.	R	New Jersey						
Neal, S.	D	North Carolina						
Lafalce, J.	D	New York						
Hubbard. C.	D	Kentucky						
Blanchard, J.	D	Michigan						

			Clusters					
Representative	Party	State	1	2	3	4	5	6
Patterson, J.	D	California						
Aucoin, L.	D	Oregon						
Derrick, B.	D	South Carolina						
Tsongas, P.	D	Massachusetts						
Lundine, S.	D	New York						
Damours, N.	D	New Hampshire						
Evans, D.	D	Indiana						
Hannaford, M.	D	California						
Moorhead, W.	D	Pennsylvania						
Annunzio, F.	D	Illinois						
Minish, J.	D	New Jersey						
Allen, C.	D	Tennessee*						
Gonzalez, H.	D	Texas*						
Green, W.	R	New York*						
Garcia, R.	D	New York*						
Badillo, H.	D	New York*						

Roll Calls = 103

*Member participated in less than 60 percent of the votes.

Mean Cluster Scores:	1	2	3	4	5	6
ACA	62	16	54	4	18	59
Party identification (percent Democratic)	0	100	100	100	100	0
Conservative coalition	89	20	63	4	28	71

Intercluster Correlation:	1	2	3	4	5
2	−.10				
3	.06	.26			
4	−.18	.16	.04		
5	−.16	.20	.06	.29	
6	.26	.09	.17	−.15	−.06

were conservative coalition roll calls (Table 2.1). Banking Committee integration was moderate, .37. Cluster analysis of the committee underscores the view of the committee as unstructured (Table 2.4). There were six clusters, each containing only two or three members; of the 44 members who took part in a minimum of 60 percent of the committee roll calls, only 16 (36 percent) were aligned with any bloc. Finally, the intercluster correlations among those factions that did appear are low: Only three of fifteen exceeded .25, indicating little voting consistency among the various clusters. In short, Banking displayed a chaotic rather than a coherent factional pattern.

RESULTS: PATTERNS OF COMMITTEE CLEAVAGE

Applying these criteria to the ten committees reveals significant variation in the patterns of panel factionalism. Table 2.5 displays our assignment of the committees to the partisan, bipartisan, or unstructured categories.[5] Note that 47 of the 48 cases (nine committees in five Congresses and the budget Committee since 1975) fall readily into one or another of the three categories; only Post Office in the Ninety-third Congress defies classification. Nonetheless, a word of caution is in order: Committee voting alignments are almost inevitably complex. Looking at all members, in separate Congresses, across the full range of issues on which committees vote does not reveal such simple lines of cleavage as Democrats versus Republicans or liberals versus conservatives. Rather, we discover that potential allies, partisans and ideologies, sometimes disagree, leading to bloc structures that are interpretable but seldom simple. Indeed, this conclusion is exactly what we should expect to characterize a decentralized legislature that makes decisions through a complicated coalition-building process that varies with the subject matter under consideration and with the passage of time. Our empirical results caution against easy generalization. We argue merely that our data do identify tendencies and that, in relative terms, committee factional alignments do differ, and often do so widely.

The first point to note is that, in keeping with the central importance of political parties in Congress, the

TABLE 2.5

Committee Factional Patterns, 92nd–96th Congresses

Committee and Congress	Factional Pattern[a]
Agriculture	
92	Partisan
93	Unstructured
94	Unstructured
95	Unstructured
96	Partisan
Armed Services	
92	Bipartisan
93	Bipartisan
94	Bipartisan
95	Bipartisan
96	Bipartisan
Banking	
92	Unstructured
93	Unstructured
94	Unstructured
95	Unstructured
96	Partisan
Budget	
94	Partisan
95	Partisan
96	Partisan
Education and Labor	
92	Partisan
93	Partisan
94	Partisan
95	Partisan
96	Partisan

(continued)

Table 2.5, continued

Committee and Congress	Factional Pattern[a]
Government Operations	
92	Bipartisan
93	Bipartisan
94	Partisan
95	Unstructured
96	Partisan
Commerce	
92	Partisan
93	Unstructured
94	Partisan
95	Bipartisan[b]
96	Bipartisan[b]
Post Office	
92	Unstructured
93	(Unclassified)
94	Partisan
95	Partisan
96	Partisan
Rules	
92	Partisan
93	Unstructured
94	Partisan
95	Partisan
96	Unstructured
Ways and Means	
92	Bipartisan[b]
93	Bipartisan[b]
94	Partisan
95	Partisan
96	Partisan

[a]The criteria for assigning each committee to these factional patterns are described in the text.

[b]The bipartisan pattern reflects the conservative coalition (see the text).

partisan factional pattern is the most common in committee
as well as on the floor. More interesting, perhaps, is that
the bipartisan and unstructured alignments also occur regularly. Specifically, slightly more than half of the time
(24 of the 47 classified cases in Table 2.5, or 51 percent)
committee divisions pitted the parties against each other.
In 11 instances (23 percent), the committee alignments
transcended party and were bipartisan in character. Finally,
12 cases (26 percent) revealed unstructured voting, with
few factions and many members unattached to any bloc. Given
the importance assigned to party loyalty, it is somewhat surprising to discover that in committee, in contrast to the
situation on the floor, members seemingly often feel free
to follow their own inclinations rather than the dictates
of party. The sort of "restrained partisanship" that Manley
(1970; see also Fenno 1973) found in Ways and Means in the
1960s may well characterize a number of committees in the
more recent period.

Second, committee factional patterns vary with the
passage of time. Only three of the ten panels displayed
consistent voting alignments during the 1970s. Two, Budget
and Education and Labor, divided along partisan lines throughout the period; Armed Services sustained a bipartisan consensus through five successive Congresses (see Table 2.5
and Appendix 2). Enduring policy concerns seem the most
plausible explanation for the persistence of voting patterns.
Both Budget and Education and Labor have been partisan-
ideological battlegrounds. In the former, Republicans and
Democrats, while proclaiming their commitment to the budget
process (LeLoup 1979), have contested vigorously the allocation of funds that such process produces. Conservatives
prefer smaller total expenditures; they favor defense out-
lays over those for social programs. Liberals are willing
to spend more, especially for domestic welfare and education
efforts (Schick 1980; Ippolito 1981). Education and Labor
has jurisdiction over many of these same issues and, not
surprisingly, divides along similar lines. Liberal Democrats
seek to expand social welfare activities; Republican conservatives strive to restrain growth of such programs if
they cannot actually reduce their scope.

Armed Services seems to have an equivalent, though
obviously different in content, consistency in policy outlook.

Here, the committee is primarily concerned with constituency matters; its members seek to locate military installations advantageously in a variety of congressional districts. As noted, the price the panel pays to secure such freedom of maneuver has been to give wholehearted support to the Pentagon's military procurement plans.[6] Thus policy consensus undergirds the committee members' ability to pursue reelection goals, and in consequence Armed Services seems to have cast policy conflict aside to preserve its primary constituency representational purposes. Programmatic agreement, along with shared goals, has created an enduring bipartisan voting alignment in the committee.

A carefully crafted committee assignment process seems to buttress the permanence of the roll call voting patterns in these three committees. In each case new members tend to reinforce rather than mitigate the prevailing alignments. Given the importance of fiscal issues, the House party leaders have come to play "an active role" in the Budget Committee "selection process." They "usually pick interested Members . . . unless an appointment would unbalance the committee or deviate from the preferred ideological makeup" (Schick 1980, pp. 98-99). In Education and Labor a self-selective recruitment appears to be at work. Given the committee's jurisdiction and the ideological polarization that characterizes these issues, the panel has been attractive to both liberal Democrats and conservative Republicans. Few southern conservative Democrats have served over the years, and the conservative coalition rarely appears on Education and Labor roll calls.

A similar self-selection process seems to be at work in Armed Services. In the 1970s, few northern or western liberal Democrats served on the committee; they presumably found more promising and productive outlets for their energies elsewhere. Moreover, many senior northerners, for example, Samuel Stratton (New York), did not dissent notably from the committee consensus. Indeed, those who did the assigning seemed to consider policy position in making their choices; they tended to select from the pool of applicants members "whose orientation most clearly matched the tradi-tional cast of the committee" (Cook 1980, p. 13). Overall, then, where there are important, long-standing policy controversies—over the budget, the government's role in social

welfare, the military--committees tend to develop persistent
cleavages that the recruitment and committee assignment
process sustains.

Three committees--Banking, Post Office, and Ways and
Means--displayed a change in their factional alignments during the 1970s, and in each case the shift was to a partisan
configuration (Table 2.5). Banking was for four Congresses
(1971 to 1978) an unstructured panel. Its diverse jurisdiction and heterogeneous environment, its high membership
turnover, and its relatively low prestige in the House seemingly, judging from committee voting, retarded growth of
consistent cleavage within the panel. In the Ninety-sixth
Congress, however, the nation's economic difficulties--
stagflation with concomitant high unemployment and high
inflation--led the Carter administration to propose numerous
social program cuts. The Democrats resisted these while the
Republicans supported the reductions, and Banking became
more polarized in partisan terms. At least, the number of
partisan roll calls rose to 70 percent (Table 2.1), and major Democratic and Republican clusters (of nine and eight
members, respectively), emerged in a committee where, in the
earlier years, no bloc had exceeded five members (Appendix 2,
Table 15). Moreover, the two clusters were regularly on
opposite sides (intercluster correlation = -.29) when votes
were counted in committee. In any case, party conflict
clearly developed in the Banking Committee during 1979-80.

Agenda change seems related to increased partisan division within the Post Office Committee as well. The creation, in 1970, of the U.S. Postal Service deprived the
committee of much of the authority it had exercised during
the previous decade. No longer able to provide constituency
benefits or to conduct more than general oversight (Fenno
1973), Post Office members appear to have been searching for
a mission. The panel was unstructured (in our terms) during
the Ninety-second Congress and defied classification (the
only such case in the analysis) in the Ninety-third. Thereafter, however, partisan cleavage characterized the committee. The number of partisan and ideological roll calls increased and major partisan clusters coalesced (Table 2.1 and
Appendix 2, Tables 30-35). This configuration, moderate to
clear partisan-ideological alignment, may reflect Democratic
and Republican views about federal employee unions, the chief

clienteles of the committee; the former defended the unions,
the latter were more critical. The pattern may be part of
the heightened partisanship that the final throes of the
nation's Vietnam adventure and the Watergate contretemps
engendered.[7] High turnover may also have contributed to the
trend toward partisan opposition. In any case, our portrait
is entirely consistent with Parker and Parker's (1979) assessment and suggests, as did their analysis, that there has
been an evolution from the relatively nonpartisan, low-
ideological posture that Fenno (1973) found characteristic
of the panel in the previous period. Post Office became an
arena for party and ideological contests.

Ways and Means, for quite obvious reasons, also became
a partisan battleground. The congressional reform movement
of the 1970s struck the committee in singularly striking
ways.[8] Virtually every aspect of the committee altered; the
panel had, after 1974, a new chairperson, many new members,
new subcommittees, and new restrictions on its activities.
New agenda items (energy taxes, for example) in an era of
economic dislocation exacerbated committee conflict. Under
Al Ullman (Oregon), who succeeded the legendary Wilbur Mills
(Arkansas) in the chair, the bipartisan consensus, featuring
"restrained partisanship" (Manley 1970) of the earlier period, gave way to rancorous party conflict. There were many
more roll calls in the Ninety-fourth and subsequent Congresses, and more of them were partisan and ideological
(Table 2.1). By the Ninety-sixth Congress there were two
large ($\underline{N}$ = 10 and 9, respectively) ideologically polarized
(ACA = 86 and 10) partisan clusters to which more than half
the committee belonged. These blocs were regularly opposed
(intercluster correlation = .35) to one another (Appendix 2,
Table 45), and epitomized the levels of partisan conflict on
the committee in the latter half of the decade.

The remaining four committees display even greater
variability in lines of cleavage, changing patterns at least
twice throughout the five Congresses. Agriculture, for instance, was moderately partisan in the Ninety-second Congress
(1971-72); there were more partisan votes than any other
type, and there was a large, 11-member Democratic bloc.[9]
In the three subsequent Congresses, however, the committee
was unstructured, with small factions to which a minority
of members belonged. During this time there was high turnover

on the panel, which also endured a collapse of leadership.
The long-time chair, W. R. Poage (Texas), increasingly came
under fire (his critics branded him a conservative autocrat)
and was ousted at the outset of the Ninety-fourth Congress
(Hinckley 1976; Parker 1979; Ornstein and Rohde 1977; see
also Chapter 4). The bargaining and compromisng needed to
pass an omnibus farm bill in the Ninety-third and Ninety-
fifth Congresses may have contributed to the lack of clear
voting alignments; the need to find common ground among
members with constituency interests in a wide variety of
crops may have inhibited the growth of permanent factional
alliances. In the Ninety-sixth Congress, in sharp contrast,
partisan cleavage appeared in Agriculture (Appendix 2,
Table 5). With no major farm bill up, attention focused on
more ideological matters—sugar price supports, grain sales
to the Soviet Union, efforts to protect farmers from dete-
riorating domestic economy. These issues tended to pit
liberal Democrats against conservative Republicans, and a
partisan-ideological alignment came to typify the Agriculture
Committee.

Government Operations displayed an equally variable
pattern of factionalism. In the Ninety-second and Ninety-
third Congresses, with Chet Holifield (D.-Calif.) as
chairman, the committee was a bipartisan, moderate body. At
least, the major blocs crossed party lines and the clusters
tended to agree with one another more often than not (Appendix 2, Tables 21-22).[10] In 1975, however, Holifield
retired, Jack Brooks (Texas) became chairperson, and the
committee took on a partisan coloration. Indeed, the conflict in Government Operations in the Ninety-fourth Congress
was one of the sharpest of the decade, with large (N = 12,
11) ideologically disparate (ACA = 10, 66) clusters regularly on opposite sides of roll call votes (intercluster
correlations = -.61). This extreme partisanship moderated
in the subsequent Congress, when committee voting revealed
an unstructured pattern. Party polarization reemerged in
1979-80, in the Ninety-sixth Congress, perhaps as part of
the general growth of partisanship that characterized the
final years of the Carter administration. Over time, then,
Government Operations evolved toward a stronger partisan-
ideological voting alignment but in an erratic and shifting
fashion.

Commerce Committee voting evolved in precisely the opposite direction from that of Government Operations, from more or less partisan configurations toward a bipartisan agreement that features the conservative coalition. During the early part of the period, in the Ninety-second to Ninety-fourth Congresses, partisan-ideological divisions dominated the committee; in the Ninety-third Congress, however, the pattern was unstructured, largely because so few members were aligned with any cluster. Before 1977, most roll calls were partisan and committee integration was quite low (Table 2.1); the blocs that formed were, with one exception,[11] partisan and there was substantial interparty conflict (Appendix 2, Tables 29-30). As noted, in 1975 and thereafter, liberal Democrats in Commerce expanded their influence, at the expense of the chairman, Harley Staggers (West Virginia); influence devolved to junior members and to the subcommittees they chaired. The result was a bipartisanship rooted in the conservative coalition. The number of conservative coalition roll calls nearly doubled, and the proportion of bipartisan votes increased as well.

The factional structure of Commerce also reveals the emergence of the conservative coalition after 1976. In the Ninety-fifth Congress (Appendix 2, Table 29) two Republican blocs (clusters 1 and 4) and a southern Democratic faction (cluster 2) emerged and voted together regularly (intercluster correlations ranged from .27 to .39). Even the liberal (ACA = 15) Democratic bloc (cluster 3) voted with the remaining factions more often than not (all the intercluster correlations were positive). Two years later, in the Ninety-sixth Congress, the trend toward conservative coalition voting was even more apparent (Appendix 2, Table 30). Two of the three main clusters were in fact bipartisan alliances of southern Democrats and Republicans (clusters 2 and 3; ACA = 87 and 81, respectively; intercluster correlation = .39). The major liberal Democratic cluster (1, $\underline{N}$ = 10 members, ACA = 11) differed only modestly from the bipartisan blocs (intercluster correlations = -.01 to -.03, respectively). This bipartisan, conservative coalition alignment may reflect conditions peculiar to the Carter presidency and its agenda or the need for liberal Democrats to forge coalitions to pass their legislation. In any case, somewhat ironically perhaps, Commerce Committee voting moved

from pure partisanship toward bipartisan ideological alignment, with the conservative coalition prominently featured.

Finally, the Rules Committee displays an equally variable pattern of voting, though partisanship is the predomi-
nant element throughout the decade. In fact, the changes
that occurred flow exclusively from the fact that in two
Congresses--the Ninety-third and the Ninety-sixth--fewer
than half the members joined any bloc, making the panel an
unstructured voting body. In the other three Congresses,
partisan politics prevailed. Even in the Ninety-second Congress, when conservative southerner William Colmer (Mississippi) chaired Rules, there were more partisan and ideological roll calls than any other variety.[12] Thereafter, these
trends were even more pronounced (Table 2.1).

It is, of course, not surprising that Rules, as an
adjunct of the party leadership (at least under ideal circumstances), acts in a partisan fashion. As expected on a
high-prestige, influential panel characterized by low turnover, there was a reasonably consistent factional structure
in the committee throughout the 1970s (Appendix 2, Tables
36-40): With the exception of the Ninety-sixth Congress,
there was always a cluster of conservative Republicans opposed to at least one group of Democrats, of varying degrees
of liberalism but always more progressive than the Republican faction.[13] A succession of northern liberal chairmen
and the new authority granted to the Speaker to nominate
Democrats (used to appoint a series of liberals) clearly
contributed to increased Democratic cohesion in Rules. On
the other hand, the emergence of separate, though supportive,
Democratic factions in the two most recent Congresses warns
that the committee may not be completely or permanently
yoked to the party leadership. Overall, however, these patterns support Oppenheimer's (1977) description of Rules as
"an arm of the leadership in a decentralized House."[14]

In sum, although partisan configurations are the most
common characteristic of House committee voting, they do not
appear as frequently as might be expected; bipartisan and
unstructured patterns are also often in evidence in these
ten committees. In addition, the lines of cleavage are not
necessarily permanent. Only three committees adhered to the
same pattern during the 1970s; the remaining seven experienced at least one shift from one alignment pattern to

another and four displayed at least two changes. Multiple causes—member turnover, agenda change that raised new issues to prominence, reform that altered structures and process in committee and in the parent House, and external events—seem to have contributed to variation over time in committee roll call voting. Conversely, stability in membership and continuing concern with a fundamental set of controversial policy questions seem to condition committees to create and maintain less mutable lines of cleavage. In any case, these committees cannot be easily categorized; they reveal an enormous variation in the ways their members line up when the roll is called.

RESULTS: COMMITTEE CLEAVAGE AND COMMITTEE PERFORMANCE

Diverse factional patterns in committee, although intrinsically interesting, take on additional and more important meaning to the extent that they contribute to an understanding of congressional committee politics. Even a preliminary assessment of this question is complicated: Changes in the external environment of the committees (events), member turnover, and congressional reform in general may affect different committees in different ways (Ornstein and Rohde 1977; Rohde and Shepsle 1978). Committee voting alignments may not be the only influence on committee performance. Still, despite these complexities, we anticipate at least one link between committee cleavage and congressional behavior, specifically between factionalism and floor success. We test this expectation with aggregate data and with an examination of individual committees.

Our hypothesis is simple: Bipartisan committees should enjoy greater floor success than partisan panels. The logic underlying this proposition is equally simple. Bipartisan committees are integrated committees; they tend, more than panels rent with factionalism, to take their legislation to the full House without significant dissent. If the members of the committee with jurisdiction, presumably the relevant experts on the issues raised, agree on the wisdom of particular amendments and acceptance of the bill, opponents will be less likely to mount persuasive arguments against specific provisions or the legislation itself. Other studies have

found that unified committees succceed disproportionately on
the floor (Dyson and Soule 1970; Matthews and Stimson 1975;
Fleisher and Bond 1983), and we predict a similar result for
these ten committees.[15] Unstructured committees should fall
somewhere between the extremes. The absence of clear alignments on committee votes should provide no precise signal
for nonmembers on the floor, leading to an indeterminant or
intermediate position for the more fluid panels.

Aggregate data support these expectations. Table 2.5
lists 11 cases (by committee and Congress) of bipartisan
factionalism. These committees were sustained on the floor
on 91 percent of the 367 votes on amendments and bills that
their recommendations presented to the full chamber. The
comparable figures for unstructured and partisan committees
were 89 and 87 percent (of 628 and 1,279 votes), respectively.[16] Moreover, student's t-test for differences of
means shows that the bipartisan-partisan difference is statistically significant, $t = -3.02$, $p < .03$.[17] In short,
although all committees do well on the floor, the bipartisan
committees, by minimizing their opponents' opportunities, do
a bit better than other factional types.

Data for individual committees lend modest additional
support to the notion that patterns of committee cleavage
influence floor success. When a committee shifts from
lesser to greater partisanship, our hypothesis predicts that
its rate of floor success should decline. Conversely, when
bipartisanship increases, so should floor success. These
relationships should be especially clear when the shift from
one Congress to the next is great; that is, when a committee
is a bipartisan panel in one session but a partisan battleground in the next, its proportion of floor wins should decline noticeably. Overall, there are twelve instances in
which changes of these types took place (Table 2.6), and
seven (58 percent) are consistent with our expectations.
To cite a single example, between the Ninety-third and
Ninety-fourth Congresses Commerce Committee voting moved
from an unstructured to a partisan cleavage, and its floor
triumphs declined, as predicted, by 6 percent (Table 2.6).

The seven successful predictions include clear cases of
major change, from bipartisan to partisan cleavage, between
Congresses. In Government Operations, for example, Chet
Holifield retired at the end of the Ninety-third Congress,

TABLE 2.6

Committee Cleavage and Committee Performance

Committee and Congress	Cleavage Category	Floor Success	
		(%)	(N)
Agriculture			
92	Partisan	85	27
93	Unstructured	77	44
94	Unstructured	80	35
95	Unstructured	91	43
96	Partisan	85	20
Armed Services			
92	Bipartisan	100	36
93	Bipartisan	91	34
94	Bipartisan	86	36
95	Bipartisan	94	31
96	Bipartisan	94	32
Banking			
92	Unstructured	81	31
93	Unstructured	85	54
94	Unstructured	89	37
95	Unstructured	86	51
96	Partisan	87	52
Budget			
94	Partisan	100	2
95	Partisan	88	8
96	Partisan	93	56
Education and Labor			
92	Partisan	71	73
93	Partisan	88	93
94	Partisan	89	46
95	Partisan	81	90
96	Partisan	80	20

| | | Floor Success | |
Committee and Congress	Cleavage Category	(%)	($\underline{N}$)
Government Operations			
92	Bipartisan	100	8
93	Bipartisan	92	25
94	Partisan	77	22
95	Unstructured	91	22
96	Partisan	85	46
Commerce			
92	Partisan	91	35
93	Unstructured	91	97
94	Partisan	84	105
95	Bipartisan	84	38
96	Bipartisan	88	80
Post Office			
92	Unstructured	100	9
93	(Unclassified)	--	--
94	Partisan	72	36
95	Partisan	93	54
96	Partisan	100	17
Rules			
92	Partisan	89	46
93	Unstructured	91	101
94	Partisan	97	87
95	Partisan	96	143
96	Unstructured	94	108
Ways and Means			
92	Bipartisan	96	24
93	Bipartisan	96	23
94	Partisan	83	78
95	Partisan	80	65
96	Partisan	90	58

Note: The calculation of floor success is described in Appendix 1.

and Jack Brooks succeeded him as chairman. Under Brooks, the committee divided along partisan lines; under Holifield, it had been a consensual panel. In the Ninety-fourth Congress the committee's floor success rate fell by 15 percent (from 92 to 77 percent). Similarly, when Al Ullman replaced Wilbur Mills in the Ways and Means chair, at the outset of the Ninety-fourth Congress, committee bipartisanship gave way to partisan factionalism, with floor success dropping from 96 to 83 percent. A third case, Commerce between the Ninety-fourth and Ninety-fifth Congresses, is more problematic. In this instance, the shift was reversed, from a partisan voting alignment to the conservative coalition form of bipartisanship. The latter, as noted, may be a special case, reflecting an ideological alliance of conservative Republicans and southern Democrats, and may not indicate any consensus among committee members. In Commerce, in any event, the move to bipartisanship saw a small, 1 percent, decline (rather than the predicted increase) in committee floor victories.

In short, aggregate and individual committee data, although hardly overwhelming, point to a modest but positive link between factionalism and committee floor success. Where committee norms and decision-making structures minimize partisanship, the committee is more likely to see the full chamber adopt its recommendations. Where partisan feelings flare up, by contrast, the committee's disagreements will be visible to all, and nonmembers who reject panel proposals may feel more confident in opposing them. The result is a lower success rate for the partisan majority of the committee.

CONCLUSION: COMMITTEE CLEAVAGE AND COMMITTEE POLITICS

This broad sketch of the aggregate patterns of committee cleavage and the effect of factional structure on committee floor success suggests some general conclusions about committee politics in Congress. First, and most obvious, voting alignments in committee are complex and variable, reflecting the numerous pressures, from both inside and outside the legislature, that play on individual members. Consideration of the full membership of each panel reveals

that frequently many legislators remain unattached to any
bloc, producing an unstructured, or fluid, voting pattern
at times on some committees. Those clusters that do appear,
moreover, although interpretable, vary widely in size and
composition. Our analysis, using different methods and
assessing a different time period, reinforces Fenno's (1973;
see also Parker and Parker 1979) insight that there is wide
divergence in patterns of committee decision making.

Specifically, we find numerous examples of partisan,
bipartisan, and unstructured roll call voting in these ten
House committees. Our expectation, derived from the volumi-
nous literature on floor voting, was that partisan divisions
would predominate in committee as well. Whereas, in fact,
partisan conflict was the most common pattern, only half
the cases fell into this category. The regular appearance
of bipartisan and unstructured alignments indicates that in
committee--perhaps because even after the reform movement
of the 1970s opened panel proceedings to public scrutiny,
less attention focuses there--members feel freer to follow
committee rather than party norms, to respond to environmental forces, or to pursue their own goals or ideologies.
This leads to a greater frequency of bipartisan and unstructured roll call voting than floor balloting would lead one
to predict. Overall, four committees--Budget, Education
and Labor, Post Office, and Rules--seemed fundamentally
partisan, though the latter two were occasionally in the
unstructured category. Armed Services was consistently a
bipartisan panel, and Agriculture and Banking can safely
be typed as unstructured. The final three committees reveal
major change in voting patterns. Two, Government Operations
and Ways and Means, moved from bipartisan to partisan alignments; Commerce evolved in the reverse direction, becoming
a bipartisan body (of the conservative coalition variety)
by the end of the 1970s.

These developments underscore an important point: the
value of longitudinal concern with committee change. Over
a ten-year span House panels show both constancy and change,
some modest, some dramatic. These alternations suggest a
need to treat individual Congresses individually; from one
Congress to the next, a committee may or may not adhere to
a given voting pattern. Some, Armed Services, Budget, and
Education and Labor, for instance, look the same at the end

of the decade as they had at the beginning. Others, however, have evolved over the period: Banking, Post Office,
and Ways and Means shifted once between 1971 and 1980; each
was by the latter date a partisan committee. And Agriculture, Government Operations, Commerce, and Rules revealed
even more fluid voting structures, and here too, with the
exception of Commerce, the shift was toward partisanship.
In short, our analysis argues persuasively that although
tendencies may be visible, it is risky to generalize about
congressional committee voting patterns. Committee cleavage
is best understood on a committee-by-committee, Congress-
by-Congress basis.

Several factors help, at least speculatively, to account for these variations in committee conflict and consensus. Most broadly, the context of American national politics altered; Vietnam, Watergate, the Carter presidency,
especially as the 1980 presidential election approached--
all seem to have heightened partisan feelings. In the
Ninety-fifth Congress (1979-80) seven of the ten committees
voted along partisan lines, and another--Commerce--was split
into ideological (the conservative coalition) camps. The
election of Ronald Reagan seems to have done little to reduce these partisan tensions, but perhaps a "centerist,"
post-Reagan administration of either party will revive an
"era of good feeling" and re-create the conditions for more
numerous committee bipartisan alliances.

Members' goals supplemented by selective recruitment
practices also contribute to variability in committee voting
cleavage. Ideologues--liberal Democrats and conservative
Republicans--find Education and Labor an attractive assignment. Hawks supportive of a strong national defense and
eager to dispense military "pork" flock to Armed Services.
Like-minded members sustain the ongoing voting alignments--
partisan in the case of Education and Labor, bipartisan in
Armed Services. Moreover, once on these panels, members
tend to retain their assignments; both these most stable
committees experienced lower than average personnel turnover
during the 1970s. In addition, the Budget and Rules Committees, both basically consistent and partisan panels, operate
in similar fashion. Their membership reflects clearly the
involvement of the party leadership in the assignment process; in each instance, the leaders seek to place ideologi-

cally sound party loyalists on the committee. Chamber procedures mandate that membership on Budget must rotate (though
the length of permissible service has been extended), but
turnover on Rules is low. Thus voting stability appears to
reflect selective assignment that overrepresents those who
"fit in," who accept the basic premises that characterize
committee outlooks, and continued service that keeps such
individuals on the panel.

Committee agendas also contribute to voting variation.
Where issues or missions persist, committee roll call configurations also seem to endure. Armed Services, Education
and Labor, and Budget fought over persistent sets of policy
issues; Rules performed its basic purpose of facilitating
Democratic legislation. In short, stability in membership,
members' outlooks, and agenda combine to create conditions
conducive to committee constancy in voting cleavage.

When such stabilizing conditions are weak or absent,
by contrast, committee factionalism seems less persistent.
High member turnover may bring new perspectives to a committee and, in turn, mandate new decision-making strategies
and factional alliances. Such turnover may occur in policy
or reelection committees, like Agriculture, Banking, or Commerce, where party leaders are less likely to invest scarce
political resources to manage the assignment process. In
the absence of leadership intervention, members will be
freer to obtain congenial assignments; indeed, leaders may
seek to earn their goodwill by accommodating their assignment preferences as much as possible (Shepsle 1978; Bullock
1979). In any case, turnover and diverse member goals and
outlooks seem likely to lead to more variable voting cleavage
in committee.

Changing agendas may produce similar results. Broad
but not necessarily recurrent policy concerns will serve to
alter voting patterns. In Banking or Commerce, for example,
different portions of the committee's jurisdiction may rise
to prominence in successive Congresses, and factionalism
may shift in consequence (Owens 1979, 1980). Agriculture
Committee alignments seem different in years when major farm
legislation comes before the panel. New issues may have a
comparable impact. The energy question may have contributed
to the shift to partisan roll call configurations on Ways
and Means in the mid-1970s. When Rules began to devote

greater attention to substantive facets of its domain
(Oppenheimer 1981), its relatively clear-cut partisanship
gave way to less structured voting. What committees consider, in sum, appears to shape members' voting responses.

Finally, reform and change may undercut the ways committees conduct their business and lead to new bloc patterns. Ways and Means, for instance, bore the brunt of the
reform impulse (see Chapter 4), and the vast array of en-
forced changes seems certain to have contributed to the decline of panel bipartisan consensus. So, too, in all likelihood, did Al Ullman's succession to the committee chair.
Likewise, a new chairman of Government Operations coincided
with increased partisan voting in the committee. When
structures and processes change, the forces that play on
committee members will also shift and induce variation in
the ways that panelists cast their votes.

Overall, comparative analysis of committee voting
cleavage reveals a mix of continuity and change in committee
politics. Constancy in membership and member goals, reflecting stability in environmental constraints, and in the
issues that a committee confronts seems to create relatively fixed voting patterns. Where the same members confront the same issues repeatedly, they develop characteristic ways to cope and cast their votes consistently. Interestingly, the content of these constancies seems less significant than the fact that they develop. That is, voting
continuity depends less on any particular set of member motivations or committee characteristics than on the persistence of those that do exist. Not all policy-oriented
committees display stable voting alignments, but those that
confront a set agenda seem most likely to do so. Not all
low turnover committees retain a basic bloc structure, but
membership stability, other things being equal, seems to
contribute to enduring patterns of roll call cleavage. Stability in predisposing conditions, whatever the specifics
of those conditions, seems to produce stability in subsequent
performance.

All this matters, of course, because voting factionalism seems related to committee behavior. The way committee
members line up on roll calls has some effect on the fate
of the bills on which they cast ballots. Specifically,
voting alignments are at least modestly associated with

committee floor success: Bipartisan committees, which back
their bills with greater unity than partisan panels, see
more of their legislation survive the trials and tribula-
tions of floor consideration. To know something about conflict and consensus within committee will provide some insight into the broader congressional process.

Committee factionalism is not the only committee attribute that may shape panel performance. Although members
have voting equality in committee, there remain other forces
at work that may enhance the influence of individual committee members. One such factor is leadership: Particular
leaders, chairpersons, or ranking minority members may be
especially well placed to put their own distinctive stamp on
committee politics. By dint of expertise or personality,
the formal leaders may steer the panel in directions they
wish it to move. Conversely, however, the same forces that
shape and constrain voting blocs may give form to the sorts
of behavior leaders display, limiting their ability to exert
more than marginal authority within the bodies they osten-
sibly lead. In the next chapter we turn to an exploration
of leadership in the ten committees.

NOTES

1. Davidson and Oleszek put the same proposition
bluntly: "Party affiliation remains the strongest single
correlate of members' voting decisions" (1981, p. 383). So
do Turner and Schneier: ". . . party appears to be more
influential than any other pressure on Congress: (1970,
p. 39).

2. Methodologically, most studies of the conservative
coalition specify that the alliance exists when majorities
of the voting southern Democrats and Republicans combine to
oppose a majority of the nonsouthern Democrats. Similarly,
partisan cleavage occurs when majorities of all Republicans
and all Democrats oppose each other. See Appendix 1 and,
inter alia, Brady and Bullock (1981) and Manley (1973).

3. If this scheme, which closely follows Fenno's
(1973) approach, provides our basic theoretical underpin-
ning, our more immediate inspiration for this chapter comes
from Glenn and Suzanne Parker's pioneering paper (1979) on

factions in committees, the first effort to supplement
participant-observational studies with the hard data that
committee roll calls provide. Because we have a broader
data base, we can extend the Parkers' work in two significant ways. First, we have roll call data for five Congresses; this enables us to include all (or nearly all)
members of each committee in our analysis and consequently
to give a fuller picture of the conflict (or consensus)
within each panel. The Parkers, by contrast, limited their
analysis largely to "holdover" members, those who served in
both the Ninety-third and Ninety-fourth Congresses (1979,
table 2, p. 87). Thus, for instance, they report data on
only 18 of the more than 50 members who sat on the House
Agriculture Committee during those two Congresses; in doing
so, they may have found greater voting structure, clearer
cleavages, on the committee than actually existed. Second,
treating each Congress separately (the Parkers merged data
from different Congresses), we are able to chart compara-
tively change across a period of extensive "reform" and
alteration in Congress. We confront this issue directly in
Chapter 4.

4. The full set of tables, one for each committee in
each Congress, appears in Appendix 2. Examples appear below
to illustrate our identification of the possible patterns
of committee cleavage.

5. All of the specified indicators do not always fall
precisely within the ranges we specify. Our assignment of
committees to a particular factional pattern reflects our
considered judgment about the weight of the evidence. The
data on roll call types and committee integration appear in
Table 2.1; the cluster analysis, including the intercluster
correlations, is in Appendix 2. We are quite confident that
our assignments are the correct ones.

6. This outlook seems to have moderated somewhat in
the 1980s. With Ronald Reagan pushing for enormous increases
in military spending in a period with record federal budget
deficits impending--in the vicinity of $200 billion an-
nually--the committee seems prepared to take a harder, more
critical look at Pentagon procurement requests.

7. Changes in leadership seem not to have affected
the emergence of partisan conflict in Post Office. The
committee, as a low-prestige, high-turnover panel, changed

chairmen in the Ninety-fourth and successive Congresses:
David Henderson (North Carolina) succeeded Thaddeus Dulski
(New York) in the Ninety-fourth Congress, Robert Nix (Penn-
sylvania) took the chair in 1977, and James Hanley (New
York) occupied the top spot two years later.

8. See Chapter 1. We take up the effects of change
and reform on Ways and Means in detail in Chapter 4.

9. We have classified Agriculture in the Ninety-
second Congress as a partisan panel, but it was not strongly
so. About one third of the committee votes were bipartisan;
committee integration was moderate (.38); and beyond the one
large Democratic faction, there were numerous, relatively
small factions. Thus the shift from partisan to unstructured alignment was not dramatic.

10. There was an ideological undercurrent beneath the
bipartisan surface in Commerce in these early Congresses.
The blocs that crossed party lines found Democrats and
moderate-to-liberal Republicans making common cause against
the more conservative elements on the committee. Thus the
transformation to partisan cleavage had its roots in this
period.

11. The one cluster that formed across party lines
during the early 1970s (cluster 6, Ninety-second Congress;
see Appendix 2, Table 26) was perhaps an anomaly, containing
two midwestern Republicans and Oklahoma Democrat John Jarman,
soon to convert to the GOP.

12. There was a strong conservative coalition component to Rules voting in the Ninety-second Congress. Bipartisan and coalition roll calls were more numerous than at
any other time during the decade, and Colmer belonged to a
southern doublet (with William Anderson of Tennessee) that
was closer to the Republican bloc than to either of the two
remaining Democratic clusters (see Table 2.1 and Appendix 2,
Table 36).

13. Interestingly, the one Republican moderate, John
Anderson (Illinois), later to launch an independent campaign
for the presidency after failing to find much support in
Republican presidential primaries, never joined the Republican faction in Rules. In the Ninety-sixth Congress, as
he undertook his campaign for president, Anderson did not
participate in 60 percent of Rules roll calls.

14. The increasing fragmentation of Rules Democrats
in the Ninety-fifth and Ninety-sixth Congresses may reflect
in part the greater attention to substantive as opposed to
procedural matters that came to characterize the committee.
These matters (for example, the content rather than the
application of House rules of procedure) seem more likely to
divide the members in a way that crafting motions to get
party programs to the floor under optimum conditions does
not (see Oppenheimer 1981).

15. Our methods differ from these other studies in
one important respect: We use committee roll calls rather
than floor votes to establish the committee's position (see
Appendix 1). Our measure of floor success includes votes
on amendments and on final passage.

16. These are small differences, to be sure, but the
range of variation across committees is also small. Our
data for the 1970s (see Table 3.5) show only four (of 46)
instances of committees that win fewer than eight of ten floor
votes, and look very much like Dyson and Soule's (1970,
tables 1 and 4) for the decade 1955-64. Even the least successful committees can count on seeing most of their legislation enacted, but within these circumstances bipartisan
committees do better than the other types.

17. In addition, the difference between the floor
success rates of bipartisan and unstructured committees was
statistically significant: $t = 1.92$, $p < .05$. The difference between partisan and unstructured committees, however, although in the right direction, did not reach statistical significance.

3
Congressional
Committee Leadership

"Leadership," James MacGregor Burns writes, "is one of
the most observed and least understood phenomena on earth"
(1978, p. 2). Nowhere is this more the case than with respect to the U.S. Congress in general and congressional committees in particular. According to the current conventional
wisdom, the latter and their subcommittees are the preeminent
legislative decision makers; yet very little is known about
the ways that committee leaders operate and the effects that
their actions generate. There are some insightful case studies of particular legislative leaders (for example, Manley
1970, chap. 4, on Wilbur Mills), but only a few systematic,
comparative analyses of committee leadership. We seek to
begin to fill this vacuum.

In the congressional context at least, leadership is a
reciprocal relationship between the leader(s) and the followers. The former presumably initiates the contacts, seeking to impel, induce, cajole, persuade, beg, influence, force,
or otherwise move the latter to behave in ways that the leader desires. The relationship is reciprocal because leaders
inevitably lack the ability to compel compliance from their
followers; their leadership efforts must, therefore, involve
consideration of what the followers will accept. The famous
"law of anticipated reactions" applies as leaders endeavor
to ask for things for which they have some reasonable expectation, given the followers' beliefs and independence, of
being able to achieve. In other words, congressional committee leadership is, to use Burns's term, "transactional,"
involving an exchange of value designed to enable both leaders and followers to gain some acceptable result.[1]

Assessing committee leadership is all the more difficult
because, as we have noted (see Chapters 1 and 2), committees
vary considerably along a number of dimensions, including
internal partisan cleavage. Because they differ, committees
impose divergent limits on their members, including their
ostensible leaders.[2] Chairpersons thus are constrained by
the particular committee setting in which they must act:
"Whatever [their] personal characteristics, temperamental
or ideological, this context puts limits on the kind of behavior [they] can engage in and still retain . . . leadership, and it sets forth positive guidelines for . . . success
and effectiveness inside the Committee" (Fenno 1973, p. 133).[3]
Ranking minority members should act within similarly constraining contexts.

Theoretically, this suggests once again the need to investigate two specific linkages. First, are there identifiable predisposing conditions--members' motives, the committee's environment, the panel's decision rules--that incline
committees to adopt particular leadership styles? For example, both Manley and Fenno convincingly demonstrate that the
House Ways and Means Committee under Wilbur Mills was a bipartisan-consensual panel. Members of Ways and Means desired influence in the House; they responded to the full
chamber itself, as the central element in their environment;
and in consequence they endeavored to write legislation that
would pass. Mills was central to this process: Under his
leadership the committee minimized divisive partisanship,
seeking to maximize unity in support of its bills. Bipartisan, consensus-building leadership was basic to committee
operations. More generally, then, we want to know to what
extent committee attributes are associated with committee
leadership patterns.

The second theoretically pertinent link flows directly
from the first. If there exist clear patterns of committee
leadership, are there equally clear consequences for committee performance associated with particular patterns? Ways
and Means during Mills's tenure is equally instructive here.
The committee's mode of doing business, its bipartisan-consensual style, was manifest in its conduct of business in
full committee rather than in an extensive set of subcommittees, in low levels of partisan controversy, in relatively
high committee integration, and in the substantial success

of its proposals on the House floor (Fenno 1973; Manley 1970).
Here, too, we ask whether other committees with particular
leadership patterns perform in distinctive ways.

A word of caution is in order at this point: Problems
of causality are rife in raising these two concerns. It is
virtually impossible, given the reciprocal character of the
leader-follower relationship in the congressional context,
to specify the direction in which influence flows. Was Ways
and Means a bipartisan body as a result of Wilbur Mills's
bipartisan leadership style, or was Mills a consensual leader
to conform to committee norms and practices? Similarly, was
Ways and Means relatively nonpartisan and well integrated
because it followed its chairman's lead, or was he a consensual leader to conform to the panel's minimal partisanship
and high cohesion?

We can note only that chairpersons and ranking minority
members are both leaders and followers. At the very least,
they lead within limits; they may try to move their committee colleagues in particular directions, but they may have
to adapt their own behavior to those colleagues' expectations. A full theoretical accounting of committee leadership would need to explain both the causes and consequences
of panel leadership patterns. In this chapter we attempt to
unravel some aspects of this theoretical puzzle. In the
previous chapter we identified patterns of committee factionalism; here we explore the place of leaders in the overall structure of committee voting, chart the changes in leadership behavior that occur over time, and assess the relationship of leadership posture to committee performance.

PATTERNS OF COMMITTEE LEADERSHIP

Our first question relates to the place of the formal
committee leaders--the chairman[4] and the ranking minority
member--in the factional structure of each committee. We
want to know whether they vote with major factions in committee or with major partisan, regional, or ideological
groupings on the panel. Drawing on studies of political parties, we anticipate three possible patterns of committee
leader behavior.

1. The extremity pattern: One leadership strategy is
to mobilize a dominant majority party faction. Leaders will,
according to this view, "tend to occupy the extreme ends of
the ideological continuum . . ." (Patterson 1963, p. 404;
see also MacRae 1956). In the congressional setting, with
Democratic majorities, the extremity hypothesis predicts
that the chairperson will rally liberal Democrats to his
cause. He should seek to assemble a majority coalition that
draws heavily on the liberal wing of his own party. Specifically, we should find the chair a member of the major voting cluster in his own party, closely aligned with any other
factions ideologically similar to the major one, and generally sympathetic to all members who share his party and ideological perspectives. Conversely, the extremity position
predicts that the chair should display only moderate agreement with any nonextreme voting blocs within his own party
and low agreement with the ranking minority member, members
of ideologically opposed voting clusters, the opposition party generally, and conservatives. Similarly, the ranking
minority member should stand with the groups at the extreme
pole within the Republican party.

2. The partisan-middleman pattern: Truman's (1959,
chap. 6) analysis of party leaders suggests a second pattern
of committee leadership: Leaders, by adopting a centerist
stance within their own parties, may seek to generate party
cohesion. By holding to the middle ground, they will unify
their own partisans to the maximum extent (for corroborative
evidence, see MacRae 1958). In our terms, the middleman may
not belong to any identifiable voting faction in the committee; if he does, he will nevertheless seek to appeal to other
partisan blocs and, indeed, to all his partisan colleagues.
The middleman is likely to eschew ideological voting and
should seek to bridge any intraparty ideological divisions.
Similarly, because the middleman tactic remains basically
partisan, the committee chair who pursues it is likely to
disagree often with the ranking minority member, opposition
representatives (as individuals and in factions), and dis-
similar ideologues. A middleman ranking minority member
should, of course, demonstrate a comparable voting posture
with his party.

3. The bipartisan-consensual pattern: A third possibility (Fenno 1973, chap. 4) is leadership through consensus.

Here the chairperson will seek to generate widespread support for committee positions, drawing votes from wherever they are available. In such circumstances, the chair may belong to a broad bipartisan faction or may avoid identification with any single bloc, preferring to work with all members. In addition, he should avoid strong commitment to any ideological element within the committee. This pattern may well reveal substantial agreement between the chair and the ranking member, who should be similarly inclined to cooperate with all groups of committee members.

In searching for the existence of these leadership patterns, we cannot resolve the problem of causality. Roll call data do not permit us to say whether leader behavior creates or reflects a committee's ways of conducting business. We must note, however, that in our data there is a clear relationship between leadership style[5] and committee liberalism. Partisan-extremist chairpersons presided over panels in which their Democratic majorities averaged 20.7 on the American for Constitutional Action scale (see Appendix 1); Democrats on committees with partisan-middleman and bipartisan leadership were less liberal, averaging 27.9 and 38.3, respectively, on the ACA measure. All we can say is that leadership and member preference are related; we do not pretend to be able to specify cause and effect clearly. Nonetheless, in the absence of any systematic, comparative evidence about leadership styles, we believe that it is valuable, as a first step, simply to describe the extent to which chairmen vote with various rank-and-file elements of their committees. In other words, regardless of the direction of influence, it is important to discover the ways that committee leaders relate to committee cleavages.

Each leadership pattern suggests a distinctive array of interagreement scores. The extremity view predicts strong (interagreement scores that approach or exceed .40) agreement between the leader and the groups that support him; it predicts low (generally negative) agreement between the leader and opposition elements on the committee. Voting in the House Education and Labor Committee in the Ninety-second Congress (Table 3.1) illustrates clearly the extremity pattern. The panel chair, Carl Perkins (D.-Ky.), belonged (IA = .50) to a 13-member (ACA = 11) liberal[6] Democratic bloc (cluster 1).

TABLE 3.1

Extremity Structure, House Education and Labor Committee, 92nd Congress

Representatives	Party	State	Clusters		
			1	2	3
Perkins, C.	D (Ch.)	Kentucky	.50		
Thompson, F.	D	New Jersey	.46		
Dent, J.	D	Pennsylvania	.54		
Daniels, D.	D	New Jersey	.46		
Brademas, J.	D	Indiana	.45		
Hawkins, A.	D	California	.59		
Scheuer, J.	D	New York	.52		
Meeds, L.	D	Washington	.47		
Burton, P.	D	California	.47		
Clay, W.	D	Missouri	.55		
Chisholm, S.	D	New York	.60		
Grasso, E.	D	Connecticut	.48		
Badillo, H.	D	New York	.48		
Quie, A.	R (RMM)	Minnesota		.59	
Erlenborn, J.	R	Illinois		.59	
Esch, M.	R	Michigan		.54	
Steiger, W.	R	Wisconsin		.42	
Landgrebe, E.	R	Indiana		.50	
Hansen, O.	R	Idaho		.49	
Ruth, E.	R	North Carolina		.49	
Forsythe, E.	R	New Jersey		.58	
Veysey, V.	R	California		.57	
Kemp, J.	R	New York		.59	
Peyser, P.	R	New York		.42	

Pucinski, R.	D	Illinois	.36
O'Hara, J.	D	Michigan	.49
Ford, W.	D	Michigan	.46
Green, E.	D	Oregon	
Mink, P.	D	Hawaii	
Gaydos, J.	D	Pennsylvania	
Biaggi, M.	D	New York	
Hicks, L.	D	Massachusetts	
Mazzoli, R.	D	Kentucky	
Bell, A.	R	California	
Dellenback, J.	R	Oregon	
Ashbrook, J.	R	Ohio*	
Eshleman, E.	R	Pennsylvania*	
Reid, C.	R	Illinois*	

Roll Calls = 99

*Member participated in less than 60 percent of the votes.

(Average) Voting Correlation Between Leaders and Voting Clusters:

	1	2	3
Party identification (percent Democrat)	100	00	100
ACA	11	68	14
Chairman	.50	-.26	.32
Ranking minority member	-.37	.59	-.35

(Average) Voting Correlation Between Leaders and Party and Ideological Groups:

	Dem	Rep	Lib	Con	CC	N Dem
Chairman	.42	-.24	.31	-.18	-.20	.43
Ranking minority member	-.31	.56	-.17	.47	.45	-.32

Voting correlation of chairman and ranking minority member = -.38.

He was associated (IA = .32) with a slightly more moderate (ACA = 14) three-member group of Democrats (cluster 3). His relations with potentially supportive factions on Education and Labor were cordial; his interagreement scores with all Democrats, liberals, and northern Democrats were .42, .31, and .43, respectively. Conversely, Perkins disagreed (IA = -.26) regularly with the 11-member conservative (ACA = 68) Republican bloc (cluster 2), with all Republicans (IA = -.24), conservatives (IA = -.18), the conservative coalition (IA = -.20), and Albert Quie (R.-Minn.), the ranking minority member (IA = -.38). In short, Perkins and the liberal Democrats fought the conservative GOP contingent in an Education and Labor committee polarized along partisan-ideological lines.

Albert Quie, the ranking Republican, was even further toward the extreme of his party during the Ninety-second Congress. He voted consistently (IA = .59) with the 11-member bloc of conservative (ACA = 68) Republicans and against (IA = -.37 and -.35) the two Democratic clusters (1 and 3). Quie supported all Republicans (IA = .56), all conservatives (IA = .47), and the conservative coalition (IA = .45); he regularly opposed all Democrats (IA = -.31), northern Democrats (IA = -.32), liberals (IA = -.17), and, as noted, Chairman Perkins (IA = -.38). Education and Labor, in short, was polarized, with extreme factions, internally cohesive, strongly opposed to one another. The committee clearly displays extremity leadership.

Similarly, the partisan-middleman pattern predicts distinctive voting alignments. Because the middleman strategy calls for mobilizing all the chairperson's partisans, the leader should display moderately positive (IA scores of .20 to .35) agreement with all his potential backers and moderately negative (IA scores from -.10 to -.20) with the opposition. In contrast to the extremity pattern, the middleman should be more centrally located within his own party and less ardently opposed to the minority members. The House Interstate and Foreign Commerce Committee in the Ninety-fourth Congress presents a typical picture of the middleman pattern (Table 3.2). Harley Staggers (D.-W.Va.), the chair, joined a small (N = 3), moderately liberal Democratic bloc (cluster 3). He maintained positive relations with a large liberal Democratic faction (cluster 2) and with a smaller, more moderate group (cluster 4) of fellow partisans. In addition, he voted regularly with all Democrats, liberals, and northern Democrats. Simultaneously he opposed the nine-member (cluster 1) conservative Republican bloc and voted against all Republicans, conservatives, the conservative coalition, and the ranking minority member--Samuel Devine (Ohio)--more often than not. In sum, Staggers was a typical middleman: centrally placed in his own party and regularly but moderately opposed to the minority.

Here, too, the ranking Republican's posture mirrored that of the committee chair. Samuel Devine joined the large conservative GOP faction; he supported all Republicans, conservatives, and the conservative coalition regularly. In contrast, he voted against each of the three Democratic clusters, all Democrats, northern Democrats, and the chairman more often than not. Like Staggers, but across the aisle, Devine was strategically positioned in the middle of his party, voting in concert with all Republican elements on Commerce and consistently but moderately against the Democrats.

Finally, the bipartisan-consensual pattern presents a contrasting picture, which the Government Operations Committee in the Ninety-second Congress typifies (Table 3.3). The committee chair, Chet Holifield (D.-Calif.), displayed precisely the predicted nonpartisan posture: moderate, positive (IA = .10 to .30) levels of agreement with all committee groupings on both sides of the aisle. Specifically, he was a member of a large bipartisan (three Democrats and nine Republicans) moderate cluster (1). In addition, he regularly voted with a second bipartisan (six Democrats and two Republicans) but more liberal faction (cluster 3). Holifield also agreed more often than not with the major moderate Democratic faction (cluster 2), with a conservative Republican pair (cluster 4), and with a three-person liberal Democratic group (cluster 6).[7] Moreover, he sided frequently with each partisan and ideological grouping within the committee (see Appendix 3), with interagreement scores ranging from .24 to .52. And, characteristic of bipartisan harmony, Holifield and Florence Dwyer (R.-N.J.), the ranking minority member, voted together on each Government Operations roll call (IA = 1.0). Overall, consensus that crossed party lines prevailed in the committee.

TABLE 3.2

Middleman Structure, House Interstate and Foreign Commerce Committee, 94th Congress

Representative	Party	State	Clusters			
			1	2	3	4
Broyhill, J.	R	North Carolina	.47			
Collins, J.	R	Texas	.46			
McCollister	R	Nebraska	.54			
Carter, T.	R	Kentucky	.41			
Brown, C.	R	Ohio	.57			
Skubitz, J.	R	Kansas	.42			
Define, S.	R (RMM)	Ohio	.45			
Madigan, E.	R	Illinois	.41			
Moorhead, C.	R	California	.47			
Adams, B.	D	Washington		.51		
Metcalfe, R.	D	Illinois		.54		
Moss, J.	D	California		.60		
Eckhardt, B.	D	Texas		.53		
Dingell, J.	D	Michigan		.45		
Scheuer, J.	D	New York		.52		
Ottinger, R.	D	New York		.58		
Waxman, H.	D	California		.44		
Sharp, P.	D	Indiana		.55		
Brodhead, W.	D	Michigan		.59		
Florio, J.	D	New Jersey		.49		
Moffett, T.	D	Connecticut		.55		
Maguire, A.	D	New Jersey		.51		
Staggers, H.	D (Ch.)	West Virginia			.45	
Rogers, P.	D	Florida			.48	
Rooney, F.	D	Pennsylvania			.38	

Symington, J.   D   Missouri   .50
Van Deerlin, L.   D   California   .38
Preyer, R.   D   North Carolina   .44
Wirth, T.   D   Colorado   .42
Carney, C.   D   Ohio
Murphy, J.   D   New York
Satterfied, D.   D   Virginia
Frey, L.   R   Florida
Lent, N.   R   New York
Heinz, J.   R   Pennsylvania
Krueger, R.   D   Texas
Hefner, W.   D   North Carolina
Santini, J.   D   Nevada

Roll Calls = 105

(Average) Voting Correlation Between Leaders and Voting Clusters:

	1	2	3	4
Party Identification (percent Democrat)	00	100	100	100
ACA	84	07	29	20
Chairman	-.25	.27	.45	.25
Ranking minority member	.45	-.27	-.26	-.21

(Average) Voting Correlation Between Leaders and Party and Ideological Groups:

	Dem	Rep	Lib	Con	CC	N Dem
Chairman	.24	-.22	-.26	-.19	-.10	.26
Ranking minority member	-.19	.43	-.20	.36	.24	-.22

Voting correlation of chairman with ranking minority member = -.26.

TABLE 3.3

Bipartisan Structure, House Government Operations Committee, 92nd Congress

Representative	Party	State	Clusters					
			1	2	3	4	5	6
Holifield, C.	D (Ch.)	California	.74					
Garmatz, E.	D	Maryland	.74					
Monagan, J.	D	Connecticut	.74					
Dwyer, F.	R (RMM)	New Jersey	.74					
Horton, F.	R	New York	.74					
Erlenborn, J.	R	Illinois	.81					
Wydler, J.	R	New York	.58					
Brown, C.	R	Ohio	.77					
Buchanan, J.	R	Alabama	.81					
Brown, G.	R	Michigan	.77					
Goldwater, B.	R	California	.63					
Thone, C.	R	Nebraska	.61					
Fountain, L.	D	North Carolina		.65				
Moss, J.	D	California		.66				
Gallager, C.	D	New Jersey		.69				
Randall, W.	D	Missouri		.65				
Wright, J.	D	Texas		.56				
Alexander, B.	D	Arkansas		.52				
Abzug, B.	D	New York		.51				
Fascell, D.	D	Florida			.79			
Reuss, H.	D	Wisconsin			.72			
MacDonald, T.	D	Massachusetts			.72			
Moorhead, W.	D	Pennsylvania			.79			

Name	Party	State	Value
St. Germain, F.	D	Rhode Island	.72
Conyers, J.	D	Michigan	.62
Gude, G.	R	Maryland	.36
McCloskey, P.	R	California	.55
Robinson, K.	R	Virginia	.96
Powell, W.	R	Ohio	.96
Rosenthal, B.	D	New York	.82
Culver, J.	D	Iowa	.82
Brooks, J.	D	Texas	.60
Hicks, F.	D	Washington	.54
Collins, G.	D	Illinois	.65
Jones, R.	D	Alabama	
Fuqua, D.	D	Florida	

Roll calls = 13

(Average) Voting Correlation Between Leaders and Voting Clusters:

	1	2	3	4	5	6
Party Identification (percent Democrat)	25	100	75	00	100	100
ACA	58	38	13	94	9	21
Chairman	.74	.12	.31	.14	-.46	.27
Ranking minority member	.74	.12	.31	.14	-.46	.27

(Average) Voting Correlation Between Leaders and Party and Ideological Groups:

	Dem	Rep	Lib	Con	CC	N Dem
Chairman	.24	.52	.32	.41	.38	.30
Ranking minority member	.28	.48	.32	.41	.35	.35

Voting correlation of chairman with ranking minority member = 1.00.

In sum, we search for the extremity, middleman, and
bipartisan—consensual leadership patterns in the ten House
committees. We explore the frequencies with which each pattern of leadership occurs, for chairs and ranking minority
members. We investigate the attributes—member goals, environmental constraints, levels of turnover, specialization,
and prestige—of the panels in an effort to account for the
emergence of particular leadership styles. We assess the extent to which leadership patterns relate to committee performance, in committee and on the House floor. These analyses should provide a preliminary portrait of the causes,
conditions, and consequences of leadership in congressional
committees.

FINDINGS: CHAIRMEN AS COMMITTEE LEADERS

Empirically, these committees and their chairmen fall
easily into one or another of the three leadership patterns.
Table 3.4, column 2, presents our categorization of each
committee chairperson.[8] In 46 of the 48 cases (nine committees in each of five Congresses and the Budget panel in the
Ninety-fourth through Ninety-sixth), the assignment of the
chairman to extremity, partisan—middleman, or bipartisan,
consensual patterns is relatively straightforward. Indeed,
only a single instance—the Post Office and Civil Service
Committee, under David Henderson (D.-N.C.), in the Ninety-
fourth Congress—did not display one of the hypothesized configurations. The other exception—the Interstate and Foreign Commerce Committee, Ninety-second Congress, under Harley
Staggers—simply reflects the methodological decision to ex-
clude leaders and other committee members with low voting
participation from the analysis (see Appendix 1). Subsequent
discussion deals with the 46 assignable cases.
These data on the committees suggest once again the
rich variety of committee behavioral patterns. Over the
five Congresses numerous examples of each of the specified
leadership postures are evident. Committee chairmen display
extremity (13 instances, 28 percent of the 46 cases), middleman (21 cases, 46 percent), and bipartisan—consensual (12
cases, 26 percent) positions relative to their committee
colleagues. They may create these alignments through lead-

TABLE 3.4

Leadership Styles

Committee and Congress/Ch./RMM	Chairman's Style	RMM's Style
Agriculture		
92 Poage/Belcher	Middleman	(Unclassified)
93 Poage/Wampler[a]	Bipartisan	Bipartisan
94 Foley/Wampler	Middleman	Middleman[b]
95 Foley/Wampler	Middleman	Middleman[b]
96 Foley/Wampler	Middleman	Extremity[b]
Armed Services		
92 Hebert/Arends	Bipartisan	Bipartisan
93 Hebert/Bray	Bipartisan	Bipartisan
94 Price/Wilson	Bipartisan	Bipartisan
95 Price/Wilson	Bipartisan	Bipartisan
96 Price/Wilson	Bipartisan	Bipartisan
Banking		
92 Patman/Widnall	Middleman	Bipartisan
93 Patman/Widnall	Middleman	Bipartisan
94 Reuss/Johnson	Middleman	Middleman
95 Reuss/Stanton	Middleman	Middleman
96 Reuss/Stanton	Middleman	Middleman
Budget		
94 Adams/Latta	Extremity	Extremity[b]
95 Giaimo/Latta	Extremity	Extremity
96 Giaimo/Latta	Middleman	Extremity[b]
Education and Labor		
92 Perkins/Quie	Extremity	Extremity
93 Perkins/Quie	Extremity	Extremity
94 Perkins/Quie	Extremity	Extremity
95 Perkins/Quie	Extremity	Extremity
96 Perkins/Ashbrook	Extremity	Extremity
Government Operations		
92 Holifield/Dwyer	Bipartisan	Bipartisan
93 Holifield/Horton	Bipartisan	Bipartisan
94 Brooks/Horton	Extremity	Extremity
95 Brooks/Horton	Middleman	(Unclassified)
96 Brooks/Horton	Extremity	(Unclassified)

(continued)

Committee and Congress/Ch./RMM	Chairman's Style	RMM's Style
Commerce		
92 Staggers/Springer	--	Middleman
93 Staggers Devine	Middleman	Bipartisan
94 Staggers/Devine	Middleman	Middleman
95 Staggers/Devine	Middleman	Bipartisan
96 Staggers/Devine	Middleman	Bipartisan
Post Office		
92 Dulski/Gross	Bipartisan	Middleman
93 Dulski/Gross	Middleman	Middleman
94 Henderson/Derwinski	(Unclassified)	Middleman
95 Nix/Derwinski	Middleman	Middleman
96 Hanley/Derwinski	Middleman	Extremity
Rules		
92 Colmer/Smith	Bipartisan	Extremity[b]
93 Madden/Martin	Extremity	Middleman
94 Madden/Quillen	Extremity	Extremity
95 Delaney/Quillen	Extremity	Extremity
96 Bolling/Quillen	Middleman	Middleman
Ways and Means		
92 Mills/Byrnes	Bipartisan	Extremity[b]
93 Mills/Schneebeli	Bipartisan	Middleman[b]
94 Ullman/Schneebeli	Middleman	Middleman[b]
95 Ullman/Conable	Middleman	Middleman[b]
96 Ullman/Conable	Extremity	Extremity

[a]Wampler (Virginia) replaced Charles Teague (California) as ranking minority member during the Ninety-third Congress.

[b]In a number of instances the ranking minority member had close connections with the conservative coalition.

ership or they may conform to existing configurations, but in any case they fit clearly into identifiable committee voting alignments.

In addition, these results reveal both the nonrandom distribution of leadership styles and the differential impact of change, intended or otherwise, on individual committees. Four panels--Armed Services, Banking, Education and Labor, and Commerce--displayed constant leadership patterns across the four Congresses. This is not unexpected for the latter two, as their respective chairs, Perkins and Staggers, served throughout the period and seemingly adhered to consistent styles of leadership. But for Armed Services and Banking, change might well have been predicted. In the aftermath of Watergate, the Republicans suffered grievously at the polls in the 1974 midterm elections, and the 75 predominantly liberal freshman Democrats who took seats in the Ninety-fourth Congress contributed mightily to their party Caucus's purge of three senior southern committee chairmen (Hinckley 1976; Parker 1979). This stunning coup, a sharp break with the virtually inviolate seniority norm, claimed Chairmen F. Edward Hebert of Armed Services and Wright Patman of Banking as victims. However, their successors, Melvin Price and Henry Reuss, assumed the same leadership postures-- bipartisan-consensual and middleman, respectively--of their ousted predecessors.

These two cases underscore the reciprocal character of committee leadership. Chairmen do not possess unrestricted influence. Rather, the leadership they exercise must be consistent with their members' goals and the committee's decision-making premises and structures; where these do not change, the chairman may find his opportunity to lead severely constrained.

Two committees show a single change over the 1971-80 period. In each instance a sitting chairperson adapted to changing circumstances--perhaps dissatisfaction with previous results, perhaps in response to new issues--by altering his leadership style. From the outset, partisan political considerations prevailed in the Budget Committee; Democrats sought to channel federal fiscal resources to social and other domestic programs, and Republicans fought fiercely both to hold down overall expenditure levels (and to balance the budget) and to increase the defense share of the smaller budget pie. Not surprisingly, in the Ninety-fourth Congress, the chairman, Brock Adams (D.-Wash.), pursued an extremity style, voting with the liberal Democrats and against the Republicans, mostly conservatives, in a polarized committee. The same pattern prevailed in the 95th Congress when Robert Giaimo succeeded to the chair.

By 1979, however, the new budgetary process had come increasingly under fire. Members of Congress at both poles of the ideological spectrum were disappointed in their efforts to reshape national spending priorities and they tended to blame the process for their failure. In addition, the phenomenal growth of budget deficits stimulated the use of the controversial reconcilition procedure, which in effect permitted the Budget Committee to constrain the choices of the authorizing panels, and this development made Budget the target of considerable hostility.[9] In consequence, perhaps seeing a need to protect the budget process itself, Giaimo, in the Ninety-sixth Congress, shifted ground, switching to a middleman stance. Presumably, he perceived that at least a more moderate, less ideological committee posture would increase the acceptability of the panel's budget resolutions.[10] Whether this shift, which was not matched on the Republican side of the aisle, will persist is, of course, a matter of conjecture.

The second instance of a single change fits this same pattern. In Post Office, the chair, Thaddeus Dulski (D.-N.Y.), was a bipartisan-consensual leader in the Ninety-second Congress (1971-72). Turnover was high in the subsequent Congress, and as noted in Chapter 1, the committee was searching for a new role in the period following the creation of the Postal Service. Dulski tried a new tack, perhaps reflecting these changes in membership and agenda, and assumed a middleman posture. Following the uncertain and unclassifiable Ninety-fourth Congress, when David Henderson chaired the panel, Robert Nix (D.-Pa.) and James Hanley (D.-N.Y.) persevered in the middleman stance, a reasonable approach in a generally increasing period of partisanship in a committee in a state of flux.

The remaining four committees reveal still more variability. Agriculture Chairman W. R. Poage (D.-Tex.) abandoned a middleman position for bipartisanship in the Ninety-third Congress, but Thomas Foley (D.-Wash.), who won the chair in

1975 following Poage's ouster, reverted to the former in the Ninety-fourth and subsequent Congresses. In Government Operations, in the latter Congresses, Jack Brooks (D.-Tex.) tried both extremity and middleman strategies after the period of bipartisan consensus that had prevailed under Chet Holifield. In Rules, in the Ninety-second Congress, William Colmer (D.-Miss.), the last of the southern conservatives to hold the chair, followed a bipartisan strategy. Following his retirement, in 1973, the chair fell into liberal hands.

Simultaneously, the Speaker of the House won new powers that enabled him to harness the committee firmly to the party (Oppenheimer 1981). In consequence, the new chairmen—Ray Madden (D.-N.Y.) in the Ninety-third and John J. Delaney (D.-N.Y.) in the Ninety-fifth—assumed extremity positions, joining the committee liberals against the conservative committee minority. In the Ninety-sixth Congress, however, Richard Bolling (D.-Mo.), long acknowledged as a major influence on the committee, finally acceded formally to the top spot. Consistent with his reputation as a consummate insider who recognized the need to "go along to get along," Bolling took a more centerist, middleman position.

The change in Ways and Means was especially dramatic. Wilbur Mills was the epitome of the bipartisan-consensual leader in the Ninety-second and Ninety-third Congresses, but even he was not immune to the reform fervor of the 1970s. The reformers had begun to chip away at committee prerogatives: Most importantly, the closed rule, long the protector of Ways and Means legislation, was modified. At the start of the Ninety-fourth Congress, after his fling with his femme fatale, Fanne Fox, Mills declined to seek reelection as chairman, and the Caucus cracked down on the committee. It transferred the party's committee assignment responsibilities to the Steering and Policy Committee, it enlarged Ways and Means from 25 to 37 members (and freshmen were appointed where only seniors had served previously), and it required the committee to create subcommittees. The committee, under its new chairman, Al Ullman (D.-Ore.), was unable to restrain partisanship; consensus eluded it. Instead, Ullman adopted a middleman position, attempting (with mixed success) to hold the committee Democrats together. In the Ninety-sixth Congress, however, Ullman shifted position, moving to the extreme pole of the Democratic continuum.

Assessing these three categories of committee leadership change leads us—speculatively to be sure—to suggest that alteration of leadership style reflects the conditions, the settings, within which the committees operate. Three of the four committees with constant leadership patterns—Banking, Education and Labor, and Commerce—are clearly policy (rather than reelection or influence) committees that operate in heterogeneous environments and that use subcommittees to a significant extent to handle their diverse work loads.[11] Apparently, these panels have developed a satisfactory modus operandi, one that permits their members to achieve their goals in a complex and politically charged context, and they cling to it, even when a new chairman takes over (in the case of the Banking Committee).[12] Low turnover may contribute to committee stability as well; three of the four committees (Banking is the exception) with unchanging leadership styles experienced considerable membership continuity over the 1970s. In sum, a policy agenda, handled by increasingly important and permanent subcommittees, in the face of a heterogeneous environment, seems to lead committees to develop an overall decision-making pattern that is resistant to change. To deal with these numerous pressures requires a routine, and these four panels seem to have settled on one and adhered to it.

The several committees where chairmen adopted new leadership styles seem to operate in circumstances that offer greater opportunities for flexibility. All six confront relatively homogeneous environments; with fewer interests to manage, it is perhaps simpler for leaders to alter their positions relative to the panel rank-and-file. If few are watching what a committee does (for example, the full chamber with respect to the Rules Committee, or the farm community in the case of Agriculture), the chair may be relatively free to take on and alter if necessary leadership postures in a flexible fashion. Similarly, high turnover and less extensive use of independent subcommittees, which tend to characterize these changing committees, may contribute to adaptability of leaders. To the extent that new members and weak subcommittees indicate a lack of vested interests on committees, their chairpersons may have greater freedom of maneuver in defining a role vis-à-vis the full committee membership.

In sum, these data reveal that identifiable extremity, middleman, and bipartisan-consensual leadership patterns regularly appear in House committees. Moreover, committees vary considerably in the extent to which their leaders adhere to particular patterns or alter their positions in response to changing committee circumstances. Member goals, environmental constraints, and subcommittee specialization seem to shape leaders' adaptation. Controversial policy agendas, heterogeneous environments, and independent subcommittees, we speculate, inhibit leadership change; other goals, more manageable decision contexts, and less use of specialized subcommittees offer leaders more behavioral freedom. In any case, leadership emerges as a complex and fluid set of interactions between chairman and rank-and-file members that reflects both factors peculiar to single committees and changes in the broader environments of the House and national politics. At the very least, these varying patterns underscore the value of Congress-by-Congress, committee-by-committee analysis.

FINDINGS: THE RANKING MINORITY MEMBERS

Like the chairpersons, the ranking minority members of the committees behave in ways consistent with our classification scheme (see Table 3.4, column 3). Only one case—Agriculture, with Page Belcher (Oklahoma) as ranking Republican, in the Ninety-second Congress—revealed an uninterpretable pattern. Two others displayed a clear but unexpected set of relationships. In the Ninety-fourth Congress the Government Operations Committee changed chairmen; Jack Brooks succeeded Chet Holifield and Frank Horton (New York) continued in the top Republican spot. In that Congress Horton assumed an extremity stance, strongly connected to conservative elements in his own party and bitterly opposed to more liberal groups across the aisle. In the subsequent Congresses—the Ninety-fifth and Ninety-sixth—however, he reversed his position dramatically; in effect, Horton appears to have been co-opted by Brooks and the Democrats. He voted in agreement with the chair (IA = .32, .75), with major Democratic factions, and with liberals in each Congress; his relations with his fellow Republicans can only be described as hostile (his interagreement score with the major GOP bloc in the Ninety-fifth Congress was -.47).[13] Because this was the only instance of "consorting with the enemy" in the data, we assign Horton to the unclassified category.

In the remaining 45 cases, the ranking minority member adopted one of the three predicted leadership styles. Among Republicans, as with Democratic chairpersons, each type is well represented. Sixteen ranking Republicans (36 percent of the 45 cases) assumed extremity postures, an equal number (16, 36 percent) were partisan middlemen, and the remaining 13 (29 percent) pursued a bipartisan-consensual strategy. Again, the evidence suggests substantial variation in the ways party leaders stake out their positions vis-à-vis their colleagues. Noteworthy here is the extent to which ranking Republicans seem to look to the conservative coalition for voting support. In addition to instances of bipartisanship, which obviously entails seeking votes across party lines, in another ten cases, on four committees—Agriculture, Budget, Rules, and Ways and Means—the ranking Republican appears to have established noticeably close connections with the coalition.[14] In committee, as on the floor, some congressional leaders look to the most sympathetic members of the opposition in their efforts to assemble a successful coalition (Manley 1973; Brady and Bullock 1980).

Leadership behavior on the minority side was somewhat more variable than that of the committee chairmen. In three of the ten panels (compared with four for chairpersons), the Republican leader adhered to the same style across the five Congresses. In Armed Services, where bipartisanship prevailed throughout the period, three successive ranking minority members were a part of that consensus (see Appendix 2). In Education and Labor, a highly partisan panel, where Perkins assumed an extremity stance, both ranking Republicans responded in kind. Albert Quie, in the Ninety-second through Ninety-fifth Congresses, and John Ashbrook (Ohio), in the Ninety-sixth, also adopted the extremity position, sustaining partisan polarization in Education and Labor (Appendix 2, Tables 16-20). Finally, Delbert Latta (Ohio), ranking minority member on the Budget Committee, persisted in the extremity posture in each of the three Congresses for which we have data, even in the Ninety-sixth, when his counterpart, Robert Giaimo, moderated his position.

Two committees witnessed a single shift in the ranking member's style during the 1970s. (Chairpersons on two committees took the same step.) In the Banking Committee (Appendix 2, Tables 11-12), William Widnall (New Jersey) countered Wright Patman's middleman strategy by making a bipartisan appeal to all members. Following Patman's ouster, Henry Reuss, the new chair, persevered in pursuing a middleman position, and Widnall's successors--Albert Johnson (Pennsylvania), in the Ninety-fourth Congress, and J. William Stanton (Ohio), in the Ninety-fifth and Ninety-sixth--shifted to the same posture. In the Post Office Committee, in the Ninety-sixth Congress, ranking Republican Edward J. Derwinski (Illinois) abandoned the middleman strategy that he, in the two preceding Congresses, and his predecessor, H. R. Gross (Iowa), in the Ninety-second and Ninety-third, had followed faithfully; he moved to an extremity style (Appendix 2, Tables 31-32).

Finally, five of the committees revealed a more variable array of ranking minority member behavior; the chair's position vacillated in this fashion on four panels. In Agriculture, for example, William Wampler (Virginia) moved progressively away from the political center. During his first years as ranking Republican, he pursued bipartisanship; then, in the Ninety-fourth and Ninety-fifth Congresses he was a middleman; finally, in the Ninety-sixth, he assumed an extremity stance (Appendix 2, Tables 2-5). Similarly, in Commerce, Samuel Devine abandoned his predecessor's middleman stance for bipartisanship in the Ninety-third Congress, reverted to a middleman style in the next Congress, and then returned to the bipartisan-consensual pattern in the subsequent two Congresses (Appendix 2, Tables 27-30). In three other committees--Government Operations, Rules, and Ways and Means--the ranking minority member's style also altered on more than one occasion (Appendix 2, Tables 21-25, 36-40, 41-45).

One other piece of evidence suggests that the ranking minority member has more flexibility than the committee chairperson. In 36 percent of the instances (9 of 25) where the same individual held the ranking Republican slot in successive Congresses, the person switched to a different leadership style. Individual Democratic chairmen changed positions vis-à-vis their rank and file from one Congress to the next only 23 percent (6 of 26) of the time (Table 3.4).

These data make clear that the ranking minority member is more than the mirror image of the full committee chairman. It is reasonable to speculate that committee cleavages and leadership styles go hand in hand. If a chairperson assumes an extremity position, then the ranking member might be expected to take a similar stance on his side of the aisle. Alternatively, where bipartisan-consensus prevails, both leaders should be a part of it and adopt bipartisan postures. In fact, the data (compare columns 2 and 3 of Table 3.4) reveal numerous exceptions to this expectation. Overall, of the 45 cases where we can specify the leadership styles of both the chair and ranking minority member, 13 (29 percent) find the two displaying variant patterns.[15] For instance, whereas Wilbur Mills pursued a bipartisan strategy on Ways and Means during the Ninety-second Congress, assiduously courting John Byrnes (Wisconsin), the ranking Republican (IA = .58), the latter took an extremity position, voting strongly in support of GOP factions and regularly against Democrats and liberals (see Appendix 2, Table 41). Byrnes seems to have sought to mobilize the conservative coalition, including Mills, to counterbalance the more liberal Democrats. In the subsequent Congress, Herman Schneebeli, Byrnes's successor, adopted a middleman stance, presumably in pursuit of the same ends.[16]

In sum, ranking members, like committee chairmen, adopt clearly identifiable leadership styles; the vast majority fall easily into the extremity, middleman, or bipartisan pattern. Moreover, as with the chairpersons, the minority leaders varied widely in their behavior; nearly one third (29 percent) of the ranking members pursued a bipartisan style, the least practiced posture. The chief distinction between the Republican minority leaders and the Democratic chairpersons appears to be the increased opportunities for flexibility available to the former. As minority members, the ranking Republicans shouldered no real responsibility for committee performance. In consequence, they probably felt less obligation to adhere to committee norms and processes. Instead, they seem to have felt free to maneuver for advantage, to seek coalitions and voting support using whatever tactics seemed appropriate.

Minority leaders' behavior, in any event, was consistent with such strategy. Much more frequently than chairmen

they made common cause in the 1970s with the conservative
coalition, voting regularly with southern Democrats as well
as their Republican colleagues. In addition, they were prepared more often than committee chairs to shift their own
positions in successive Congresses; if a new leadership
style seemed more promising, they adopted a new stance. As
a result, their behavior was far more than simply an "equal
and opposite" matching of the chairperson's position. At an
aggregate level, minority leadership was less constant than
that of the Democratic chairmen. In only three committees
did the ranking minority members persist in a single leadership style across these five Congresses; by contrast, the
minority leadership of five panels changed position on two
or more occasions. In short, ranking Republicans acted in a
variety of ways, contributing once again to a wide mix of
committee behavioral patterns and warning once again against
easy and oversimplified generalizations about the congressional committee system.[17]

RESULTS: COMMITTEE LEADERSHIP
AND COMMITTEE PERFORMANCE

Differing leadership patterns take on added significance to the extent they help explain committee behavior.
Does it really matter whether committee chairpersons adopt
extremity, middleman, or bipartisan-consensual positions
within their panels? Even a preliminary answer is a complicated matter. As noted, external events (such as the subcommittee bill of rights) and personnel turnover (for example, the large, liberal class of 1974) may affect individual
committees in different ways (Ornstein and Rohde 1977; Rohde
and Shepsle 1978). Despite these complexities, we can for-
mulate some expectations about the relationship between
leadership style and committee performance, specifically between the chairperson's stance and committee partisanship,
committee integration, and committee floor success (for our
measures of these factors, see Appendix 1). We test these
expectations both with aggregate comparisons and with an examination of individual committees.

One obvious hypothesis links leadership and partisanship. The extremity posture and strong partisanship should

be closely related. A chairman voting with partisan ideologues is likely to evoke strong reactions from the opposition; the committee should operate in an atmosphere of extreme partisanship. The middleman stance is also partisan,
but because it is more moderate, encompassing a broader ideological range, it should be accompanied by less violent partisan animosity. Bipartisan-consensual committees, of course,
mute party considerations and should be characterized by
still lower levels of partisan conflict. In short, moving
from extremity through middleman to bipartisan leadership
styles should lead to a diminution of interparty cleavage.

Aggregate comparisons support this view. In the 13 instances of leadership extremism (Table 3.4, column 2), the
level of party conflict, as measured by the proportion of
partisan roll calls, averaged 78 percent. Comparable figures
for the partisan-middleman panels ($\underline{N}$ = 21) and the bipartisan-
consensual committees ($\underline{N}$ = 12) were 69 and 42 percent. Moreover, Student's $\underline{t}$-test for difference of means reveals that
these differences are statistically significant: extremist-
middleman, $\underline{t}$ = 5.10, $\underline{p}$ < .001; extremist-bipartisan, $\underline{t}$ = 12.41,
$\underline{p}$ < .001; middleman-bipartisan, $\underline{t}$ = -10.08, $\underline{p}$ < .001.

The data for individual committees also indicate a clear
relationship between leadership style and committee partisanship (Table 3.5, column 3). In general, committees with
stable leadership patterns should see only marginal shifts
in levels of partisanship from Congress to Congress; this
appears to be the case for Education and Labor, Commerce,
and Banking, although there are some fluctuations from one
year to the next.[18] By contrast, changes in leadership style
and partisanship should covary; that is, less extreme leadership (change from extremity to middleman, or from middleman to bipartisan, patterns) should go with reduced partisan
voting, and conversely. Government Operations, Post Office,
Rules, Ways and Means, Budget, and Agriculture perform consistently with the hypothesis.

More specifically, there were 11 instances of change in
leadership style in a subsequent Congress. In ten of them,
levels of partisan voting in committee rose or fell in keeping with our prediction (Table 3.5). For example, when
Thomas Foley replaced W. R. Poage as Agriculture chairman
at the outset of the Ninety-fourth Congress and adopted a
middleman stance, in contrast to his predecessor's bipartisan

posture, we expect an increase in panel partisanship. This
is exactly what occurred: Under Poage, in the Ninety-third
Congress, 52 percent of Agriculture roll calls saw partisan
majorities opposed to one another; the figure rose, two
years later, to 68 percent with a more partisan middleman
in the chair. Similarly, when Jack Brooks moderated his
leadership style, from extremist to middleman, in Government Operations in the Ninety-fourth to Ninety-fifth Congresses, the level of partisanship declined, as predicted,
by 11 percent. In short, the weight of the evidence strongly sustains the direct link between committee leadership
patterns and committee partisanship.

We can also test a related hypothesis concerning committee party unity. For reasons analogous to those underlying the committee partisanship proposition, we predict that
leadership style will relate to majority party (Democratic)
cohesion. Extremity leadership seems to require a solid
core of majority party ideologues; the middleman stance
spans a wider partisan spectrum, and the bipartisan pattern
actually crosses party lines. Moreover, the extremism pattern posits greater partisan polarization than others, which,
in turn, should stimulate majority (and minority) unity. If
so, then moving from extremity through middleman to bipartisan leadership styles should lead to decreasing Democratic
party unity. Again, the aggregate data sustain the hypothesis: The Democrats on committees characterized by extremist
leadership averaged an integration score of .62, those on
panels where the chairman assumed a middleman posture averaged .52, and the majority on bipartisan panels averaged .46
on the integration measure.[19]

Here, too, the performance of individual committees
provides evidence that sustains the proposition (Table 3.5,
column 4). The consistent integration scores of the panels
(Education and Labor, Commerce, and Banking) varied little
from Congress to Congress.[20] Committee change also provides
supporting evidence, but there are some exceptions. Rules
presents the clearest case: The shift from Colmer's bipartisanship to the extremity stance of his more liberal successors was accompanied by the predicted rise in Democratic
unity. The same tendency appears in other committees experiencing leadership change, particularly in Budget, Government Operations, and Ways and Means, but also, with occasional

TABLE 3.5

Committee Leadership and Committee Performance

Committee and Congress/Ch.	Leadership Style	Partisan Votes (%)	Committee Performance	
			Democratic Party Integration	Committee Floor Success (%)
Agriculture				
92 Poage	Middleman	55	.68	85
93 Poage	Bipartisan	52	.59	77
94 Foley	Middleman	68	.45	80
95 Foley	Middleman	70	.55	91
96 Foley	Middleman	56	.62	85
Armed Services				
92 Hebert	Bipartisan	12	.57	100
93 Hebert	Bipartisan	16	.46	91
94 Price	Bipartisan	23	.32	86
95 Price	Bipartisan	32	.31	94
96 Price	Bipartisan	30	.35	94
Banking				
92 Patman	Middleman	61	.53	81
93 Patman	Middleman	44	.53	85
94 Reuss	Middleman	77	.66	89
95 Reuss	Middleman	50	.55	86
96 Reuss	Middleman	70	.68	87
Budget				
94 Adams	Extremity	85	.53	100
95 Giaimo	Extremity	78	.60	88
96 Giaimo	Middleman	77	.46	93
Education and Labor				
92 Perkins	Extremity	80	.66	71
93 Perkins	Extremity	69	.70	88
94 Perkins	Extremity	84	.76	89

95	Perkins	Extremity	75	.70	81
96	Perkins	Extremity	94	.78	80
Government Operations					
92	Holifield	Bipartisan	77	.35	100
93	Holifield	Bipartisan	72	.60	92
94	Brooks	Extremity	100	.61	77
95	Brooks	Middleman	89	.57	91
96	Brooks	Extremity	81	.53	85
Commerce					
92	Staggers	(Unclassified)	—	—	—
93	Staggers	Middleman	78	.50	91
94	Staggers	Middleman	86	.63	85
95	Staggers	Middleman	83	.50	84
96	Staggers	Middleman	69	.43	88
Post Office					
92	Dulski	Bipartisan	43	.64	100
93	Dulski	Middleman	74	.71	100
94	Henderson	(Unclassified)	—	—	—
95	Nix	Middleman	66	.57	93
96	Hanley	Middleman	100	.71	90
Rules					
92	Colmer	Bipartisan	48	.40	89
93	Madden	Extremity	71	.56	91
94	Madden	Extremity	76	.59	97
95	Delaney	Extremity	85	.64	96
96	Bolling	Middleman	77	.67	94
Ways and Means					
92	Mills	Bipartisan	34	.37	96
93	Mills	Bipartisan	55	.43	96
94	Ullman	Middleman	74	.46	83
95	Ullman	Middleman	62	.34	80
96	Ullman	Extremity	75	.50	90

Note: The measures of the committee performance variables are described in Appendix 1.

deviation, in Post Office and Agriculture. For example, when Giaimo of the Budget Committee moderated his stance from extremist to middleman in the Ninety-sixth Congress, Democratic party integration declined to .46, from .60 in the previous Congress. Of eleven instances of such change in leadership style, the shift in majority party integration was consistent with the hypothesis in eight (Table 3.5). The sum of the evidence thus strongly suggests a clear link between leadership style and Democratic party cohesion.

A third hypothesis relates leadership to extra-committee performance, victory on the floor. Dyson and Soule (1970) find cohesive (integrated) committees to be the most successful on the floor (see also Fleisher and Bond 1983), and we have suggested that leadership style is associated with party cohesion. It seems reasonable, in consequence, to infer that style may relate to floor performance—on amendments and final passage—as well. If party conflicts are not resolved in committee, they may spill over onto the floor and lower the prospects for victory there. We predict, therefore, that partisan leadership—extreme or middleman variety—will be less successful on the floor than bipartisan strategies.

Once again, the aggregate figures tend to sustain our expectation: Bipartisan committees "win"—that is, have their position supported by a majority of the full House—on 91 percent of all roll calls; the committees with extremity and middleman leadership succeeded on 88 percent.[21] In addition, the Banking, Commerce, Armed Services, and Education and Labor Committees (those with invariant leadership patterns) had, as expected, quite stable records of floor success, although each of the latter two deviated once from the committee norm. Among committees that underwent change in leadership style, Government Operations and Ways and Means showed a concomitant drop in floor victories when they shifted to more partisan leadership. On the other hand, the single instances of bipartisan leadership in Agriculture and Rules did not produce the clear-cut superiority in floor wins that the hypothesis predicts. On the level of individual committee predictions, there are an equal number, five of ten, of confirmations and failures (Table 3.5). Again, though the evidence is certainly mixed, the relation of leadership style and committee floor success seems worthy of serious consideration.

Overall, leadership does seem to relate to committee performance. Leadership style seems incontrovertibly linked to committee partisanship, more than modestly to Democratic party integration, and at least minimally to committee victories on the House floor. Leadership style, in short, tells us more than the place of the chairperson in committee factional alignments; it contributes to an understanding of various aspects of committee performance.

CONCLUSION: COMMITTEE LEADERSHIP
AND COMMITTEE POLITICS

Conceptualizing leadership as a transactional relationship between leader and followers, we have suggested that congressional committees can be characterized by identifiable leadership patterns or styles that are associated with both committee attributes (member goals and committee norms) and panel performance (partisanship and floor success). Acknowledging the problems of establishing causality, we have used committee roll call data to begin to define the place of leadership in committee politics. We have asked, first of all, whether there is any identifiable pattern of leader-follower relations in congressional committees. We have found clear evidence of three leadership patterns—extremity, partisan-middleman, and bipartisan-consensual—and discovered that leaders can readily be assigned to them. Moreover, each style had a sizable number of practitioners among both chairmen and ranking minority members. Among the former, the least frequent pattern, the bipartisan-consensual style, appeared at one time or another in six committees and constituted 12 of the 46 classifiable committee settings. The extremity style appeared in five committees, but occurred in 13 instances. The ranking minority members vary similarly in their adoption of leadership styles; in their ranks, the least common stance, again the bipartisan posture, turned up 13 times (out of 45 classifiable cases) on five different committees. Leadership, in short, like voting cleavage, appears in diverse forms on both sides of the committee aisle.

Moreover, leadership variation is not random; it seems to reflect the conditions present in particular panels at particular times; where conditions change, so too will lead-

ership postures. Where committees develop long-standing
ways to conduct their business, these operating procedures
seem to constrain leadership options. Thus, the four committees—Armed Services, Banking, Commerce, and Education
and Labor—that displayed constant leadership styles are
characterized, in general, by members' pursuit of multiple
but recurring policy goals in a heterogeneous environment.[22]
These panels, for the most part, have experienced low turnover (Banking is the single exception here) and have made
use of autonomous subcommittees to a considerable extent.
They are, in a sense, "institutionalized" committees, and as
such their leaders tend to adopt persistent patterns of relations with the rank-and-file members. If such relatively
immutable conditions are lacking, committee leaders retain
greater flexibility to respond to issues and events with altered positions vis-à-vis their committee colleagues. These
constraining conditions appear on the majority side of the
aisle, where basic decisions are most frequently made more
often, and thus chairpersons seem to have less room for maneuver than their ranking minority counterparts.

Again, it is less important for leadership stability
that a committee adopt any particular leadership pattern
than that it have some regular mode of action. The four
committees that had invariant leadership styles over the
1970s included two with middleman leaders and one each with
extremity and bipartisan chairmen. Similarly, one case of
minority leader consistency was an extremity style (Education and Labor) and the other (Armed Services) was bipartisan-
consensual. Leadership thus displays both change and continuity. The latter flows from more or less fixed attributes:
membership stability, pursuit of policy goals, and a complex
but regular issue agenda that independent subcommittees come
to treat continuously. Where those conditions do not develop, or do not impinge immediately on particular leaders
(such as the ranking minority members), constraints are lower
and change will be more common. The rich variety of committee leadership patterns, and their explanations, thus reflect both institutional continuities and committee-by-
committee, Congress-by-Congress differences in those continuities.

A second general question, the "so what?" of the skep-
tics, asks whether knowledge of committee leadership styles

reveals anything about committee politics and performance. The data suggest an affirmative answer: Leadership style seems directly related to committee partisanship and, with a few exceptions on a few committees, to majority party integration and committee success on the floor. Despite the difficulty in establishing definitively the direction in which influence flows as well as in distinguishing the impact of leadership from that of other forces that affect committees, these data, particularly those on change over time, permit the inference that leadership helps shape committee performance. In the preponderance of instances (Table 3.5) where leadership became less extreme, committee partisanship and majority party integration declined as committee floor success increased. Where leadership became more extreme, precisely the reverse relationships regularly appeared.

In addition, though we do not bring data directly to bear on the matter, our findings suggest, at least speculatively, that committee attributes and committee leadership are reciprocally related. On the one hand, member goals and panel norms and process may structure committee leadership. For example, in Armed Services and Banking, new chairmen, relatively liberal northerners replacing southern conservatives (Berg 1978), adopted leadership styles identical to those of their predecessors. Similarly, where committee conditions change, leadership change may follow directly: In Ways and Means, dramatically restructured (especially in terms of a greatly enlarged contingent of liberal Democrats), Al Ullman was unwilling or unable to sustain Wilbur Mills's bipartisan-consensual leadership.[23] On the other hand, Jack Brooks, succeeding to the chair of Government Operations, a committee only moderately influenced by broader change in the House, seems to have consciously abandoned Chet Holifield's bipartisanship (Ornstein and Rohde 1977).

In general, then, our results sustain the view that leadership in the congressional committee context is transactional and highly variable in form. Committee chairpersons do have leadership resources, for example, influence over subcommittee structures and recruitment of committee staff. But their success in securing their followers' support may well be limited by their own leadership skills and by the committee settings in which they seek to lead. Committee-specific factors—followers' personal goals, the aggressive-

ness of the now formally dominant majority party committee
caucus, the committee's relations with actors in its environment, and the extant committee norms and decision-making
process--all impinge on the leaders' opportunities. Individual chairmen, our data suggest, respond to these circumstances in distinctive ways; they may, we infer, seek to
lead within these constraints or, alternatively, conform to
them. Most often, our speculations suggest, their leadership posture is limited by ongoing committee processes. However, the leadership style that chairmen do assume, whether
by choice or necessity, appears to relate directly to committee performance. Finally, these relationships may alter
as conditions change. If Wilbur Mills was the leader of Ways
and Means, then Al Ullman, operating in a quite different
committee setting, was much more a follower. Committee leadership, in short, is patterned, but the patterns are neither
simple nor immutable.

Analysis of committee voting cleavages and committee
leadership styles indicates that panel politics transcends
simple generalizations about the committee system. Individual committees display numerous forms of behavior; both factionalism and leadership vary both from committee to committee and from Congress to Congress. We have suggested that
such variations reflect differences in the extent to which
specific committees continue to meet their responsibilities
in relatively constant decision-making settings. When new
pressures come to play on committee members, they adapt to
them, altering the ways they cast their votes as well as the
ways they lead or respond to their leaders. The 1970s, of
course, was an era notable for broad "reform" and change,
and as such may prove, from hindsight, to be a period of unusually profound alteration in congressional politics in general. Whatever the ultimate verdict of history, the decade
provides an opportunity to explore change, intentional or
otherwise, and its impact on legislative committees. In the
next chapter we take up this topic directly, building on the
analyses of voting and leadership presented to this point.

NOTES

1. For a full discussion of leadership in general and in the legislative setting, see Burns 1978, chaps. 1 and 13. See also Gibb 1968; Bass 1981; and especially Peabody 1982.

2. We are well aware that there may be substantial differences between the formal and nominal leaders, the chairperson and the real leader(s) on any committee. For instance, Richard Bolling (D.-Mo.) was clearly the de facto leader of the House Committee on Rules long before he became the de jure leader, by acceding to the chair in 1979. Yet there is ample precedent for treating formal (positional) leaders as the leaders (Peabody 1976) and, moreover, if the form of analysis we attempt works for the official leaders, it can be used with equal facility to study the informal leadership.

3. Fenno's generalization (for other versions, see Peabody 1976, p. 7; Jones 1981) is probably even more accurate in the postreform period in Congress, that is, after 1975, when the formal authority of full committee chairs was sharply curtailed (see, inter alia, Ornstein 1975; Welch and Peters 1977; Rieselbach 1978).

4. The use of the masculine form here intends no slight to women. It is simply realistic: All 20 individuals who chaired the committees were men; of the 22 ranking minority members who served during this period, 21 were males.

5. We use "leadership style" in a restricted sense here: to refer to the voting alignment--extremity, middleman, or bipartisan--that links a committee's chairperson to its rank-and-file. We recognize fully that leaders who display the same style, as we use the term, may possess quite different personal qualities or quirks (Wright Patman and Henry Reuss on the Banking Committee come readily to mind). In addition, there may be intracommittee variation in leadership--across different issues, with respect to a particular subcommittee's products, or in consequence of the chair's relations with the ranking minority member. Yet our purpose, for now, remains limited: We want merely to map the patterns, the styles, of committee leadership in general and to explore some broad effects of such patterns on committee performance.

6. For expository convenience, we categorize blocs ideologically according to their members' mean Americans for Constitutional Action score (see Appendix 1), as follows: liberal, 0–33; moderate, 34–66; and conservative, 67–100.

7. In the single exception to Holifield's bipartisan leadership strategy, he disagreed sharply (IA = −.46) with an extremely liberal (ACA = 09) doublet (cluster 5). He was feuding with one of the pair, Benjamin Rosenthal (New York) (see Ornstein and Rohde 1977, p. 210), but his relationship to the other dissenter, John Culver (Iowa), was also negative (IA = −.27).

8. The raw data--the chairman's correlations with each voting cluster on his committee and with each of the party and regional groups--on which the categorization of leadership style rests appear in the individual committee tables in Appendixes 2 and 3.

9. For more on these matters, see Chapter 1 and the sources cited in note 14.

10. Giaimo himself acknowledges this point, at least implicitly, noting that if "those that follow one political persuasion to the exclusion of others ever gain control over the budget process . . ., an enormous evil will be inflicted on the American people" (1982, p. 133).

11. These committee attributes are summarized in Table 1.4.

12. Even the fourth stable committee, Armed Services, is not a complete exception to this line of argument. While we categorize it as a reelection committee, given the members' stress on district military installations, the panel does have formal jurisdiction over a significant policy matter, military procurement. Adding the Pentagon to the constituency interests the committee serves makes its environment far more heterogeneous. Finally, Armed Services does make extensive use of specialized subcommittees. Thus, to the extent that the committee does pursue policy goals in a complex environment using autonomous subcommittees, it resembles the other three committees whose leadership patterns also remained constant. In any case, our point is that in the face of conflicting pressures, policy-oriented committees may find it necessary to establish behavioral patterns that minimize their leaders' ability to change styles readily.

13. The data on Horton and Government Operations for these Congresses appear in Appendix 2, Tables 24–25.

14. We have indicated these instances in Table 3.4, column 2.

15. The number of "mismatches" rises to 15 (32 percent of 47 cases) if we include the two instances of Frank Horton's "defection" to the majority Democrats on Government Operations. For the reasons noted, we have designated these as unclassified cases, but they surely illustrate a lack of symmetry between the leadership styles of chairman and ranking minority member.

16. The behavior of these ranking Republicans on Ways and Means is consistent with Manley's (1970; see also Fenno 1973) description of the "restrained partisanship" norm on the panel. The minority, and their leader, during this period struggled to carry the day within the committee but tended in more bipartisan fashion to rally behind the committee's decision once the roll had been called.

17. Interestingly, none of the attributes of the committees (for example, member goals or environmental constraints) helps to explain these wide variations. Perhaps minority status in all committees creates conditions conducive to ranking member freedom and flexibility.

18. In Armed Services, however, when a new chairman, Price, took over, there occurred a clear and persistent increase in partisanship.

19. Student's t-test demonstrates the statistical significance of these differences: extremist–middleman, $t = -7.83$, $p < .001$; extremist–bipartisan, $t = -8.63$, $p < .001$; middleman–bipartisan, $t = 3.77$, $p < .001$.

20. Again, Armed Services does not quite meet expectations. Hebert and Price were both bipartisan leaders, but committee integration, higher than expected under the former, fell to more reasonable levels during the latter's tenure.

21. These, too, are small differences; they take on meaning, however, in the context of high overall success rates for all committees. The t-tests comparing committees with bipartisan leadership to those with other styles approach but do not quite achieve statistical significance: bipartisan–extremity, $t = -1.84$, $p < .07$; bipartisan–middleman, $t = -1.15$, $p < .25$. Within a narrow range, bipartisan

leaders can expect their committees to win on the floor somewhat more often than extremity or middleman chairpersons.

22. Even Armed Services, at first blush the exception
to this generalization, does not fall entirely outside this
line of reasoning. The committee does have a strong secondary concern with weapons procurement policy (for recent
evidence, see Smith and Deering 1983), surely an abstruse
and persistent set of issues. If the Pentagon and the defense community are added to constituency interests concerned
with local military installations, Armed Services' environment seems far more heterogeneous than it appears initially.

23. We take up the question of chairmanship change in
detail in Chapter 4. Here we point out that new chairpersons may well find themselves severely constrained: Traditional ways of conducting committee business may limit the
extent to which a new chair may put a personal stamp on committee behavior and legislation.

4
Change, Reform, and Committee Politics

The decade 1965-75 was a period of extraordinary change in the country and in Congress. Most broadly, a series of crises, foreign and domestic, wracked the nation: Vietnam, the energy crisis, Watergate and the resignation of Richard Nixon, and such emotion-laden social issues such as school prayer and abortion. These and other developments made "politics as usual" difficult if not impossible. More specifically, this period, beginning with the 1964 Republican electoral debacle that brought a cadre of liberal Democrats to Congress, witnessed the emergence of a congressional reform movement. The House of Representatives in particular consciously sought to alter its structures and processes in ways designed to respond to and remedy the chamber's alleged shortcomings.

More narrowly still and less intentional, more "normal" or evolutionary change affected the national legislature. Congressional turnover was high (Cooper and West 1981; Hibbing 1982a, 1982b), bringing significant numbers of younger members--in effect a new generation, with new ideas and new commitments to reform and policy change--to Capitol Hill. As these men and women rose to positions of consequence in Congress, they gave a distinctive coloration to its activities, particularly in the latter half of the 1970s. These developments, outside and within Congress,

intended or unanticipated, of course affected different committees in different ways. Some panels took on new issues,
others continued to treat old ones. Turnover was high in
some committees and far less dramatic in others. New leaders emerged in some committees and old leaders endured in
others. In this chapter we seek to assess the cumulative
impact of these changes, broad and narrow, on congressional
committee politics, particularly on committee cleavage,
leadership, and performance.

CHANGE AND REFORM IN CONGRESS

In this context we distinguish change from reform.
Change, the broader of the concepts, refers to any shift,
whether or not intended, in fundamental organizational patterns. It may reflect extralegislative forces such as major unforeseen events (the Arab oil embargo of 1973 or
Watergate, for example) or national political tides (such
as Democrat Jimmy Carter's emergence and the defeat of
Republican Gerald Ford in 1976). It may reflect, alternatively, congressional developments such as legislative election swings (as in 1964 and 1974) or scandals (for instance,
Wilbur Mills's disgrace and eventual departure from his
powerful position as chairman of the Ways and Means Committee). Change, in short, often unpredictable, may raise new
matters for congressional consideration and may confer the
responsibility for dealing with an altered agenda on new
individuals.

Reform, in contrast to change, connotes an intentional
effort to reshape institutional structures and processes.
Thus it is one facet of change, although not necessarily the
most important one; indeed, change broadly conceived may
induce reform by indicating where and why an institution
like Congress has failed to perform adequately. For example, although reform proposals percolated in the 1960s, and
a few were adopted in the Legislative Reorganization Act of
1970, the recent reform movement gathered momentum under
the press of basic change. An executive-legislative confrontation over foreign policy (especially Vietnam) and
domestic spending (the budget) dominated the Nixon presidency
and highlighted congressional shortcomings. A Watergate-

weakened presidency provided Congress (its ranks altered
visibly after the 1974 midterm elections) with the challenge
to put its houses in order, both to contest the executive
for control over policy and to improve its own capacity to
make wise policy.

In the 1970s, Congress rose to this challenge, adopting four sets of specific reforms that affected in various
ways congressional committees.[1] One set of reforms sought
to counter an increasingly hostile public opinion. A series
of scandals—from Adam Powell to Abscam, featuring nontyping
typists, aquatic exhibitionism in the Tidal Basin, and FBI
agents disguised as arab sheiks, as well as ordinary, old-
fashioned corruption—and apparent conflicts of interest
combined to reduce the prestige of Congress. To restore
popular approbation, the legislature adopted a series of
reforms designed, in large part, to expose its operations
to public scrutiny. It enacted codes of ethics and campaign
finance limitations intended to permit attentive observers
to discover the sources of legislators' income and election
funds. Availability of such information, the reformers
hoped, would make it more difficult for lawmakers to place
personal interests above national needs.

More important for present purposes, members of Congress concluded that they should conduct the public's business in public. The committee process was opened up; all
sessions, including markups and conference committee meetings, were to be open to the public, unless a majority
voted, in public, to close them. The Legislative Reorganization Act of 1970 decreed that members vote publicly.
Committee roll calls and teller votes on the floor were to
be recorded; these requirements reduced the likelihood that
members could avoid "going on the record," individually,
during committee deliberation or floor consideration of
legislation. These developments meant, in sum, that con-
gresspersons were more exposed to interest groups, executive
branch personnel, and the public generally in their activity. In consequence, the influence of political parties
may have been reduced: The more visible any action, including that in committee, the greater the difficulty party
leaders have in controlling it (Froman and Ripley 1965).

A second set of reforms aimed directly at the executive branch, seeking to reassert atrophied legislative

powers. The "imperial presidency," symbolized by Vietnam
and Watergate, suggested that the legislature had lost, or
ceded, much of its traditional authority: to declare war,
to control the federal purse strings, and to oversee the
bureaucracy. Reform would allow Congress to reclaim its
rightful role in the policy process, imposing its preferences on the presidency when it seemed sensible to do so.
Acting on this assumption, Congress took a number of steps
to buttress its position relative to the executive. It enacted, over Richard Nixon's veto, the War Powers Resolution
(1973) to circumscribe the commander in chief's authority
to commit military forces to combat. It acknowledged its
inability to exercise effective control over federal expenditures and passed the Budget and Impoundment Control
Act (1974) to enable it to impose fiscal discipline on an
archaic budgetary process.

In addition, to remedy disadvantages in information
and analytic capacity, Congress moved to enlarge its data
resources. It established two support agencies--the Congressional Budget Office (CBO), as part of the new budget
process, and the Office of Technology Assessment (OTA), to
advise on the impact of scientific programs--and strengthened two old ones--the Congressional Research Service (CRS)
of the Library of Congress and the General Accounting Office (GAO). It also greatly enlarged members' personal and
committee staffs and sought to harness computers to its
information needs. Finally, the legislature began to assert
more forcefully already established powers: the legislative
veto, which reserved to Congress (or some part of it) the
opportunity to block or delay executive actions, and more
generally broad legislative oversight of administration.

These steps strengthened Congress's overall position
vis-a-vis the executive, but they also had varying implica-
tions for particular congressional committees. For the
whole legislature these reforms enabled Congress to promote
its own priorities with more formal authority and with the
support of enlarged expertise that enhanced staff and information resources provided. Individual committees, however, were in no way obligated to take advantage of the
opportunities reform afforded them. Given the variations in
member goals and environmental constraints, some might be
reluctant to step up oversight activities or to exercise

the legislative veto. Differing committee structures and
decision-making premises might also lead to divergent asser-
tions of the revived congressional prerogatives. Finally,
some reforms had direct impact on particular panels. The
Budget Act, for instance, created the Budget Committee and
made it a contender for power and policy influence within
the House. The traditionally dominant fiscal committees,
Appropriations and Ways and Means, accordingly were faced
with a diminution of their budgetary authority.

A third cluster of reforms was a response to a perceived inefficiency in congressional performance. A decentralized decision-making process impeded coherent policy
formulation, and the reformers professed a desire to make
it easier for Congress to act. Specifically, the House majority party—the Caucus and its leader, the Speaker—was
granted additional authority, and the committees, allegedly
the chief roadblocks to legislative responsibility, were in
some ways brought to heel. The Caucus won the right to
determine who would chair the committees, breaching the
seniority principle that had automatically placed the majority member with the longest continuous committee service in
the chair. In addition, the Democrats created a Steering
and Policy Committee that eventually came to make committee
assignments as well as to advise on party policy positions.
Finally, the Caucus assumed the power to instruct the Rules
Committee, to prevent favored programs from expiring in that
sometimes defiant body.

The Speaker's new authority included personal power
to name Rules Committee members, to yoke that panel firmly
to the leadership. He was given a major voice in the new
Steering and Policy Committee; half its members were his
appointees and, presumably, loyal supporters. Also, the
Speaker received new ability to regulate the flow of legislation to and from committees and to create ad hoc committees to facilitate coherent treatment of complex policy
issues. Finally, the leadership began to supplement existing techniques of vote gathering with the use of an increasingly sophisticated whip system and informal task forces as
means to increase party cohesion (see Dodd and Sullivan 1981;
Sinclair 1981a, 1981b; Vogler 1981). To the extent that
such steps increased centralization in the House, the independent role of the committees could be expected to decline.

Moreover, because party leaders would single out specific matters for special attention, their new authority might well impinge more forcefully on some committees than on others.

It is important to note in this connection that the House resisted strenuously, and ultimately rejected, most efforts to realign the overall committee system. Defenders of the status quo managed to remove all but the most routine features of the 1974 Select (Bolling) Committee on Committee's reform proposals (Davidson and Oleszek 1977). They substituted a much milder set of committee changes that the Caucus's (Hansen) Committee on Organization, Study, and Review suggested. The resulting reform was more cosmetic than anything else, indicating that House members retained considerable vested interests in the existing distribution of power among the committees. As Davidson and Oleszek put it:

> The Select Committee's . . . package threatened too many careers and political relationships to gain passage. So many legislators and staff . . . were adversely affected by the proposed changes that the plan immediately encountered bitter, personal opposition. . . . [M]embers . . . quickly singled out those provisions affecting their own committee and subcommittee assignments. (1977, p. 264)

If there was any doubt about the members' commitment to promoting their personal political power, a fourth and final set of reforms--aimed at enhancing individual influence--made clear their priorities. Many legislators, especially the liberals and junior members, chafed under the restrictions that a committee-dominated Congress imposed on their full participation and policy influence. Strengthening the parties through centralization was one way to circumvent recalcitrant committee leaders, but the reformers were not content to rely exclusively on such steps. They quickly seized on the reform mood to make changes that improved their personal positions. They adopted decentralizing ("democratizing") reforms that frequently ran counter to other changes; much influence that previously rested with committee chairpersons now devolved to autonomous subcommittees.

Substantial pieces of House committee power were re-
allocated to the rank-and-file. Members were limited to one
subcommittee chair each; no individual could select a second
subcommittee assignment until each full committee member
had secured one subcommittee position. In 1973, the Democratic Caucus adopted a subcommittee bill of rights to protect the independence of subcommittees. The bill of rights
required that subcommittees have fixed jurisdictions and
that legislation on these subjects be referred automatically
to them. It permitted subcommittees to meet at the pleasure
of their members, to write their own rules, and to control
their own budgets and staffs. Two years later the Caucus
mandated that all committees with more than 20 members
create a minimum of four subcommittees. The upshot of these
changes was to establish "institutionalized" subcommittees--
permanent, independent, and often active. These decentralizing reforms had differential effects on individual committees, however (Stanga and Farnsworth 1978). Where subcommittees were strong and seats on them equitably allocated
(for instance, Agriculture), these reforms produced few
visible changes; where senior members dominated the subcommittees (Education and Labor) or operated without subcommittees (Ways and Means), the potential for altered patterns
of influence and performance was far greater.

In short, four sets of House reforms--to regain public
approval, to restore a competitive position against the
executive, to render internal operations more efficient,
and to reallocate internal influence--altered legislative
politics in general and committee politics more particularly. So did more general change--new members and new
issues. In this chapter we attempt to assess the impact of
change and reform on our ten committees. We identify three
groups of committees: those where change was relatively
great, those where it was evolutionary rather than fundamental, and those where it was minimal. We ask whether
change and reform altered factionalism and leadership style
in these panels and whether, in consequence, committee performance (partisanship, integration, and floor success)
shifted as well.

"REVOLUTIONARY" CHANGE: OUSTING THE OLIGARCHS

Perhaps the most publicized development among the multitude of profound changes of the 1970s was the startling breach of the seniority principle in the House at the start of the Ninety-fourth Congress. The newly elected cadre of 75, mostly liberal freshman Democrats joined forces with the returning reformers to oust three elderly southern oligarchs--W. R. Poage (Texas), 75 years old, of the Agriculture Committee; F. Edward Hebert (Louisiana), 74, of Armed Services; and Wright Patman (Texas), 81, of Banking and Currency--from their committee chairs. The reformers' intentions are not entirely clear. Many apparently considered the deposed leaders too "autocratic" (Congressional Quarterly 1977, p. 766; Parker 1979; but see Ornstein and Rohde 1977, p. 206). Thus a change of chairmen might have been aimed at altering the committee's decision-making practices and as a result the content of their policies. Hinckley (1976) suggests that the three were vulnerable for a combination of reasons: Each was old and southern and faced with an acknowledged challenger within his committee's ranks. From this perspective, the removals may have been more symbolic than policy related; for by eliminating those who epitomized the ancien regime, the reformers proclaimed their freedom to alter the old order, at little or no cost in policy terms.

Multiple motives also generated a fourth committee chairmanship change in 1975. Ways and Means, with jurisdiction over critical revenue matters, had long been a target of liberal reformers. Chairman Wilbur Mills (Arkansas), "often cited as the single most powerful person in the House" (Rudder 1978, p. 33), was widely acknowledged to possess extraordinary skills, both substantive and parliamentary, that he used to protect the power of his committee and to produce relatively conservative policy outcomes (Manley 1970; Fenno 1973). Indeed, in 1973, reformers succeeded, at least slightly, in circumscribing Ways and Means's ability to protect its legislation from floor amendment using the "closed rule." During the Ninety-third Congress Mills's bizarre behavior--a series of widely publicized events that culminated in his hospitalization for alcoholism--undermined his position. The reformers were prepared to move

against Mills, and recognizing that he could not be re-
elected, Mills resigned as committee chair.

Whatever the causes, four prominent House committees
experienced highly visible and extensive change. They not
only felt the force of the general reform movement but also
were abruptly compelled to adapt to new leadership. Thus
these panels are particularly well suited to an effort to
assess the impact of change and reform; they provide excel-
lent "laboratories" for gauging the effects of reform. Because each suffered substantial change, of several vari-
eties, each should offer some significant clues about the
consequence of change. If altered conditions affect committees at all, the results should be readily apparent in
these four; if the performance of these committees shifts
only modestly, even under the cumulative impact of procedural and leadership change, we may conclude that at least
some aspects of legislative activity are largely immune to
the sorts of institutional tinkering in which reformers
typically engage (Jones 1977). We use a before-and-after
approach to compare the two Congresses prior to the three
that immediately follow the dramatic removal of four senior,
established committee chairpersons. We look specifically
for change in the factional alignments within the committee,
the place of the chairman in that factional structure, and
committee behavior or performance.

Our data for these four committees reveal the basic
stability of congressional committee politics. In three of
the panels changing chairpersons, as well as the other
alterations that occurred during the 1970s, produced shifts
of degree, at most, not of kind. Only Ways and Means, the
object of a wholesale assault that far transcended ousting
the sitting chairman, displayed significantly different
structures and behavior in the aftermath of reform. Generally, committees, as ongoing political institutions with
relatively fixed member motivations and internal organiza-
tions and processes and with established relationships with
environmental actors, seem highly resistant to the prag-
matic, piecemeal, politically inspired change typical of
the reform movement.

Agriculture: _Plus ça change, . . ._

As noted in Chapter 1, the Agriculture Committee is
basically a constituency-oriented panel that seeks to provide for farmers, using a commodity-focused subcommittee
system to produce legislation satisfactory to its clientele.
In recent years, as the absolute number of rural representatives declined, the panel sought to broaden its political
base, to preserve a working majority in the House for its
farm package. It folded the food stamp program, with its
obvious appeal for urban, liberal lawmakers, into the farm
bill and logrolled explicitly with these same interests,
supporting minimum wage legislation in exchange for votes on
the farm law (Barton 1976; Peters 1978). Given these circumstances, we expect to find (and do; see Chapter 2) a
loose, fluid, relatively unstructured set of factional
alignments in Agriculture; the bargaining needed to assemble
a coalition in support of the farm program seems to require
flexibility rather than partisan or ideological purity. The
chairperson's job has been to organize these crop-oriented,
constituency-based elements into a coalition sufficient to
carry the day for the omnibus farm bill.

W. R. Poage pursued this goal with shifting leadership
in the face of changing patterns of cleavage in the Ninety-
second and Ninety-third Congresses. In the former, he confronted a moderately partisan factional alignment with a
middleman leadership style. He belonged to a large, 11-
member bloc of moderate Democrats and had positive associations with four of the remaining five small clusters (Appendix 2, Table 1).[2] He apparently sought to mobilize all
elements of the majority Democrats and to extend his reach
across the aisle. Thus his associations with all Democrats,
northern Democrats, and liberals were strongly positive; his
relationships with all conservatives and potential members
of the conservative coalition were also positive but much
more modest (Appendix 3, Table 1). His major opposition
came from a dissenting conservative Republican cluster that
included Charles Teague (California), the ranking minority
member, and from all Republicans.

Poage confronted an unstructured setting in the
Ninety-third Congress (1973-74). Again six distinct clusters appeared, all small and encompassing fewer than half

the committee members (Appendix 2, Table 2). He belonged
to a three-member, moderate southern Democratic cluster and
sustained positive, though occasionally modest, relationships with each of the remaining five factions. In this
setting, and perhaps because the farm bill was up for renewal and because there were many newcomers on the committee
(turnover was 30 percent), Poage shifted somewhat to the
center and apparently pursued a bipartisan leadership style,
in contrast to his middleman posture of the previous Congress. He had positive but low relationships with each partisan, regional, and ideological grouping on the panel.[3]
Lacking a firm supporting cluster or coalition, Poage seems
to have cast his net more widely, seeking votes from all
segments of the committee. His strategy succeeded, and the
House enacted a farm bill satisfactory to Poage and the
Agriculture Committee (Barton 1976).

In 1975, however, the waves of change swept over the
committee. The Democratic Caucus ousted Poage and replaced
him with Thomas Foley (Washington), a more liberal and accommodating chairman than his predecessor (Ornstein and
Rohde 1977; Berg 1978). High turnover and implementation of
the House subcommittee reforms altered the character of the
committee, but despite this substantial transformation,
little substantive change in committee alignments and behavior occurred after 1975. In the Ninety-fourth through
Ninety-sixth Congresses (Appendix 2, Tables 3-5), Agriculture
continued to be characterized by a chaotic factional structure. In the first two of these Congresses there were few
clusters, of small size, and most members remained unaligned;
in the Ninety-sixth there were six small factions, encompassing 64 percent of the members. Foley belonged to no
faction in the Ninety-fourth Congress; two years later he
joined a six-member, moderate Democratic bloc; in the
Ninety-sixth Congress, however, he reverted to an unaligned
position. Without a solid supporting coalition, he seemingly was left to bargain for committee members' votes.

In so doing, Foley assumed a middleman stance, appeal-
ing to the center-liberal elements within the Democratic
party. He apparently had some difficulty in implementing
this strategy in the Ninety-fourth Congress. He won
support from the two liberal Democratic factions, but differed regularly with a conservative southern Democratic bloc

and more often than not with a moderate cluster of southern Democrats. His most vigorous opposition came from a five-member conservative Republican faction. The interagreement scores reinforce the same point: Foley drew backing from all Democrats, northern Democrats, and liberals, but was opposed by all Republicans, including the ranking minority member, conservatives, and potential conservative coalition supporters. In short, Foley positioned himself securely in the center-left segment of his own party, a typical middleman location.

In the subsequent Congresses Foley's middleman posture was even more readily visible. In the Ninety-fifth, with the farm program again up for renewal, he shifted modestly toward the center and broadened his appeal (just as Poage had done at the time of the previous renewal). He belonged to the largest Democratic cluster; he also maintained strong ties to the remaining clusters (Appendix 2, Table 4). His interagreement scores also indicate his centrist position: Not only did he vote with all Democrats, northern Democrats, and liberals, but also the conservatives and the conservative coalition gave him modest backing (see Appendix 3). Only all Republicans and the ranking minority member, William Wampler (Virginia), opposed him regularly. In the Ninety-sixth Congress Foley displayed vintage middleman behavior: He sustained moderate, positive associations with all four Democratic factions and with all Democrats, northern Democrats, and liberals, and he regularly opposed both Republican blocs as well as all members of the GOP, the ranking member, conservatives, and the conservative coalition.

Overall, then, Foley appears to have paralleled Poage's posture. He accommodated the liberal Democrats whenever possible but moved toward the middle of the ideological spectrum (though without abandoning the middleman style) when necessary to ensure passage of basic farm legislation. The internal alignments and patterns of leadership in the Agriculture Committee, in sum, look very similar during the Poage and Foley chairmanships.[4]

Committee performance data tell basically the same story: Agriculture under Foley behaved much as it had under Poage. Table 4.1 presents the pertinent measures of committee performance and indicates that although there was a somewhat

TABLE 4.1

Congressional Committee Performance, 92nd-96th Congresses:
Committees Experiencing Major Change

| | Committee Attributes | | Committee Performance | | | |
Committee and Congress/Ch.	Voting Cleavage	Leadership Style	Partisan Votes (%)	Committee Integration	Chair "Wins" (%)	Floor "Wins" (%)
Agriculture						
92 Poage	P	M	55	.38	91	85
93 Poage	U	B	52	.35	77	77
94 Foley	U	M	68	.25	73	80
95 Foley	U	M	70	.30	89	91
96 Foley	P	M	56	.33	91	85
Armed Services						
92 Hebert	B	B	12	.57	94	100
93 Hebert	B	B	16	.55	92	91
94 Hebert	B	B	23	.39	80	86
95 Price	B	B	32	.43	57	94
96 Price	B	B	30	.36	48	94
Banking						
92 Patman	U	M	61	.31	67	81
93 Patman	U	M	44	.38	79	85
94 Reuss	U	M	77	.31	83	89
95 Reuss	U	M	50	.37	75	86
96 Reuss	P	M	70	.34	85	87
Ways and Means						
92 Mills	B	B	34	.40	88	96
93 Mills	B	B	55	.32	81	96
94 Ullman	P	M	74	.22	78	88
95 Ullman	P	M	62	.25	80	80
96 Ullman	P	E	75	.23	75	90

Notes: P—Partisan/Ideological; B—Bipartisan; U—Unstructured; E—Extremity; M—Middleman; B—Bipartisan. The measures of committee performance are described in Appendix 1.

more partisan cast to the committee after the new chairman
took over, continuity was more characteristic than change.
For instance, in the immediate postreform period, there were
an increase (from 55 and 52 percent to 68 and 70) in partisan votes and a concomitant decline in committee integration. However, these trends were in large part reversed in
the Ninety-sixth Congress, which looks very much like the
Ninety-second, a decade earlier, in terms of these indicators of performance. More importantly, perhaps, the new
chair "won," that is, secured the voting support of a committee majority, on about the same proportion of votes as
had his predecessor. Similarly, the committee carried the
day on the House floor to a comparable extent, with the exception of the Ninety-fifth Congress when it was unusually
successful in sustaining its positions. These shifts in
behavior no doubt reflect Foley's greater liberalism and
more central location within Democratic party ranks but
hardly define dramatic departures from the committee's behavior when Poage was chairman.

To summarize, given the extensive changes that hit the
Agriculture Committee in 1975 and thereafter, the degree of
committee continuity seems extraordinary. Under both Poage
and Foley the panel was most often unstructured in factional
terms; both pursued centrist, most often middleman, leadership styles, moving to extend their appeal when necessary
to ensure renewal of the basic farm programs. Although
Foley was a somewhat more mainstream Democrat,[5] committee
behavior became only slightly and temporarily more partisan
after he assumed the chair. Fundamentally, despite all the
shifts in personnel, structure, and chairmanship, Agriculture
members continued to pursue the same goal throughout the
1970s: passage of farm legislation that protected the com-
modity interests of their constituents (Ornstein and Rohde
1977). Both chairmen, operating in a similar committee environment, appeared to maneuver with similar strategies and
with equal success to achieve this end. Change and reform
seemingly did little to alter the committee's ability,
under Foley, to attain its basic purpose.

Armed Services: The Hawks Still Have It

Like Agriculture, the Armed Services Committee is,
for the most part, a reelection-oriented committee (Bullock
1976). Although its jurisdiction includes most major military matters and gives members a secondary but clear set of
programmatic concerns, Armed Service has not often imposed
its own views on the Pentagon (see Chapter 1). Thus, traditionally, the committee has been a "hawkish" panel, where
consensus in support of a strong defense and a focus on the
distribution of military projects among the constituencies
have prevailed. This was certainly the case in the Ninety-
second and Ninety-third Congresses, when F. Edward Hebert
was chairman. The committee's factional structure before
1975 was clearly one of bipartisan consensus (Appendix 2,
Tables 6-7). Of the ten clusters that formed in this period
(six in the Ninety-second Congress and four in the Ninety-
third), seven were bipartisan and nine were moderate to conservative in outlook. Overall, the voting patterns in Armed
Services are entirely consistent with the view of the committee as united by common ideology in support of a powerful
military establishment.

Hebert was certainly central to this consensus; his
bipartisan leadership style is obvious in both Congresses.
In the Ninety-second, he joined three Republicans, including the ranking minority member, Leslie Arends (Illinois),
in a bipartisan conservative bloc and maintained the support,
often substantial, of each cluster in the committee (Appendix 2, Table 6). His associations with all party, regional, and ideological groups were positive (Appendix 3,
Table 1). In the Ninety-third Congress the picture was
identical. Hebert belonged to the dominant, 13-member, bipartisan, conservative coalition cluster, which included
the ranking Republican, William Bray (Indiana). As before,
he won support regularly from all factions and from all partisan, regional, and ideological elements. In both Congresses, in short, Hebert was part of a powerful bipartisan
voting agreement.

The reform movement altered Armed Services, although
perhaps with less impact than it had on Agriculture. Hebert

fell victim to the purge that the Democratic Caucus conducted at the outset of the Ninety-fourth Congress; Melvin
Price of Illinois, second in committee seniority, replaced
him in the chair. Price was less conservative and a more
national Democrat than Hebert, but as a product of Armed
Services he differed only slightly on military affairs (Berg
1978). In addition, the 1970-75 reforms were largely in
place in Armed Services when Price took over. On the other
hand, despite the Republican debacle in the 1974 midterm
elections, turnover in the committee was a relatively low
22 percent. It is not surprising in these circumstances
that committee politics under Price differed only slightly
from the previous period.

The bipartisan bloc structure of Armed Services persisted during Price's chairmanship (Appendix 2, Tables
8-10). In the Ninety-fourth Congress six clusters formed,
four of which crossed party lines and five were moderate to
conservative. Five clusters are evident in the Ninety-fifth
Congress: four bipartisan and four at the moderate-
conservative end of the ideological spectrum. Similarly,
two years later there were six factions, five crossing party
lines and all save one falling within the moderate to conservative ideological range. One hint of change, however,
did intrude on the clear survival of the committee's
pro-military consensus. In each of the postreform Congresses there appeared a "dovish" cluster of northern liberal Democrats that dissented from the dominant point of
view. Thus, in the Ninety-fourth Congress Les Aspin (Wisconsin), Ronald Dellums (California), Bob Carr (Michigan),
and Thomas Downey (New York) formed a discernible faction.
Two years later Patricia Schroeder (Colorado), another liberal Democrat, joined Carr and Downey in a bloc that frequently opposed the majority. And, in the Ninety-sixth
Congress, Carr, Schroeder, and Lucien Nedzi (Michigan) constituted an equivalent cluster.

The new chairman, although fundamentally a liberal
Democrat, did not join the dissenters. Rather, he persisted
in the bipartisan-consensual leadership tradition (Appendix
2, Tables 8-10). In 1975-76, he belonged, together with
his predecessor, to a six-member, bipartisan, moderate-
conservative bloc. He sustained positive but relatively low
associations with four of the five remaining factions, and

he maintained positive, but again modest, relationships
with most party, regional, and ideological groups (except
for liberals and northern Democrats) and with the ranking
Republican member, Bob Wilson (California) (see Appendix 3).
In the next Congress a similar situation obtained. Price
joined no faction but steered a middle course among those
that formed, voting regularly with four of the five clusters. In addition, his interagreement scores with committee element--party, regional, and ideological--were positive, although his association with the ranking minority
member was slightly negative. In the Ninety-sixth Congress
Price was a member of a five-member, bipartisan, moderate
cluster. His associations with the four remaining factions
were positive, if small, although his negative interagreement score with the committee's most conservative cluster
suggests that Price moved somewhat toward the left in
1979-80. His associations with the party, regional, and
ideological groups were positive, although low, but that
with the ranking member remained slightly negative. In sum,
Price seemingly sought and won votes from the moderate-
conservative, bipartisan committee majority.

Committee performance under Price points to continuity
rather than change (Table 4.1). The new chairman, despite
his greater loyalty to his national party, seems to have
introduced only modest shifts, toward partisan behavior, in
the panel's performance. There was an increase in partisan
votes, coupled with a decrease in committee integration.
The emergence of the dissenting doves certainly contributed
to this development.[6] The chair "won" in committee somewhat
less frequently in the Ninety-fifth and Ninety-sixth Congresses, but the committee's floor success rate was not
lower in the later period. In short, Armed Services performed similarly before and after chairmanship change.

The weight of the evidence--committee factional alignments, the chair's leadership style, and committee behav-
ior--suggests, then, that change and reform altered Armed
Services less than might have been expected. Although Price
was a more national Democrat than Hebert, and despite the
appearance of a liberal minority--which combined to produce
somewhat more partisanship on the panel--the pro-military
bipartisan consensus emerged largely unscathed after 1975.
The old values survived, in part because Price shared them

and in part because a "selective recruitment" phenomenon (Cook 1980; Ray 1980) guaranteed that the hawks would retain their majority on the committee. Again, as in the case of Agriculture, the moral seems clear: Committee members' motives and goals are paramount; where they remain intact, the impact of reform and change, intended and otherwise, is likely to be peripheral, not central. Unless lawmakers want to transform their committee, traditional modes of be-havior are likely to survive, even in the face of external pressure for institutional modification.

Banking: Small Change on the Margin

The Banking, Finance, and Urban Affairs Committee is a policy committee whose members seek to shape public programs that concern financial institutions as well as numerous urban policy matters (see Chapter 1).   These subjects do not offer an easy opportunity for Banking members to pro-mote their own reelection; they also compel the committee to confront a heterogeneous environment. Given these con-ditions, it seems reasonable to predict a relatively fluid factional structure in Banking, and that was precisely the case during Wright Patman's chairmanship (Appendix 2, Tables 11-12). In the Ninety-second Congress fewer than half the members were aligned with any cluster; only two small blocs--one Democratic and liberal, the other Republican and conservative--formed. Similarly, in the next Congress the four small blocs that surfaced included fewer than half the members, were partisan clusters, and tended to vote along party lines. Overall, then, the committee seems to have been characterized by loose, shifting coalitions that differed from issue to issue and that precluded any stable factional pattern.

Patman, despite his reputation as a "populist" and a bit "erratic," steered a careful middleman course through the Banking Committee shoals. He belonged to no faction in the Ninety-second Congress but regularly won the votes of the liberal Democratic cluster. His associations with all Democrats, northern Democrats, and liberals were positive, and those with all Republicans, conservatives, potential members of the conservative coalition, and the ranking

minority member, William Widnall (New Jersey), were con-
sistently negative. In the next Congress little changed.
Patman was, in this instance, a member of the most liberal
Democratic cluster, but he also voted with the other Democratic faction consistently. He also commonly captured the
backing of a pair of eastern, urban, liberal Republicans—
Margaret Heckler (Massachusetts) and Matthew Rinaldo (New
Jersey). As in the previous session Patman's allies were
Democrats, northern Democrats, and liberals, and his foes
were drawn from Republican and conservative ranks. In sum,
in each Congress Patman pursued a middleman strategy to
mobilize all segments of his partisan majority.

Patman's removal was the most visible reform of the
committee. After considerable maneuvering the Caucus replaced him with Henry Reuss (Wisconsin), fourth on the
panel's seniority roster. Here, too, the choice fell on a
somewhat more liberal, more mainstream national Democrat.
On matters within Banking's domain, however, the differences between the two chairmen were negligible (Berg 1978).
In other ways Banking Committee reform was not particularly
tempestuous. Although half the members in the Ninety-fourth
Congress were new to the committee, they did not differ significantly from those they replaced. The general House reforms, including the subcommittee bill of rights, were
adopted in ways consistent with trends operating in the full
chamber.

Reflecting these conditions, committee politics under
Reuss differed only a little from the Patman period. In
the Ninety-fourth and Ninety-fifth Congresses there were
six small, exclusively partisan clusters in Banking (Appendix 2, Tables 13-14). In the former, 58 percent of the
members were aligned, but in the latter once again only a
minority of the panel were bloc members. These factions
tended to adopt partisan voting stances. In the Ninety-
sixth Congress (1979-80) partisanship increased, and the
factional cleavage in Banking moved from unstructured to
partisan (Appendix 2, Table 15). Two-thirds of the members
belonged to one or another of the six exclusively partisan
clusters that appeared. The underlying conflict between
Republicans and Democrats, implicit in the first four Congresses of the decade, became more overt in the Ninety-
sixth, perhaps reflecting the heightened partisanship of

the final days of the Carter administration. On balance, however, voting alignments in Banking from 1975 on differed only modestly from the pattern of the earlier period.

Reuss's behavior paralleled Patman's; he persevered in a middleman leadership posture. In each Congress he joined a liberal cluster and maintained positive associations with the other Democratic clusters and negative associations with the Republican blocs.[7] In each he won support from all Democrats, northern Democrats, and liberals but was regularly opposed to all Republicans, the ranking minority member, and committee conservatives. Reuss, in sum, positioned himself centrally within the ranks of his party. In addition, committee performance varied very little between the two periods (Table 4.1). On all four measures—partisan votes, committee integration, chair victories in committee, and panel floor success—Banking's performance with Reuss in the chair strongly resembled that during the Patman period.

Once again, reform, including chairmanship change, led to little meaningful alteration in committee behavior. The Banking Committee's factional structure, the chairman's place in it, and panel performance are all but indistinguishable before and after 1975. For most of the 1970s, members appeared to pursue policy individualism, shifting pragmatically from issue to issue and seldom voting consistently with any committee bloc. For his part, Reuss, like Patman, seems to have been unwilling or unable to assemble a cohesive majority. Neither his newly acquired status nor the more generally applicable House reforms seem to have allowed Reuss to move the committee far from its conventional path. Member goals, interests, motivations, and values seem to acquire a momentum of their own, one that institutional change may alter only rarely.

Ways and Means: Après Mills le déluge

Ways and Means epitomizes the influence-oriented committee (see Chapter 1). Under Wilbur Mills's chairmanship the panel minimized partisanship in order to maximize its members' power inside the House. Its broad jurisdiction over taxation matters enhanced its authority; the committee used its position to write finance legislation that, first

and foremost, would pass the House. Its decision-making
process, which Mills guided with consummate skill and sen-
sitivity, featured a search for accommodation and agreement.
If the committee was unified, the full House, trusting and
deferring to Ways and Means's expertise, would accept the
committee's legislation. The consensus that Mills and a
supportive panel majority forged was a moderate-conservative
one; the few liberals on the committee might dissent, but
the remaining moderate members were capable of compromise.
The result was a committee, integrated and carefully consid-
erate of the full chamber's sentiments, that wrote legislation that regularly and readily passed.

The data for the Ninety-second Congress are entirely
consistent with this portrait of Ways and Means (Appendix
2, Table 41). There was some minimal partisanship in the
panel. Four factions emerged, two conservative and two
liberal; three of the four were exclusively partisan.
Mills, however, followed a classic bipartisan-consensual
leadership style. He joined no faction but sustained positive associations with three of the four clusters, particularly with the 11-member, conservative coalition cluster.[8]
More importantly, Mills maintained cordial, and substantial,
relations with all party, regional, and ideological elements, including John Byrnes (Wisconsin), the ranking Republican. This style enabled Mills to "win" on 88 percent of
all committee roll calls and led to a committee floor success rate of 96 percent.[9] This performance was vintage
Mills: bipartisan consensus created amid restrained
partisanship.

In retrospect, we can see that Mills's decline developed during the Ninety-third Congress. The reform movement hit Ways and Means hard: Its sessions were now to be
public, and it lost the protection, in theory if not regularly in practice, that the closed rule had given its
legislation on the House floor. Simultaneously, Mills's
personal problems grew, seemingly distracting him from his
usual close attention to committee business. Accordingly,
panel politics shifted modestly but visibly (Appendix 2,
Table 42). During 1973-74, there were three factions; one
eight-member conservative coalition faction regularly opposed two smaller, liberal Democratic blocs. Thus, underlying partisanship, constrained somewhat by conservative

coalition alignments, continued to characterize the committee. It was Mills's behavior that shifted during this
Congress. As before, he belonged to no faction, but now
his relationships with the more moderate elements in Ways
and Means were attenuated, and his major support came from
his Democratic colleagues. Specifically, he won the backing
of the two Democratic clusters and had positive associations
with all Democrats, northern Democrats, and committee liberals. By contrast, his interagreement scores with the
bipartisan cluster, all Republicans (including the ranking
member), conservatives, and the conservative coalition were
essentially zero (Appendix 2, Table 42, and Appendix 3).
Thus Mills's bipartisan leadership style produced few out-
right enemies but only moderately strong supporters.

Mills's long and distinguished tenure ended abruptly
in the Ninety-fourth Congress. HIs personal problems became
public, and he gave up the Ways and Means chair. The liberal Democrats were quick to impose new restrictions on the
committee. The Caucus added 12 new members, many of them
liberals, to the panel and required that the committee
create subcommittees. Mills had dominated a small group
that conducted its business in full committee sessions. In
addition, the Democrats transferred their committee assignment role, traditionally a strong basis for Ways and Means's
members' inside influence in the House, to the Steering and
Policy Committee. In sum, genuine revolution hit Ways and
Means; the committee in 1975 differed dramatically from
what it had been only two or three years previously.

To succeed Mills, the Democrats chose Al Ullman (Oregon), second in committee seniority. The new chair faced a
formidable challenge: He needed not only to assume the top
leadership spot but also to find ways to manage a vastly
altered committee. His ostensible followers were younger,
more liberal, more independent, and more likely to represent
competitive rather than safe districts than the members Mills
had managed so adroitly (Rudder 1977, 1978). Moreover, the
committee's prestige had been successfully challenged, and
numerous nonmembers—the full House and lobbyists, who had
access to the committee both in the required open meetings
and through their electoral influence on the more marginal
new members—were in a position to participate in committee
deliberations, many of which took place at the subcommittee
level.

It is not clear how Ullman would have preferred to proceed. Perhaps, as a product of the committee, his preference was to carry on in the bipartisan-consensual tradition. Perhaps, as a more mainstream national Democrat than his predecessor, he was content to permit the increased partisanship that the reforms produced to prevail. Whatever his intent, Ullman presided over a distinctly more partisan panel. In the Ninety-fourth Congress the number of roll calls—less than 75 per Congress under Mills—soared to 235, indicative of the breakdown of consensual committee politics. The four clusters were, in contrast to the previous Congresses, now exclusively partisan. On the right flank there appeared a five-member Republican bloc, a faction of three southern Democrats, and one of three moderate Republicans. An 11-member liberal Democratic faction provided the opposition (Appendix 2, Table 43). The shifting combinations of these groups contributed to the rise in partisan-ideological conflict in the committee: When the parties did not oppose one another, cleavage fell along conservative coalition lines.

This pattern continued in the Ninety-fifth and Ninety-sixth Congresses. In the former, once again, a conservative Republican cluster of seven members aligned regularly with a pair of southern Democrats—Omar Burleson (Texas) and Joe Waggonner (Louisiana)—and/or a group of three more moderate Republicans, including Barber Conable (New York), the ranking member (Appendix 2, Table 44). The Democratic majority was fragmented, consisting of two similar liberal blocs and a more moderate doublet of Andrew Jacobs (Indiana) and Martha Keys (Kansas).[10] In the Ninety-sixth Congress the partisan pattern was equally clear. A ten-member, conservative Republican faction opposed a liberal Democratic cluster of nine members and an equally progressive, four-member bloc of Democrats; the two Democratic elements voted together commonly (Appendix 2, Table 45). In the three postreform Congresses, then, partisan-ideological conflict clearly superseded the consensual politics that Mills had cultivated so assiduously.

Ullman's behavior reflected this heightened partisanship. He seems, in the Ninety-fourth and Ninety-fifth Congresses, to have pursued a middleman leadership strategy to mobilize his heavy Democratic majority. In 1975-76, he

belonged to no cluster but won the support of the liberal
bloc in his party; he was opposed often by the conservative
Republican faction and on occasion by the smaller GOP and
the dissident southern Democratic groups (Appendix 2,
Table 43). More generally, his relations with Democrats,
northern Democrats, and liberals were positive, while those
with Republicans and conservatives were not (Appendix 3).
The same circumstances existed in the Ninety-fifth Congress.
Ullman voted with a liberal Democratic cluster, won support
from the two other similar blocs, and opposed the Republican
and southern Democratic factions (Appendix 2, Table 44).
In addition, he sustained positive agreement with Democratic
and liberal elements in the committee but was frequently
at odds with the Republican-conservative groups. In these
two Congresses Ullman's position was entirely consistent
with middleman leadership.

In the Ninety-sixth Congress, however, perhaps because of Ways and Means's travails on the House floor,
Ullman moved toward an even more partisan leadership style,
taking an extremity position. He joined no faction but
voted regularly with the major liberal Democratic cluster
(Appendix 2, Table 45) and a second, smaller but almost
equally liberal bloc; his connections with the more moderate
Democrats were positive but more modest. Moreover, during
1979-80, the chair maintained strongly positive relations
with Democrats, northern Democrats, and liberals and negative associations with Republicans, conservatives, and the
conservative coalition (Appendix 3). In short, when he
encountered problems, Ullman's response was to become more
partisan; he seems to have made no effort to restore the
bipartisan-consensual alliance of the previous period.

The performance of Ways and Means also highlights the
shift from consensus to partisan conflict (Table 4.1). The
committee divided along partisan lines far more frequently
after 1975, up from 34 and 55 percent to a high of 75 percent party line votes when Ullman adopted an extremity
posture in the Ninety-sixth Congress. Likewise, full
committee integration declined visibly. Ullman's strategy,
presumably geared to the political realities of a given
Congress, enabled him to "win" committee roll calls almost
as often as did Mills. If he could hold his party together,
his position tended to triumph. But on the floor he fared

considerably less well. Lacking the support of a cohesive
committee--Mills's forte--Ways and Means's floor success
rates fell precipitously, from well over 90 percent to about
80, in the Ninety-fourth and Ninety-fifth Congresses; committee victories did rebound in part when Ullman moved to
an extremity leadership style at decade's end. In general,
as its partisan conflict spilled over onto the House floor,
Ways and Means found its recommendations rejected more
regularly.

Reform and change battered Ways and Means mercilessly
in the 1970s. In contrast to Agriculture, Armed Services,
and Banking, virtually every aspect of the committee altered.
Enlargement and ordinary turnover combined to create a committee quite distinct in personnel. Its organizational and
structural attributes were also vastly different, particularly the requirement that it use subcommittees. Its relations with its environment--not only the more liberal House
but also extralegislative participants--differed dramatically after 1975. Finally, the committee's issue agenda,
especially with the emergence of the energy crisis that followed the 1973 Arab oil embargo, shifted significantly. The
new chairman had to confront all these changes.

Although it is difficult, if not impossible, to iso-
late the effects of these factors singly, there can be little doubt about their cumulative impact. What had been a
bipartisan-consensual committee under Mills became a
partisan-ideological panel when Ullman assumed the chairmanship. The most important consequence of this change was the
committee's reduced capacity to sustain its legislation on
the House floor.[11] Over the long run, if the committee
cannot recoup its position, it risks permanent loss of its
status and power in the House.[12]

The twin tremors of reform and change rocked Congress
during the 1970s. The shock approached earthquake proportions for four House Committees when the Democratic Caucus
toppled the entrenched senior leaders, the chairmen. In
three of the four cases the consequent change in committee
factional alignments, in the chairman's place in the factional structure, and in committee performance suggests continuity not radical reorientation of committee politics.
Agriculture, Armed Services, and Banking looked in most ways

very similar throughout the 1970s. This implies, for one
thing, that chairmanship change was more symbolic than
policy related in these instances. The three new chairmen
were northern, mainstream Democrats, in clear contrast to
those they replaced; but they were also committee members
with long service, presumably well versed in committee
norms and routines. Their accession to the top leadership
positions signaled the ability of the Democratic majority,
riding high in the post-Watergate period, to impose its
will on committees, but sent the message without disrupting
the ongoing processes that each panel's members seemingly
valued.

In addition, these three cases, and that of Ways and
Means as well, imply an important role for political partisanship as a deterrent to chairmanship change. Each of
these panels, in sharp contrast to other House committees,
had unstructured or bipartisan lines of cleavage before
1975. Lacking a firm supporting partisan coalition, the
sitting chairmen of these committees, vulnerable on other
grounds, may have emerged as prime targets for Democratic
liberals' discontent.

Ways and Means is equally instructive. Unlike the
other committees, reform and change touched every aspect--
membership, structure, environment, and leadership--of the
committee. The result was dramatic; each attribute of
committee politics took on new forms. Restrained partisanship, featuring consensual leadership that produced committee integration and substantial floor success under Mills,
gave way to partisan factionalism, abetted by Ullman's more
partisan leadership style, that undermined Ways and Means's
clear dominance on the House floor. The committee was
fundamentally altered after 1975.

The lessons of these cases seem straightforward. Committees differ, and reform and change, in their various
guises, touch varying committees in varying fashions. Beyond new chairmen, Armed Services and Banking changed only
modestly during the reform era, Agriculture endured somewhat
more extensive alterations, but only Ways and Means suffered
genuinely radical transformation. Second, the consequences
of these shifts suggest that reformers may be hard-pressed
to achieve their purposes. Unless they can perform major
surgery, as they did in Ways and Means, they may find that

old ailments resist marginal tratment, as they did in the
other three instances. Conversely, and most importantly,
committees seem to develop customary modes of behavior--con-
sistent with members' goals and values and with their customary ways of dealing with their agendas--that reforms can
alter only with great difficulty. If members prefer "business as usual," because it serves the purposes they seek,
traditional behavior is likely to survive in the face of all
but the most major forms of change.

Finally, the seeming triumph of continuity and stability over substantial change puts the place of the committee
chairperson in perspective. Ousting the oligarchs, however
dramatic, may be of relatively little significance. Leadership may involve reciprocal relations between chairs and
followers, but the latter may have the upper hand. Chairmen
may operate in a far broader, far less mutable context than
is generally recognized; their options may well be severely
limited by the ongoing, widely accepted modes of managing
committee affairs. So long as followers remain content with
the old ways, their leaders may be hard-pressed to steer them
along new courses. The road to reform is arduous and unpredictable; even changing chairpersons is, at best, only
a short and uncertain step toward reaching reformers'
goals.[13] That three of these four committees, each singularly subjected to reform, emerged unscathed from the experience attests to the hardy persistence of committee
politics.[14]

EVOLUTIONARY CHANGE: IMPERSONAL FORCES

A second set of committees experienced reform and
change in less dramatic and immediately personal ways.
Budget, Government Operations, Post Office, and Rules were,
like all House panels, obliged to respond to the general
reform movement of the early 1970s. But each was spared the
trauma of forced leadership change; each, in fact, had more
than one chairperson during the decade, but the mantle
passed in these instances in evolutionary fashion, through
resignation, retirement, or defeat at the polls. In every
instance the succession was determined traditionally: The
surviving senior member took the chair in the subsequent

Congress with minimal controversy. Evolutionary, impersonal change of this sort should be less likely than the intentional assaults on sitting chairpersons and particular panels to undercut conventional committee procedures. If so, there should be greater behavioral continuity in these committees than in those where reform and change impinged more directly. On the other hand, even where change was evolutionary, new leaders did assume responsibility, and the forces for change--reform in general, personnel turnover, environmental shifts, and agenda alterations--did operate. Perhaps such developments are sufficient to undercut committee stability and to change the contours of comittee activity as much as more radical reform. In this section we examine these instances of more gradual change.

Budget: A Shakedown Cruise

The House launched the Budget Committee with the passage in 1974 of the Budget and Impoundment Control Act. As noted in Chapter 1, the committee undertook two roles: to establish and protect the new, presumably preferable process of producing budgets and to determine the allocation of federal funds within that process. The latter task quickly came to structure committee cleavage; partisan confrontation--with Republican conservatives attempting to limit expenditures in general and to commit more relatively to defense than to domestic programs and Democratic liberals stressing social spending--soon became the Budget Committee's order of the day. The controversy over size and focus of the budget regularly appeared in committee and on the House floor. Republicans, almost unanimously, voted against the panel's resolutions in both places, and the budget frequently came perilously close to sinking in the full chamber.

These circumstances created conditions that set Budget on a partisan course from the Ninety-fourth Congress on. In each of the three Congresses after 1975, classic partisan cleavage patterns were clearly visible (Appendix 2, Tables 46-48). Party polarization was high, with large, ideologically distinct, and strongly opposed blocs contesting the budget each year. For instance, in the Ninety-fourth

Congress, all eight Republican members joined a conservative
cluster that regularly voted against two liberal Democratic
factions. The parties fought fiercely over fiscal priorities in the subsequent Congresses as well.

   This partisan battle survived a change in chairmen and
one chairperson's shift in leadership style.[15] Brock Adams
(Washington) gave up his seat to join the Carter administration cabinet at the start of the Ninety-fifth Congress,
and Robert Giaimo (Connecticut) took over. The new chair
was slightly less liberal than his predecessor: Adams's
ACA ratings for 1975 and 1976, when he was Budget chairperson, were 7 and 8 percent; Giaimo's were 25 and 10 percent;
during his first year as leader Giaimo earned an ACA rating
of 24 percent. More fundamentally, however, the difference
was of marginal import. Lke Adams, Giaimo displayed the
extremity leadership style that strong polarization along
party and ideological lines seemingly dictates. As his
predecessor had, he belonged to the major Democratic cluster
and maintained close relations with all Democrats, northern
Democrats, and liberals (Appendix 3, Table 1). As expected,
he opposed the Republican and conservative elements in
Budget. In short, the change in leaders produced no visible
signs of new committee alignments or leadership styles.

   In the Ninety-sixth Congress, however, with the committee's budget resolutions increasingly in danger of being
swept away on the floor, Giaimo seems to have shifted strategy. A small southern-border state Democratic faction that
differed noticeably from one group of Democratic liberals
and sailed at some distance from the other (which included
the chairman) appeared. Giaimo may have felt he needed to
take some action to hold the Democrats together; in any case
his position moderated and he assumed a middleman posture
during 1979-80. He did belong to the largest Democratic
cluster, and he maintained positive associations with liberal Democratic groupings and mainly negative relationships
with the Republican, conservative opposition. These relationships were attenuated, however; for example, Giaimo's
agreement with northern Democrats was .49 in the Ninety-
fifth Congress and .28 two years later, and over the same
interval his association with the conservative coalition
rose from -.09 to .01. Within continued partisan cleavage,
strategic considerations seem to have dictated to the

chairman that he move toward the center; loss of his most
moderate party colleagues threatened to jeopardize the
committee's budget resolutions as well as his leadership
and he acted to avert such possibilities.

Committee performance (see Table 4.2) shifted only
slightly in consequence of these changes. When Giaimo succeeded Adams there was a small decline in partisan votes,
with a concomitant increase in committee integration; the
chair won a little more often in committee, but the panel
lost slightly more frequently on the floor. The new leader's switch to a middleman style two years later made no
difference at all in partisanship or integration and
saw a diminution in the chair's proportion of committee
"wins," partially offset by a gain in floor success. Overall, however, these changes seem modest, seemingly reflecting substantive politics--the need to pass a budget resolu-
tion--far more than reform or changes in committee outlooks,
personnel, or practices.

Government Operations: Charting a New Course

Government Operations experienced substantial change
in the 1970s. House reforms touched it as they did other
committees; in this case, two effects appear to have impinged importantly on Government Operations. General concern with legislative oversight, a major charge of the committee, grew greatly after Vietnam and Watergate. Although
the (Bolling) Select Committee on Committee's 1974 reform
proposals were largely rejected, they did highlight the need
for more serious congressional surveillance of the executive
branch, and the committee seems to have responded, becoming
substantially more active. In addition, the committee assumed jurisdiction over some significant policy issues--rev-
enue sharing and countercyclical economic programs, for
example. These developments made the committee more attractive to policy-attentive members, and the committee's
stigma as an undesirable, duty assignment faded markedly by
decade's end. Finally, new leadership took over in Government Operations: Jack Brooks succeeded Chet Holifield in
the chair, when the latter retired at the end of the
Ninety-third Congress.

TABLE 4.2

Congressional Committee Performance, 92nd–96th Congresses:
Committees Experiencing Evolutionary Change

| | Committee Attributes | | | Committee Performance | | |
Committee and Congress/Ch.	Voting Cleavage	Leadership Style	Partisan Votes (%)	Committee Integration	Chair "Wins" (%)	Floor "Wins" (%)
Budget						
94 Adams	P	E	85	.18	70	100
95 Giaimo	P	E	78	.25	94	88
96 Giaimo	P	M	77	.25	77	93
Government Operations						
92 Holifield	B	B	77	.27	100	100
93 Holifield	B	B	72	.42	83	92
94 Brooks	P	E	100	.24	69	77
95 Brooks	U	M	89	.30	76	91
96 Brooks	P	E	81	.26	81	85
Post Office						
92 Dulski	U	B	43	.49	95	100
93 Dulski	(Unclassified)	M	74	.34	(95)	(100)
94 Henderson	P	(Unclassified)	75	.23	(67)	(72)
95 Nix	P	M	66	.34	90	93
96 Hanley	P	M	100	.23	100	90
Rules						
92 Colmer	P	B	48	.28	67	89
93 Madden	U	E	71	.27	73	91
94 Madden	P	E	76	.28	78	97
95 Delaney	P	E	85	.27	85	96
96 Bolling	U	M	77	.34	84	94

Notes: P—Partisan/Ideological; B—Bipartisan; U—Unstructured; E—Extremity; M—Middleman.
The measures of committee peformance are described in Appendix 1.

These developments produced a substantial change in committee politics. Bipartisan consensus gave way to partisan conflict after 1975: Committee cleavage, the chair's leadership style, and panel performance indicated heightened Republican-Democratic antagonism. In the first years of the decade, moderate, bipartisan factions dominated the committee; there were smaller, more ideologically extreme Republican and Democratic factions in both the Ninety-second and Ninety-third Congresses, but the centerists controlled the committee helm (Appendix 2, Tables 21-22). The cumulative effect of the various changes and reforms altered the committee's course in the Ninety-fourth and subsequent Congresses. After 1975, the largest clusters were partisan alliances, although in 1977-78, few factions formed and the alignment was basically unstructured. In general (see Appendix 3, Tables 23-25), the middle-of-the-road bipartisanship of the earlier period foundered and the partisan contingents drifted toward opposite ends of the ideological spectrum.

The chairman's behavior was consistent with these general developments. Holifield had been a member of a moderate bloc in each Congress; he had Republican allies in each instance. Moreover, his associations with each partisan, ideological, and regional grouping were positive in each Congress (see Appendix 3). Brooks, by contrast, was far more partisan, at least in the committee setting.[16] In the Ninety-fourth Congress he was not a member of the liberal, 12-member Democratic faction, but he maintained a strong voting alliance with it (Appendix 2, Table 23). In the two Congresses thereafter he belonged to a liberal Democratic cluster. When the committee was most chaotic, in the Ninety-fifth Congress, Brooks was a middleman leader, perhaps seeking an optimum strategy to hold his divided crew together (Appendix 2, Table 24). When partisanship was stronger, he took on an extremity style (Appendix 2, Table 25). Throughout his chairmanship, Brooks's relations with liberal Democratic elements on the panel were positive and those with Republicans, conservatives, and the conservative coalition were negative (Appendix 3). From the perspective of the chair, Government Operations steered a more partisan course after Brooks's accession.

Committee performance suggests the same conclusion (see Table 4.2). Under Brooks's leadership the committee took more partisan votes. The new chair commanded a majority in committee less frequently. Intracommittee divisions reduced prospects on the floor, and, as expected, Government Operations' success rates declined during its more partisan period. Its victories were fewer during each Congress when Brooks chaired the panel than when Holifield occupied the top spot.

In short, over the 1970s, Government Operations evolved from a bipartisan panel to a more partisan body. Committee cleavage, leadership, and performance reveal greater partisanship in the period after 1975. A confluence of forces seems to account for the committee's new course. Agenda change is one. As new concerns energized the committee, new modes of activity became attractive and necessary. The need to root out bureaucratic "waste, fraud, and abuse" in periods of economic adversity and the obligation to make policy in areas added to the panel's jurisdiction may well have altered members' outlooks. Although turnover was low, continuing members appear to have become more active and more policy oriented. These developments, in turn, may well have induced environmental actors to pay more heed to committee activity, requiring committee adaptation. In consequence, subcommittees began to assume more responsibility (Ornstein and Rohde 1977; Deering 1982), especially for oversight, abetted of course by the subcommittee bill of rights.

These rather extensive changes make Government Operations resemble Ways and Means more than, say, Agriculture or Banking. Although there was neither open hostility toward the committee nor a forced change in chairmen--that is, change was evolutionary not revolutionary--Government Operations felt the force of substantial changes, and its processes and performance altered accordingly. Its ongoing procedures appear to have been disrupted, as those on more stable committees were not, and it adapted of necessity to its new circumstances. Should these current circumstances-- a recurring, complex, policy-focused agenda, treated in a heterogeneous environment by autonomous subcommittees--

continue to develop and become permanent, Government Operations should adhere to its present forms of behavior.   Future changes in chairperson, or increased membership turnover, might then have little or no impact on committee
patterns as relatively fixed routines retard and constrain
shifts in panel practices to a greater degree than has been
the case in recent years.

Post Office: Cast Adrift

The single most salient fact about the Post Office
Committee is the blow that the creation of the U.S. Postal
Service delivered.   The committee lost control over the
policy that had been its concern throughout the 1960s (see
Chapter 1).   In the ensuing decade, Post Office continued
to be a "duty" committee, whose members did not relish
service there.   With important postal matters (rates and
regulations) determined elsewhere, the panel operated in a
relatively homogeneous political environment.   Federal
employee unions constituted the committee's clientele;
others (the full House and the executive branch) seemed
largely indifferent to the committee.   In the previous period Post Office was largely a consensual, nonideological
panel (Fenno 1973); in the 1970s, its evolution, under a
succession of four chairmen and in the face of the general
reform tides, was a drift toward partisan-ideological
conflict.

The sharpest break came between the Ninety-second and
Ninety-third Congresses, unaccompanied by a change in leadership.   In the former, lines of cleavage were blurred; the
panel was unstructured (Appendix 2, Table 31).   There were
only three small but partisan factions.   The chair, Thaddeus
Dulski (D.-N.Y.), although a member of the largest faction
(five northern liberal Democrats), also maintained positive
associations with all party,   ideological, and regional
groups in Post Office.[17]   In keeping with the bipartisan-
consensual pattern, there were few partisan votes and committee integration was high; the chair commanded a majority
on 95 percent of the committee roll calls and the House
accepted the panel's position on every floor vote (Table
4.2).

Beginning in 1973, the committee took on a partisan coloration. Although its factional structure is unclassifiable by our criteria (see Chapter 3) in the Ninety-third Congress, in the three ensuing Congresses the alignment was partisan, with a liberal Democratic cluster in opposition to a conservative Republican bloc (Appendix 2, Tables 33-35). A succession of middleman chairmen, moreover, led the Democratic majority. Dulski moved toward the center of the political spectrum in the Ninety-third Congress, perhaps because an unstructured factional alignment dictated an effort to appeal to all fellow partisans. David Henderson (D.-N.C.) displayed no clear leadership style in the Ninety-fourth Congress, but his successors, Robert Nix (D.-Pa.) and James Hanley (D.-N.Y.), continued the middleman pattern in the subsequent Congresses. Dulski, Nix, and Hanley won the backing of Democrats, northern Democrats, and liberals, and each found Republicans, conservatives, the conservative coalition, and the ranking minority member regularly in opposition (Appendix 3).

Committee performance also altered in the Ninety-third Congress and thereafter (Table 4.2). Most visible were increases in the proportion of partisan votes and declines in committee integration, precisely the developments that enhanced partisanship predicts. On the other hand, except for the Ninety-fourth Congress, when Henderson took no clearly definable leadership position, the chair won in committee and the committee succeeded on the floor to the same extent in both the bipartisan-consensual and the more partisan-ideological periods. Dulski's shift to a middleman leadership style was accompanied by more partisanship in Post Office, and the changes persisted under Nix and Hanley. In the latter instances, new leaders did not introduce much change.[18] In addition, neither Dulski's "conversion" nor the accession of new leaders had much noticeable impact on either the chairman's internal or the committee's floor victories. In short, evolutionary trends, including agenda change, construction of the committee's environment, regular but not forced leadership change, and high membership turnover, produced mixed results, most clearly a more partisan voting pattern in Post Office. By 1980, the committee had shifted considerably from its bipartisan-consensual pattern of a decade previous.

Rules: Steady as She Goes

The Rules Committee plays a special role in the House. As the chamber's "traffic cop," it regulates the flow of legislation from the authorizing committees to the floor. Its ability to define the conditions under which the House will consider bills gives Rules and its members substantial influence over much of what the full chamber does (Matsunaga and Chen 1976). This central position confers considerable prestige on the panel; it is a powerful committee on which members have been eager to serve. Rules's importance also gives party leaders reason to care about it and its composition; they need a reliable gatekeeper to aid in promoting party positions (see Chapter 1). They hope and expect Rules to facilitate party goals.

This hope, however, has not always been easily realized. In the 1950s and 1960s, under conservative southern Democratic chairpersons—"Judge" Howard Smith (Virginia) and William Colmer (Mississippi)—Rules often thwarted the majority leaders. Two defecting Democrats voting with all the Republicans deadlocked the 12-member (eight Democrats and four Republicans) panel, 6-6, defeating leadership initiatives (under committee procedures a tie vote kills a motion). In 1961, after a bitter battle, the committee was enlarged to 15 members (ten Democrats and five minority members) to produce a more reliable, but often shaky, 8-7 Democratic majority after any southern conservative defections (Peabody 1963). In the 1970s, to obviate any possible recurrence of recalcitrance in Rules, another majority member was assigned to the committee, giving the Democrats an 11-5 edge, and the Speaker was empowered to nominate majority members of the committee, thus making Rules a functioning component of the majority crew (Oppenheimer 1981).

In light of Rules's institutional connection to majority party leadership, we would expect partisan-ideological conflict to characterize the panel more or less independently of changes in personnel or procedures. This, in fact, is what we find, with minor deviations, throughout the 1970s, particularly later in the period as the explicit reforms took hold. Even with Colmer in the chair, in the Ninety-second Congress, committee cleavage fell along partisan lines, although the conservative coalition was often

visible. Two Democratic clusters—one liberal, the other
moderate—regularly opposed a conservative Republican bloc
(Appendix 2, Table 36). Colmer and his fellow conservative,
William Anderson (D.-Tenn.), formed a separate bloc, and
with some support from John Young (D.-Tex.) voted with the
minority frequently. But the basic alignment pitted Democrats against Republicans. In the subsequent Congresses
partisan cleavage predominated. Colmer and Anderson left
Rules in the Ninety-third Congress and a northern liberal,
Ray Madden (Indiana), took the chair. We have described
the pattern as unstructured because a minority of members
belonged to any faction, but the two clusters that did form
were partisan-ideological opposites. A similar circumstance
developed in the Ninety-sixth Congress, and in the Ninety-
fourth and Ninety-fifth clear partisan conflict emerged.
In short, although its intensity seems to have ebbed and
flowed, Republican-Democratic cleavage constituted the underlying dimension of Rules Committee politics throughout
the 1970s.

After Colmer, leadership style was consistent with
basic committee partisanship. The Mississippi Democrat
pursued, as expected, a bipartisan style. Although he
maintained positive associations with each cluster and all
party, regional, and ideological groups except northern
Democrats, he was closer to the Republican and conservative
elements in Rules (Appendix 2, Table 36, and Appendix 3).
With Madden and his successors—John Delaney (New York) and
Richard Bolling (Missouri)—as chairpersons, leadership became avowedly partisan.[19] Madden and Delaney displayed
extremity styles, whereas Bolling was a more moderate middleman in the Ninety-sixth Congress. After Colmer's departure partisan leadership coincided with partisan factionalism in the committee (Appendix 2, Tables 37-40).

Colmer's leadership and conservative coalition behavior did dampen partisan conflict somewhat in the Ninety-
second Congress but not as much as might have been expected.
Thus, when liberal, partisan chairmen took over committee
performance altered in degree rather than kind (Table 4.2).
Party roll calls increased, from fewer than half to three
fourths or more; the chair commanded a committee majority
more frequently. But, by contrast, committee integration
remained constant, although, as expected, it rose somewhat

in the Ninety-sixth Congress when Bolling assumed a middleman leadership style. Floor success remained high through
the period. In short, partisanship, slightly submerged with
southern conservative Colmer in the chair, surfaced clearly
when more national Democrats succeeded to the top post in
Rules.

Overall, Rules Committee patterns and performance
seem consistent with the panel's place as an adjunct of
the majority party in the House. Its main function remained
to facilitate favorable treatment of Democratic party programs. Colmer, as it turned out, the last of the southern
conservative chairmen, was able to mute but not eliminate
committee partisanship. Indeed, he made no serious effort
to subvert his party systematically. Matsunaga and Chen
(1976) report that he, as an astute politican attuned to
House mores saved his fire for issues of singular significance to him, compromising or deferring on other matters to
promote harmonious relations with the majority of his Democratic colleagues. When he left the committee, and when
simultaneously party leaders successfully asserted control
over assignments to the committee,[20] Rules, under more liberal leadership, became a more visibly partisan body. The
change in chairmen from Colmer to Madden facilitated this
development, as did the general House reforms of the 1970s.
Subsequent accession of new leaders and further reforms
after 1973 merely reinforced the partisan cast of committee
politics. Evolutionary change, in other words, had some
but hardly a decisive impact on the Rules Committee.

More broadly, natural, impersonal evolution of the
sort that these four committees experienced suggests that
stability rather than change is the dominant feature of House
committees. Any number of factors in given committee settings seems to contribute to change, but none appears to
be either a necessary or sufficient condition for such
change. Rather, the cumulative impact of numerous changes,
if it disrupts ongoing committee patterns, is likely to
induce shifts in the ways committees go about their business.
Each of these committees experienced change and reform. Each had more than one chairman; each had chairs who
pursued differing leadership styles. The reforms of the
decade, in principle, affected each committee equally. In

fact, however, these forces of change and reform touched the different committees in different ways and to different degrees, and committee behavior evolved accordingly.

Government Operations, we suggest, was most forcefully affected. Its agenda changed in two ways: New responsibilities were added to its jurisdiction and its traditional concern, oversight, became a "hot" topic, stimulating increased activity on the part of the subcommittees chaired by liberals who had amassed substantial seniority. These developments seem to have enlarged the policy concerns on what had previously been an undesirable committee and to have broadened the range of environmental forces concerned with panel activity. In addition, the chair changed hands when Jack Brooks succeeded Chet Holifield. The cumulative impact of these events, most pronounced at the outset of the Ninety-fourth Congress, was to move the committee from a bipartisan-consensual to a partisan-ideological mode. Single shifts after 1975, in panel cleavage and in chairman's leadership stance, produced no dramatic alterations in committee performance.

Post Office and Rules experienced less extensive change during the 1970s. Creation of the U.S. Postal Service truncated the former's agenda, narrowing its environmental focus. Turnover remained high on a committee that continued to be an unwanted, low-prestige assignment for many members. After a period of uncertainty--unstructured bipartisanship and unclear, almost aberrant patterns under two chairmen--Post Office politics evolved into a partisan-ideological conflict under two new chairs in the Ninety-fifth and Ninety-sixth Congresses. This gradual change produced a committee quite distinct from the picture Fenno (1973) portrayed for the 1960s.

The principal development in Rules was its subordination to the Democratic party leadership, marked by the departures of Colmer and William Anderson after the Ninety-second Congress and by the Speaker's assertion of new powers over assignments to the committee. Under a succession of three chairmen--Ray Madden, John Delaney, and Richard Bolling--the committee's basic partisan character, suppressed but still apparent during Colmer's tenure, appeared more clearly. It remained visible, though with variations in intensity, in the face of new leaders and of changes in leaders' style. Consistent with the committee's role in the House, evolutionary change and reform led to rather modest changes in Rules's performance.

Budget evolved least of all. Throughout its six years of existence, it was the scene of intense partisan-ideological conflict over budgetary size and priorities. Neither high turnover nor changes in chairmen and leadership style altered the basic antagonism between Budget's Democrats and Republicans.

The experience of these committees, where evolution less than revolution characterizes their circumstances, suggests once again the tendency toward committee continuity. No single form of change or type of reform seems capable of moving committees from their conventional practices. It is, rather, the extent of change that matters. Where new pressures--environmental shifts, new members, altered agendas, changed chairpersons--converge, committee politics is likely to reflect these new conditions. Government Operations and, to a lesser extent, Post Office are cases in point. Conversely, as Budget Committee behavior illustrates, minimal change of one or another sort is unlikely to force a committee to adopt new forms of activity. It takes, in sum, strong winds of change to propel committees of Congress on to new courses.

MINIMAL CHANGE: CONSTANT PERFORMANCE

The remaining two committees, especially Education and Labor, experienced less upheaval in the 1970s than the other panels. The broad events of the era had potentially no less effect on these committees. The reform movement in Congress similarly carried with it the promise for change in Education and Labor and in Commerce. What distinguishes these two committees, however, is that these occurrences seemed to have less impact on them, perhaps because their chairpersons served throughout the decade and adhered to a single leadership style over the five Congresses. In consequence, more than the committees previously treated at least, committee politics, particularly as seen in terms of committee performance, remained quite constant.

Commerce: Continuity Despite Internal Upheaval

Interstate and Foreign Commerce presents a somewhat anomalous situation. Congressional reform and shifting internal considerations introduced clear and important changes in the committee. Significantly, the panel's Democrats restructured the body (see Chapter 1); they wrote new rules, they seized control of an increasingly autonomous set of subcommittees, and they circumscribed the powers of the chairman while permitting him to retain his position. The liberal-dominated Democratic Caucus, however, did deprive Harley Staggers of the top spot on the prestigious Oversight and Investigations subcommittee. Given these changes, and despite Staggers' continuing status as presiding officer, fundamental shifts in committee performance might have been expected. Few alterations, however, actually appeared over the ten-year interval we consider.

In fact, the one basic change was an evolution in Commerce Committee cleavage from partisan-ideological alignment to a bipartisan configuration featuring the conservative coalition. By the Ninety-fifth and Ninety-sixth Congresses there existed close collaboration between Republican and southern Democratic blocs, and in the latter specific conservative coalition clusters crossing party lines appeared for the first time (Appendix 2, Tables 29-30). Staggers, however, remained a faithful middleman leader despite the reorientation of committee factionalism. In the Ninety-third and Ninety-fourth Congresses he belonged to a liberal Democratic cluster; after 1977, however, he was unaligned. Throughout the period, he sustained mostly positive associations with Democratic blocs and with Democrats, northern Democrats, and liberals;[21] conversely, his relations with Republican clusters, Republican members, conservatives, the conservative coalition, and the ranking minority member were consistently negative (Appendix 2, Tables 29-30 and Appendix 3). The chair, it seems, fell increasingly outside the committee's main currents as the decade unfolded.

Most importantly, however, committee performance remained basically unchanged over the period (Table 4.3). With the exception of a decrease in partisan roll calls, expected as cleavage came increasingly to cross party lines,

TABLE 4.3

Congressional Committee Performance, 92nd-96th Congresses:
Committees Experiencing Minor Change

| Committee and Congress/Ch. | Committee Attributes | | Committee Performance | | | |
	Voting Cleavage	Leadership Style	Partisan Votes (%)	Committee Integration	Chair "Wins" (%)	Floor "Wins" (%)
Education and Labor						
92 Perkins	P	E	80	.30	80	71
93 Perkins	P	E	69	.34	83	88
94 Perkins	P	E	84	.39	83	89
95 Perkins	P	E	75	.37	84	81
96 Perkins	P	E	94	.30	86	80
Commerce						
92 Staggers	P	(Unclassified)	84	.21	--	(91)
93 Staggers	U	M	78	.21	48	91
94 Staggers	P	M	86	.25	85	85
95 Staggers	B	M	83	.20	72	84
96 Staggers	B	M	69	.24	77	88

Notes: P—Partisan/Ideological; B—Bipartisan; U—Unstructured; E—Extremity; M—Middleman.
The measures of committee performance are described in Appendix 1.

in the Ninety-Sixth Congress roughly eight of ten votes saw
the parties opposed to one another. After a poor showing
in the Ninety-third Congress, when the voting pattern in
Commerce was unstructured, the chair was consistently on
the winning side in committee. Moreover, committee integration and panel floor success were strikingly constant in
the face of the changes in organization and factionalism
that took place. In short, internal upheaval induced only
modest changes in committee performance.

Education and Labor: The Triumph of Continuity

Little needs to be said about Education and Labor.
Its politics proved remarkably durable. On the whole, although the committee did readjust and strengthen its subcommittees' structure and although its prestige declined,
reform and change did not require basic reorientation of
committee patterns (see Chapter 1). Carl Perkins, moreover,
chaired the committee in all five Congresses. Neither the
panel's partisan-ideological factionalism nor the chairman's
extremity style of leadership changed at all. Democrats
and Republicans contested social issues, and Perkins led
the former as a member of a strongly liberal bloc in each
Congress (Appendix 2, Tables 16-20). The chair's relationships with liberal elements were always strongly positive
and those with conservative groups almost always equally
negative (Appendix 3).

Committee performance reflects the stability in internal committee politics. Partisan roll calls fluctuated
somewhat,[22] but committee integration, the chairman's success in securing the support of a committee majority, and
(with the partial exception of the Ninety-second Congress)
the committee's floor "wins" were basically unchanged for
ten years (Table 4.3). In the case of Education and Labor,
in sum, marginal adjustments to the times produced no
alteration in committee politics; stability in committee
cleavage and leadership went hand in hand with continuity
in committee performance.

Commerce and Education and Labor, alone among our
committees, did not suffer a change of chairpersons between

1971 and 1980. The latter displayed great stability, and the former, although intracommittee turmoil seems to have produced an unsettled pattern of voting cleavage, performed in a rather consistent fashion across the decade. These results underscore the continuity of committee politics and buttress our argument that a marked set of changes rather than any single shift seems required to induce new forms of committee performance. These two panels operated in a steady fashion, we suggest, because they had developed a customary way to conduct business that was never sufficiently disrupted to mandate change in performance. Both are policy committees that dealt, in a heterogeneous environment, with a range of complex issues that persisted over the years. Both had low turnover and a rather well-articulated set of increasingly autonomous subcommittees. The result seemingly is that both had well-established routines from which there was no compelling reason to depart significantly.

CONCLUSION: CHANGE AND CONTINUITY IN COMMITTEE POLITICS

We have assessed the effects of three types of change, broadly defined, on ten House committees. Congress and its committees act in a world that events outside its halls shape to a major degree; the legislature can do little more than respond, as it sees fit, to international crises and domestic controversies. The legislature can, however, seek to reform its own structures and processes with a conscious effort to create "better" procedures or to produce "superior" policies. Congress did so extensively during the early 1970s. Finally, politics proceeds according to its own seemingly inexorable logic--members come and go, to and from Congress and committee; committee leaders assume and relinquish authority within the individual panels.

These three sets of forces--external events, congressional reform and "ordinary" politics--impinge on legislative committees in different ways and, we find, produce different results. We reach this conclusion after examining three groups of committees. Four panels seem to have confronted major change, not only the impact of broad trends

but also the direct attention of congressional reformers who
ousted the sitting chairpersons. Another four committees
experienced more moderate, or evolutionary, change; they
also acted in a context that events and reform altered, but
their new leaders assumed authority in more normal fashion.
The final two committees seem even less the object of specific pressures; beyond the general developments that affected the House, they received little attention from those
outside their committee rooms.

We expected that change would affect these committees
to different degrees. Because the forces promoting change
hit the first set most heavily, their performance should
have been more likely than that of other committees, which
suffered lesser disruptions of conventional patterns, to
alter over the decade of the 1970s. These expectations
were only partially met, however. It is the case that the
extreme instances of change and continuity were in the predicted categories. Ways and Means falls at one pole of the
continuum. Almost every feature of the committee was dramatically altered. Its agenda changed in response to external events; reforms dramatically altered its membership,
structures, and procedures; a new chairman took over following the forced resignation of his predecessor. By 1980,
what had been a bipartisan-consensual committee of substantial influence had become a partisan-ideological panel of
reduced power and effectiveness in the House. At the other
pole Education and Labor·was least affected by events of
the period and its lines of cleavage, leadership patterns,
and committee performance were remarkably consistent.

Between these polar cases, however, were deviations
from our predictions. Agriculture, Armed Services, and
Banking each had leadership change imposed on it, and
Agriculture and Banking experienced high turnover. Yet
each continued to behave, in terms of voting cleavage, leadership styles, and committee performance, in much the same
fashion as it had early in the 1970s. A major change did
not, in these cases, have much noticeable impact on their
activities. Similarly, the Government Operations Committee,
where change was evolutionary in our scheme, was altered
considerably, perhaps more than any other committee save
Ways and Means. New agenda items and a heightened concern
for old issues coupled with a significant, though not forced,

change in leaders led Government Operations to abandon its early bipartisan-consensual politics, under Chet Holifield, and to move to a partisan-ideological posture, with concomitant shifts in committee performance, after Jack Brooks took the chair.

These cases indicate, in sum, that change comes in differing ways, in consequence of differing developments, to individual committees. We again caution against sweeping generalizations about congressional committees and the committee system. Committees must, we believe, be treated as individual bodies and assessed in terms of their particular locations in congressional politics, as well as in light of their particular membership, organizational, and procedural attributes.

On balance, the weight of our evidence suggests that, ceteris paribus, continuity is a central aspect of committee politics in Congress. Forces of stability, that is, impose considerable constraint on the possibilities for dramatic change in the ways committees act. Of the ten committees, only three--Ways and Means, Government Operations, and Post Office--displayed substantial change in performance during the 1970s. The other seven performed with considerable consistency. This is not to argue, of course, that these latter panels, although we label them as "stable" committees, did not exhibit changes of consequence. Voting cleavage in the Commerce Committee, for instance, evolved from partisan to bipartisan (conservative coalition), despite Harley Staggers' continuing chairmanship. Similarly, Rules displayed shifts in both factionalism and leadership style. In neither case, however, did these developments produce vastly different patterns of committee performance.

Such continuity seems to reflect the durability of committee politics. Any number of factors--low turnover, constant member goals and motives, a fixed policy agenda, a stable environment, acceptable procedural routines featuring autonomous subcommittees, and leadership continuity--seem to contribute to the persistence of committee behavior. Change in any of these dimensions might require new forms of committee activity, but this does not appear to be the case. As our data indicate, several panels did experience high turnover (Budget, Agriculture), or structural alteration (Education and Labor), or even forced leadership

succession (Armed Services, Banking) without major consequent change in performance. No single change, in other
words, seems sufficient to disrupt regular committee
routines.

By contrast, where there occurs some combination of
multiple changes in these dimensions, committee performance
change seems much more likely to follow. Thus the enlargement of Ways and Means put new members with new goals on
the committee; public sessions exposed it to new environmental forces concerned with new issues (for example,
energy); imposition of subcommittees disrupted ordinary
procedures; the ouster of Wilbur Mills brought Al Ullman to
the chairmanship. It was the cumulative impact of this set
of changes that altered Ways and Means Committee performance,
that reduced the committee's policymaking effectiveness.
Similarly, the combination of changes and reforms explains
the more pronounced behavioral variations in Government
Operations and Post Office. The former experienced agenda
change and an increased stress on policy; it altered its
subcommittee patterns somewhat and leadership change.
Each witnessed the emergence of new forms of activity.
A series of major changes rather than any particular shift
of any particular type appears best to explain the emergence
of altered committee behavior. In the absence of cumulative change and reform, the old order prevails, and
continuity characterizes committee politics.

Some circumstances, however, do seem associated with
change; at least they seem to increase a committee's vul-
nerability to dislocation of its conventional modes of
doing business. Member goals are one such factor. Two
of the least stable committees (Government Operations and
Post Office) were duty committees, whose members presumably,
preferring to serve elsewhere or committing their energies
more fully to other assignments, were less wedded to committee routines. Second, agenda change seems critical;
where a panel must confront new issues (Government Operations, Ways and Means) or refocus its attention on a more
limited menu (Post Office), old patterns are more likely to
require adjustment. Third, changes in environmental forces,
which may flow directly from agenda shifts, may require
adaptation to new pressures; each of these three less
stable committees was confronted with an altered environment.

In addition, two of the changing committees experienced high turnover (Ways and Means, Post Office); new members, less socialized in conventional procedures, may take
on new roles more readily. In the same vein, two of these
these three committees (Post Office is the exception) made
relatively modest use of their subcommittees. As less
"institutionalized" bodies, their members had fewer vested
interests in panel procedures, and in consequence may have
been less reluctant to adopt new structures in the face of
altered committee circumstances. Finally, the winds of
change swept more forcefully over bipartisan or unstructured
panels. Given that party loyalty is a major influence on
members of Congress, it is reasonable to surmise that where
partisan sentiments are high, where committee politics reflect party commitments, flexibility will be reduced. The
most changeable committees all featured minimal or nonpartisan alignments; each thus seems more susceptible to abandoning old political patterns.[23]

Old ways change slowly in congressional committees.
It takes a singular combination of forces—new members, new
agendas, a changed environment, new leaders—to force a
committee to reshape its politics. Where continuing committee members confront a recurring and often complex
policy agenda in a heterogenous environment, where they
use standard procedures, especially independent subcommittees, to do so, and where leadership style remains constant,
change is less likely. Simply put, the more complicated the
committee's politics, the more resistant to change it remains. Because such complex patterns are more common than
simpler arrangements, committee politics in Congress in-
clines toward continuity rather than change.

NOTES

1. Writing about reform has been a growth industry
for scholars concerned with Congress. General treatments
of the reform movement include Davidson, Kovenock, and
O'Leary (1966), Huntington (1973), Ornstein (1974, 1975),
Welch and Peters (1977), Rieselbach (1977, 1978), Patterson
(1978), and Sundquist (1981). On change more generally,
consult Dodd and Oppenheimer (1981), Dodd and Schott (1979),

Mann and Ornstein (1981), and Hinckley (1983). For a list-
ing of pertinent studies, see Rieselbach (1983).

2. As in previous chapters, for ease of presentation,
we refer the reader to Appendixes 2 and 3, where the full
array of data--factional structures, the intercorrelations
among those blocs, and the chairperson's relationships to
the clusters and other committee groups--is presented.

3. Poage's only negative association (IA = -.29) was
with the ranking minority member, Charles Teague, who was
replaced midway through the Ninety-third Congress by William
Wampler. Poage's association with the new Republican leader
was positive (IA = .24).

4. Even when each leader confronted a partisan rather
than an unstructured factional pattern (Poage in the Ninety-
second Congress, Foley in the Ninety-sixth), the proportion
of partisan roll calls (Table 4.1) was relatively low,
slightly more than 50 percent. In each instance there was
no major farm bill to pass, and in each case the committee
endured some additional party conflict with little or no
visible effect on its performance.

5. Foley became majority whip in the Ninety-second
Congress, at least in part because, as a mainstream Democrat,
he was broadly aceptable within the party.

6. The rise of this antimilitary faction seems to
have stimulated the conservative coalition within the committee. The proportion of coalition roll calls rose in the
Ninety-fourth and Ninety-fifth Congresses, to 41 and 46 percent, but declined somewhat, to 26 percent, in the Ninety-
sixth, under Price (see Table 2.1).

7. The single exception to this generalization is
trivial; in the Ninety-sixth Congress Reuss's agreement with
a relatively moderate Republican faction (Appendix 2, Table
15, cluster 1) was positive (IA = .02) but insignificant.

8. Mills did differ, although modestly, with the
liberal Democratic doublet of Charles Vanik (Ohio) and
James Corman (California). (See Appendix 2, Table 41.)

9. These success rates are at least equal to those
that Manley (1970) and Fenno (1973) describe for Mills and
Ways and Means in previous decades.

10. This coupling shows conclusively that bedfellows
need not make strange politics.

11. Most dramatically, the committee's 1975 energy tax legislation was decimated on the House floor. Similarly, in 1977, Speaker Thomas P. O'Neill felt obliged to use an ad hoc committee on energy to hold together an energy package, which included tax provisions over which Ways and Means had jurisdiction, during floor consideration. On these and other instances, see Rudder (1977, 1978) and Oppenheimer (1980). See also, more generally, Vogler (1981).

12. Al Ullman lost his 1980 reelection bid and was succeeded as Ways and Means chair by Daniel Rostenkowski (Illinois). Lacking roll call data, we cannot be sure of the new chair's position in the committee; however, impressionalistically at least, it appears that he has been cautious, preferring to protect his panel's position rather than to advance innovative tax policies and risk floor rejection of them. See Fessler (1983).

13. For instance, liberal reformers, it seems safe to speculate, were probably disappointed with both the performance of the finance panel under Ullman and the increasing power of the Budget Committee that Ways and Means's decline seemed likely to occasion.

14. For a study of an entirely separate aspect of congressional committee change, using an entirely independent data base, see Hammond and Langbein (1981). Specifically, the authors find that "reform had no direct impact" (p. 28) on committee activities once other factors were controlled.

15. High turnover, which House rules requiring membership rotation on the Budget Committee mandated, seems to have had no impact on panel partisanship. Each party's recruits reflected the same ideological outlooks as those they replaced.

16. In fact, in general, Brooks was less liberal than Holifield. His ACA scores for the Ninety-third Congress, when he was second in committee seniority, were 38 for 1973 and 25 for 1974; Holifield's were 20 and 14, respectively. The implication, once again, is that committee norms and processes constrain leadership behavior. When confronted with the overall circumstances of the committee, Brooks, we may infer, felt a need to behave in a more partisan fashion than his predecessor.

17. Dulski's only negative interagreement was with a very conservative (ACA = 93) Republican pair--John Rousselot (California) and Edward Derwinski (Illinois)-- and it was quite low (IA = -.04). (The data for the Ninety-second Congress are in Appendix 2, Table 31, and in Appendix 3.)

18. The succession of chairmen of Post Office varied somewhat ideologically. Dulski was a moderate-liberal with ACA scores of 33 and 14 in 1973 and 1974 (the Ninety-third Congress). Henderson was much more conservative (ACA scores of 57 and 60 in the Ninety-third and 69 and 71 in the Ninety-fourth Congress). Nix was a sharp contrast, with ACA ratings ranging from 0 to 17 for the Ninety-fourth Congress, before he became chairman, and the Ninety-fifth, when he occupied the top rung of the committee ladder. Hanley was, like his fellow New Yorker, Dulski, a moderate-liberal, with ACA ratings between 17 and 32. All this suggests, once more, the constraining influence of committee politics. Henderson was, in effect, out of touch with the committee majority, and assumed an idiosyncratic stance. The other chairs produced similar results despite their variations in liberalism.

19. The chairpersons who followed Colmer were all substantially more liberal than he. The contrast between Colmer and Madden was particularly stark; in the Ninety-second Congress, when both served, the former's ACA ratings were 88 and 95 for 1971 and 1972, while the latter's were 7 and 9. Delaney and Bolling consistently scored in the liberal range, below 31. That Colmer's extreme general conservatism did not appear so strongly in committee indicates once more the constraining role of committee norms and processes.

20. For example, in the Ninety-third Congress, when Colmer and William Anderson were no longer in Congress, the Democratic leaders engineered the appointment of more dependable southern, relatively conservative lawmakers--Clem McSpadden (Oklahoma) and Gillis Long (Louisiana). They continued to nominate more loyal Democrats to Rules throughout the decade. Thus, while adhering to norms like regional balance, the leadership ensured that Rules would follow the party line.

21 Staggers did oppose a three-member southern Democratic conservative cluster in the Ninety-fifth Congress and a six-member, extremely conservative (ACA = 84) conservative coalition bloc in the Ninety-sixth (Appendix 2, Tables 29-30). These were the least liberal clusters that attracted Democratic members in the entire period, and Staggers' modest antagonism to them (IA = -.12 and -.17, respectively) seems consistent with the middleman posture that saw him maintain positive agreement with all other elements in his party.

22. The Ninety-third Congress reveals what little variation there is in Education and Labor politics. In 1973-74, perhaps reflecting a low floor success rate in the previous Congress or in light of the specific issues before the committee in the Ninety-third, Perkins did sustain slightly positive interagreements (IA = .01 and .07) with Republicans and the conservative coalition. Each other aspect of his behavior, however, is consistent with stable extremity leadership on a partisan-ideological committee.

23. We acknowledge that we cannot demonstrate conclusively the importance of these factors. But they do reflect tendencies in the ten committees. Thus, for instance, two of the three most changed committees experienced high turnover, but only three of the remaining seven did. Likewise, all three altered committees began basically as bipartisan or unstructured committees in the Ninety-second Congress, while one of the seven more stable panels was a bipartisan body. Finally, all of the policy committees with heterogeneous environments were among those that changed least. The factors discussed in these paragraphs, then, seem at least speculatively related to the incidence of committee change.

5
Conclusion:
Committee Politics
in the 1970s

In a very real sense, congressional politics is committee politics. For a century, and particularly since the
1910–11 House revolution against Speaker Joseph Cannon
undercut strong political parties, committees have been
the central loci of legislative decision making. They have
the expertise necessary to dominate consideration of issues
within their jurisdictions; in consequence, they have won
the respect, sometimes reluctant, or at least the deference
of nonmembers. Committee views have tended to become congressional policies. The highpoint of committee government
in Congress may have come in the 1960s, when the individual
panels constituted the basic feature of a highly "institutionalized" legislature (Polsby 1968). Congressional rules
and norms protected the committees' positions; autonomous
panels were at the core of a decentralized decision-making
process in the House of Representatives.

Committee power, not surprisingly, evoked a reaction
from members of Congress who shared insufficiently in the
exercise of that power. Agitation for reform began in the
mid-1960s and, when coupled with major events that multi-
plied the pressures on Congress and with substantial membership turnover, led to modifications in committee, and thus
congressional, politics in the subsequent decade. Indeed,
the first formal set of changes, which the Legislative Reorganization Act of 1970 contained, included the requirement

that committees record and make available their roll call
votes. In this book we have used these newly available
data to chart some aspects of committee behavior: lines of
cleavage within ten House panels, patterns of leadership
in these committees, and the changes that occurred in them
during the 1970s. These analyses have led us to some general conclusions about congressional committees and about
legislative politics more generally that we summarize and
extend in this concluding chapter.

CONCLUSIONS: CONGRESSIONAL COMMITTEE POLITICS

Our investigation of varying attributes of ten House
committees has produced some broad conclusions about committee conflict, leadership, and change.

Committee Distinctiveness

Paradoxically, perhaps, a first generalization about
congressional committees is that it is dangerous to generalize about congressional committees. Committees are distinctive entities; no two are quite alike. To be sure,
House panels share basic features, defined by chamber rules
and congressional practices and expectations. These broad
contours—for example, the requirement that committees have
subcommittees or the conventional organization along party
lines—however, reveal very little about real committee
politics. Within the context such regularities define, we
discover a rich variety of congressional committee patterns.
Member motivations, committee agendas, environmental conditions, and committee norms and processes combine in varying ways to produce distinctive forms of committee factionalism, leadership, and performance.

Moreover, no single predisposing condition seems
decisive in determining the shape of committee politics.
For instance, one panel where reelection concerns motivated
members was basically fluid and unstructured in its voting
alignments (Agriculture), and another (Armed Services),
whose members pursued the same goal, retained a bipartisan
factional pattern. Nor does any other committee attribute

account for political configurations. In short, Fenno
(1973) is certainly correct that congressional committees
vary and vary widely, but our analysis of a ten-year period
suggests that it is difficult to categorize committees
with complete accuracy. There are some regularities, more
precisely some tendencies in the data, but in general, observers should be cautious in discussing the "committee
system" in Congress. Our analysis of change underscores
this point: Congress-by-Congress comparisons reveal that
individual panels may take on new forms as time passes. We
do not want to overemphasize committee change; in fact, we
find and stress a considerable continuity in committee politics. We do, however, believe that stability reflects
combinations of conditions peculiar to particular committees more than the impact of any individual influence on
all panels. In this sense, continuity and distinctiveness
are entirely compatible aspects of committee politics. The
study of committees should start from the premise that individual panels are the appropriate units of analysis.

Committee Cleavage

One committee feature that helps to define committee
politics is the nature of voting cleavage. Committees prove
to be clearly distinguishable in terms of partisan factionalism. We predicted three possible forms of committee conflict: partisanship, which pits the Republicans against
the Democrats; an unstructured alignment characterized by
small clusters and substantial fluidity; and bipartisanship,
which features cross-party alliances. In 47 of 48 instances
a particular committee in a given Congress fit one or another of these hypothesized categories. Although the partisan pattern predominated (half the cases revealed party
cleavage), the others appeared regularly (see Table 2.5),
more often than floor voting would lead one to expect. Committee distinctiveness, then, rests in part on the existence
of diverging lines of cleavage in individual committees.

Committee variation also reflects differential mixes
of stability and change over the 1970s. Some committees
(for example, Education and Labor) displayed constant lines
of cleavage; others (Government Operations) developed

entirely new factional alignments over the course of the
decade. There was, in addition, substantial variation for
single committees from Congress to Congress. The overall
trend was toward an increase in partisan conflict by 1980.
These developments seem to flow from a number of forces.
On the one hand, national political trends and events may
induce change: The politics of the Nixon, Ford, and Carter
presidencies (Vietnam, Watergate, energy, recession) seem
to have heightened party conflict between 1971 and 1980.
On the other hand, constant committee member goals, which
low turnover and selective assignment and recruitment practices sustain, and fixed policy agendas seem to deter change
in voting behavior. Where likeminded members treat the same
issues repeatedly, within a relatively constant set of norms
and decision-making procedures, committee factionalism is
likely to endure; where these conditions do not exist,
variable voting is a more likely result.

Finally, and perhaps most important, committee cleavage contributes to understanding committee performance.
Among these ten committees bipartisanship is at least modestly associated with floor success. Panels that take
legislation to the full chamber with the unified support of
a cross-party coalition are more likely to see that legislation survive, unamended, than those bodies that are unable
to find consensus in committee. All in all, then, House
committees are distinctive in part because their members
line up differently when the committee roll is called;
these factional variations, in turn, bear a relationship to
committee performance.

Committee Leadership

Committee leadership also contributes to committee
distinctiveness. House committees differ substantially in
terms of the places their leaders--chairperson and ranking
minority member--assume in their voting alignments. We
specify three possible positions, or styles, that committee
leaders may adopt: extremity leadership, where the leader
joins those at the ideological pole of the party; middleman
leadership, where the leader's position is more central
within the party; and bipartisan-consensual leadership,

where the leader draws substantial support from both his own and the opposition parties. Here, too, the committees and their leaders fell easily into these categories; both committee chairs and ranking minority members almost always adopted one of the three styles we identify (see Table 3.4).[1] In short, committees vary in the ways the formal leaders relate to the rank-and-file. Moreover, leader-follower associations shift as time passes; only four of the ten panels displayed invariant patterns.

Certain conditions seem to influence committee leadership; committee distinctiveness does not reflect random variations in leadership. Those panels that have standard routines—stable membership pursuing complex but recurring policy matters in a heterogeneous environment, using fixed procedures—resist change. Those that lack such stable modes of operation impose fewer restraints on leaders, who in consequence seem freer to alter their relationships with their committee colleagues. Because these constraints affect the majority, which has the responsibility to process legislation, more intensely than they affect the minority, which can act as the "loyal opposition," the chairs exhibit more consistent links with ordinary committee members than do the ranking minority members. Leadership, in sum, is a reciprocal relationship: Individual leaders both influence and are influenced by conditions on the committee.

Committee leadership matters, our analyses suggest, because leadership style relates to committees' performance. Committees with extremity leaders as chairpersons are internally more partisan and less integrated; externally, they tend to succeed less often on the floor. As leadership changes—that is, as leaders come and go or as they shift their behavioral styles from one Congress to the next—committee performance shifts accordingly. Committee distinctiveness, then, flows from variation in the transactional interactions between leaders and followers and from the behavioral consequences that such relationships appear to produce.

Committee Change

If voting cleavage and leadership style contribute to committee distinctiveness, so does the differential

impact of change and reform on individual panels. We have
suggested that three forms of change, broadly defined to
encompass intentional alterations in political organization
(reform), affect legislative committees. First, major international and domestic events raise issues with which
some committees must deal; the energy crisis, for instance,
mattered more to the Commerce Committee than to, say, the
Agriculture Committee. Second, "reform" may be directed at
some panels more fundamentally (Ways and Means) than at
others (Education and Labor, for instance). Finally, evolutionary politics--chairmanship change and member turnover--
will touch some committees (Rules) more immediately than
others (Armed Services). These possibilities, and particularly the forced removal of four senior sitting chairmen,
led us to speculate about change and committee performance
in three sets of committees: those that experienced revolutionary, evolutionary, or minimal alterations during the
1970s.

Comparative analysis of these three groups of committees revealed that no single factor--member goals, turnover,
agenda change, or shift in pattern of cleavage or leadership style--entirely accounts for change in committee behavior. In particular, ousting an oligarchic chairperson
does not guarantee altered committee performance. Three of
the four committees that endured this "reform" looked virtually the same under new leaders as they had under the
deposed chairpersons. Nor does either internal upheaval
(as in Commerce) or leadership evolution (Rules, Budget)
seem to incline panels toward more than marginal deviation
from standard performance levels. As expected, minimal
change (Education and Labor) is unaccompanied by meaningful
modifications in committee behavior. In short, no specific
change of the sorts we consider seems adequate, taken
alone, to induce, much less compel, a committee to depart
from its customary modes of activity.

When significant performance change does come, as it
did to Government Operations, Post Office, and Ways and
Means, it appears to flow from the cumulation of several
forces. Although no particular factor seems necessary and
sufficient to induce committee change, a combination of
major developments that disrupts conventional operating procedures apparently can require new patterns and altered

performance. High turnover that brings new members with different motives to a committee, new agenda items that alter environmental pressures on a panel, new leaders, and "reformed" decision-making procedures may merge to jar committees out of old ways of conducting business. The three panels that revealed the greatest behavioral change, and especially Ways and Means, were subjected to major shifts; all experienced change in factional alignment, leadership style, and most importantly committee performance.

Change, we suggest, is the exception rather than the rule; continuity is more common for congressional committees. Seven of the ten panels, despite some shift in some aspect of their political circumstances, showed at most modest movement in their levels of performance. For a variety of reasons, related to member goals, environmental forces, and committee norms and procedures but not dependent on any specific one of them, committees seem to become "institutionalized," to develop satisfactory forms of activity. It seems to matter less what the precise bases of such satisfaction are than that members are, in fact, content with "the way things happen." They tend to remain so, we speculate, unless a combination of cataclysmic forces hits them. Because stability, predictability, accommodation, and personal courtesy are central congressional values to which most members subscribe, the conditions conducive to basic behavioral change rarely occur. Most committees operate in ways that satisfy most of their members most of the time, and consequently continuity comes to characterize much of congressional committee politics.

COMMITTEE CONTINUITY AND CHANGE: AN OVERVIEW

Looking at the basic dimensions of committee politics, cleavage and leadership, in combination reinforces the picture of committee distinctiveness within a context of committee continuity that the previous discrete analyses have revealed. Tables 5.1 through 5.5 present cross-tabulations of cleavage and leadership style for the Ninety-second through Ninety-sixth Congresses.[2] They indicate both the array of factional-leadership combinations and the alterations in these patterns that took place across the 1970s.

TABLE 5.1

Dimensions of Committee Politics, 92nd Congress

Leadership Style

	Extremity	Middleman	Bipartisan
Partisan	Education and Labor	Agriculture	Rules
Unstructured		Banking	Post Office
Bipartisan			Armed Services Government Operations Ways and Means

Voting Cleavage

N = 8.

TABLE 5.2

Dimensions of Committee Politics, 93rd Congress

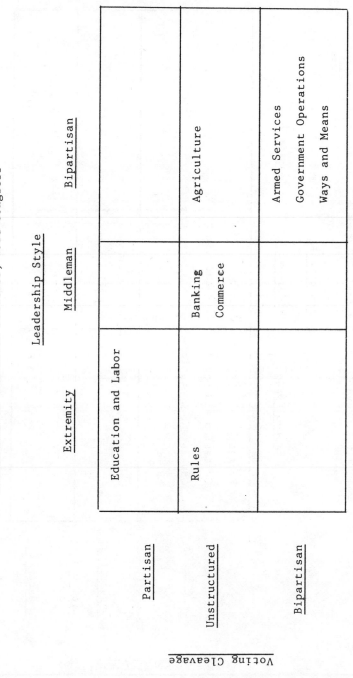

	Leadership Style		
Voting Cleavage	Extremity	Middleman	Bipartisan
Partisan	Education and Labor		
Unstructured	Rules	Banking Commerce	Agriculture
Bipartisan			Armed Services Government Operations Ways and Means

N = 8.

167

TABLE 5.3

Dimensions of Committee Politics, 94th Congress

Voting Cleavage	Leadership Style		
	Extremity	Middleman	Bipartisan
Partisan	Budget Education and Labor Government Operations Rules	Commerce Ways and Means	
Unstructured		Agriculture Banking	
Bipartisan			Armed Services

N = 9.

TABLE 5.4

Dimensions of Committee Politics, 95th Congress

	Leadership Style		
Voting Cleavage	Extremity	Middleman	Bipartisan
Partisan	Budget Education and Labor Rules	Post Office Ways and Means	
Unstructured		Agriculture Banking Government Operations	
Bipartisan		Commerce	Armed Services

N = 10.

TABLE 5.5

Dimensions of Committee Politics, 96th Congress

Leadership Style

Voting Cleavage	Extremity	Middleman	Bipartisan
Partisan	Education and Labor Government Operations Ways and Means	Agriculture Banking Budget Post Office	
Unstructured		Rules	
Bipartisan		Commerce	Armed Services

N = 10.

The first thing to note about these classifications is that over the five Congresses eight of the nine possible combinations occur at least once. Only the bipartisan factionalism—extremity leadership pattern never appears. More important, most cases fall along the main diagonals of the tables. Thirty-nine of the 45 classifiable cases indicate voting cleavage—leadership patterns of the expected sort; in 21 instances partisan voting and partisan——either extremity or middleman——leadership characterizes a committee. Another nine cases pair unstructured voting alignment with middleman leadership, entirely reasonable given a leader's need to hold together a disparate majority. Finally, nine cases match bipartisan voting and bipartisan-consensual leadership, again a quite comprehensible combination.[3] These frequencies sustain the view that voting cleavage and leadership style combine to create an array of distinctive patterns of committee politics.

Second, the frequencies of occurrence indicate the incomplete dominance of partisan politics in congressional panels. Slightly fewer than half the cases (22) involve partisan cleavage; more (33; 73 percent of the 45 classifiable cases) involve partisan leadership styles.[4] Moreover, the trend of the 1970s was toward increasing partisanship. In the Ninety-second and Ninety-third Congresses there were two instances of partisan voting—extremist leadership committees and one of the partisan cleavage—middleman leadership pattern. In the Ninety-fifth and Ninety-sixth there were six cases of each. In the most recent (Ninety-sixth) Congress there appeared one bipartisan panel (cleavage and leadership); there had been three such committees in both the Ninety-second and Ninety-third Congresses. Indeed, by 1979-80 seven panels had partisan-factional alignments, and nine revealed partisan (extremity or middleman) styles of leadership. Events of the decade, legislative change (especially high personnel turnover occasioned by exceptional levels of retirement; see Frantzich 1978; Hibbing 1982a) and reform, and the recession of the late 1970s seem to have combined to fuel the fires of congressional partisan conflict. What is surprising, perhaps, is that the heating up of party battles produced so little overall alteration in committee performance (see Chapter 4).

Tables 5.1 through 5.5 also highlight the "mix" of stability and change that characterizes congressional committees. The tables permit 34 comparisons of a committee's position in consecutive Congresses, for example, a comparison of the Agriculture Committee's location in the Ninety-second and Ninety-third Congresses. In 16 of these instances (47 percent), a given panel changed its location from one Congress to the next. Of the 16 cases, seven involved relatively minor shifts--a move reflecting a change in either voting cleavage or leadership style. Thus, for example, between the Ninety-fifth and Ninety-sixth Congresses, Banking Committee voting became partisan when it had been unstructured while its chairman persisted in pursuing middleman leadership (compare Tables 5.4 and 5.5). In five cases a particular panel moved on both voting cleavage and leadership style: Agriculture was a partisan cleavage-middleman leadership committee in the Ninety-second Congress but an unstructured bipartisan body two years later (Tables 5.1 and 5.2). These 12 cases involve shifts of one row or one column or both; because they entail movement into an adjacent cell in the tables, they can be considered minimal, or evolutionary, change.

The remaining four (of the 16) cases of change can, in contrast, be considered major. Each saw a committee move to a nonadjacent cell in an immediately subsequent Congress. One instance--Commerce between the Ninety-fourth and Ninety-fifth Congresses--involved a shift of voting cleavage only. When the committee's Democratic Caucus clamped down on Harley Staggers in 1975 (see Chapter 4), constraining him with new rules and removing him from a prestigious subcommittee chairmanship, partisan voting cleavage gave way to bipartisan factionalism. There may have been less to the change than meets the eye, however, for the cross-party alliance that emerged featured the conservative coalition. The liberal Democrats' takeover drove their moderate southern colleagues to vote with the Republicans in committee, leaving an ideological cleavage basic to committee alignment. Importantly, as noted, panel performance did not alter significantly in the wake of this internal committee upheaval.

The other three cases of major inter-Congress change in committee voting-leadership patterns entail movement on

both dimensions. Thus, for example, in Rules in the Ninety-
second Congress, William Colmer pursued a bipartisan chairmanship strategy on what was a fundamentally partisan
committee. When he left the chair, a more "normal" configuration appeared: His successor, Ray Madden, took an
extremity leadership stance and the committee's voting
cleavage shifted to an unstructured alignment. A partisan
pattern, cleavage and leadership, persisted throughout the
remainder of the 1970s, producing rather stable committee
performance.

The last two instances of significant change involve
committees that, we have argued, did become dramatically
different as a result of a set of several dramatic developments. In Government Operations, by the start of the
Ninety-fourth Congress (1975), an altered agenda and resulting changes in environmental pressures, a revamped
decision-making process featuring enhanced subcommittee
autonomy, and a new chairperson (Jack Brooks replacing Chet
Holifield) were in place. The committee promptly abandoned its bipartisan voting and leadership configuration in
favor of a pure partisan--party line voting and extremity
leadership--pattern and its performance altered measurably.

Finally, Ways and Means demonstrated equally dramatic
change. Under Wilbur Mills it had been a bastion of bipartisanship. After the wholesale assault on its prerogatives, personnel, and procedures, and with Al Ullman in
the chair, the committee quickly became a partisan panel.
Its votes revealed, in the Ninety-fourth Congress and thereafter, a classic Republican-Democratic confrontation, and its
chair pursued partisan leadership tactics. This shift, too,
was accompanied by substantial changes in levels of committee performance.

In short, change in the combination of cleavage and
leadership in congressional committees is common (occurring
in almost half the cases) but mostly minor (involving a
small shift on one or the other dimension). Committee politics (as in Commerce) or leadership change (as in Rules)
can cause shifts of significance, but once again only
major movements on multiple dimensions (Government Operations, Ways and Means) seem to produce the massive changes
necessary to alter committee performance--partisanship, integration, and floor success--in important ways. Our major

theme, stressing continuity of distinctive, individual committee patterns, thus reappears here. Congressional committees develop their own ways of accomplishing their tasks.
They adjust these, from Congress to Congress, apparently
in response to changes in their circumstances--new members,
new issues, House reforms, new leaders--but unless these
alterations cumulate in ways that undercut the conventional,
accepted modes of action, change is likely to remain modest
and marginal. Such combinations of significant shifts occur
rarely, and, in consequence, stability in voting, leadership, and most importantly committee performance is more
visible than change.

EPILOGUE: CONGRESSIONAL COMMITTEES IN THE 1980s

The safest, but probably most accurate, extrapolation
of these findings from the 1970s into the 1980s is to predict more of the same. In the absence of some singular set
of circumstances, war or worldwide economic collapse, that
requires abandonment of "ordinary politics," Congress is
highly unlikely to alter its fundamental operating procedures. Committees thus should remain the central loci of
legislative activity and decision making. If so, there is
no reason to believe that the individual panels will be
inclined to surrender their autonomy; they will, we expect,
continue to chart their own courses, responding differen-
tially to the particular circumstances in which they are
required to act at any specific time. Because these circumstances will vary from one committee to another, the
committees should preserve their own individuality. They
will adapt, probably only modestly and slowly, to the conditions they face. In short, the future appears to offer
distinctive committees marching to their own drummers, more
often changing at the margins than in any revolutionary
fashion.

This is likely to be the case, we predict, because the
fragmentation of authority within Congress that promotes
committee stability within diversity will in all probability
persist. The contingencies that might promote centralization of legislative activities, thus curbing the committees,
seem remote. One possibility, enhanced political parties

that would dominate policy making, runs against the congressional grain and 75 years of congressional evolution.
Members value their individual independence, which finds
frequent expression in the committee rooms, and show no
willingness to cede it to the parties, or any other agency.
The grudging way in which the reform movement added to party
power in the 1970s testifies to members' reluctance to increase party discipline. Only some grave crisis producing a
deep and widespread feeling of legislative incompetence
might generate structural change that strengthens the party
machinery; short of such a catastrophe, decentalization
rooted in independent committees and constituency politics
seems virtually certain to survive.[5]

A second possibility that might, in a somewhat nar-
rower fashion, undercut committee sovereignty flows from
budgetary politics. Fiscal problems, especially extraordinary budget deficits, that seem intractable have led to a
review of practice under the 1974 Budget Act. A series of
reform proposals—most fundamentally, a suggestion that all
financial decisions be incorporated in a single omnibus
budget bill—has emerged from a Democratic Caucus task
force, but little more than minor adjustments seems prob-
able. Chairpersons of the authorizing committees remain
vigilant, prepared to resist Budget Committee encroachment
on their turf. They are unlikely to acquiesce in reforms
that would centralize budgetary decisions in the hands of a
more prominent and powerful Budget Committee at the expense
of their panels (see Cohen 1983).

Thus, neither enhanced party discipline nor enlarged
Budget Committee authority appears likely, in the short run
at least, to impose discipline on a decentralized Congress.
The far more likely script calls for continued committee
distinctiveness. Each panel, responding to forces that
impinge on it, will adapt as necessary—and we expect as
minimally as possible—to the developments that affect it.
These forces for change, moreover, will continue to touch
individual committees in varying ways. Indeed, by the
Ninety-eighth Congress (1983-84), committee circumstances
had altered visibly. Most importantly, the election of 1980
brought Republican Ronald Reagan to the White House and gave
him a majority in the Senate but not in the House. The
administration's conservative program—smaller government,

lower domestic expenditures, and a stronger national de-
fense--confronted House committees with a new agenda.

Although there were no events with the drama and impact of Vietnam, Watergate, or the energy crisis, the Reagan
years did witness some major developments. On the domestic
front, the new administration had to deal with the most
serious and persistent recession since the Great Depression.
Giving high, almost exclusive, priority to the economy, the
administration proposed a "supply side" solution--simulta-
neous tax and expenditure reductions intended to stimulate
productivity--to the twin difficulties of inflation and unemployment that plagued the nation. In the House, the main
burden of dealing with these matters fell on the Budget and
Ways and Means Committees. Conversely, the Reagan policies
challenged the Banking and Education and Labor Committees,
the chief House defenders of the besieged social programs.
"Reaganomics" succeeded significantly in reducing inflation,
made substantial but less than desired cuts in social spending, achieved only a small diminution of the unemployment
rates, and, as a result of its economic "mix," left behind
enormous and unprecedented budget deficits.

Internationally, the administration's program was
simple: Confront the Soviet Union around the world, especially with a military buildup of major proportions. House
Budget and Armed Services committees were obligated to deal
with Reagan's initiatives. New weapons of staggering cost
would consume a much larger share of the federal budget.
More broadly, as detente diminished in consequence of arms
development and as American advisers and armed forces became
increasingly involved in Central American revolutionary politics and Middle East peacekeeping, Congress's concern to
keep presidential authority in check grew apace. And while
the recession retarded the energy crisis (demand for oil
declined as a result of conservation and economic dislocation), the nation, executive and legislative branches, retained a lively interest in Arab-Israeli relations.

Congress, and more particularly its individual committees, dealt with these matters in its usual fashion, its
circumstances marked by ordinary political evolution. As
the 1980s opened, the congressional retirement rate, high
in the previous decade, returned to its lower levels,
promising greater membership stability. Turnover among

committee chairmen, however, was great; of the ten committees examined here, only three--Armed Services, Government
Operations, and Education and Labor--had the same chair in
the Ninety-eighth Congress as in the Ninety-sixth. The accession of new leaders was accomplished without struggle,
in keeping with the seniority principle, and at the same
time there was little, if any, significant alteration in
committee rules or practices. The changes of the 1970s remained in place largely because the reform fervor that had
animated the earlier decade diminished. Only the startling
Supreme Court decision overturning the constitutionality of
the legislative veto--a major weapon that committees used
to challenge administrative actions--altered the balance
between the branches, depriving Congress of a significant
source of authority.[6] On balance, these developments seem
modest in their impact on Congress. The legislature in the
mid-1980s looks very much as it did at the conclusion of the
period we analyzed.

Given this general continuity, it would be rash indeed
to predict much change in committee politics. We expect,
then, barring the cumulative upheaval that seems to produce
substantial change, congressional politics to continue to be
committee politics and individual committees to continue to
operate in stable but distinctive fashion. Some will vote
along party lines; others will find bipartisanship more conducive to accomplishing their purposes. Different leaders
acting in different committee contexts will pursue partisan--
extremity or middleman--or bipartisan styles as they seek to
build winning coalitions for the legislative results they
seek to attain. Change, when it comes, will be modest and
gradual, reflecting marginal modification of the circumstances in which individual committees find themselves. In
addition, our analyses suggest the importance of party conflict as a stabilizing force: Where committee cleavage and
leadership revolve around party considerations, change comes
more slowly. The heightened committee partisanship that
evolved during the Carter presidency, and that seemingly
persists in the Reagan administration, thus implies enduring
committee patterns.

On the whole, then, we expect little dramatic change
in committee politics under ordinary conditions, and ordinary conditions show a strong tendency to survive all but

the most forceful sets of changes in membership, agenda,
environment, and committee norms and processes. What committees enact may well change, and change substantially,
but the ways the panels achieve these outcomes are likely
to persist. Characteristic modes of conducting business
should continue, and the chore of the analyst, in the 1980s
as in the 1970s, is to chart the contours of committee
politics. To do so will reveal distinctive but enduring
patterns of performance for particular committees. This
picture of institutionalized chaos may be disquieting or
difficult to decipher, but it is likely to reflect the
realities of committee politics and thus of a significant
portion of congressional politics as well.

NOTES

    1. Forty-six chairs and 45 ranking members fit our
assignment criteria easily (see Chapter 3). In fact, only ·
one instance for each leader category truly defied classifi-
cation--Post Office in the Ninety-fourth Congress, David
Henderson (D.-N.C.), chairman, and Agriculture, Ninety-
second Congress, Page Belcher (R.-Okla.), ranking member.
Commerce, in the Ninety-second, Harley Staggers (D.-W.Va.),
chairman, was excluded because he failed to vote often
enough to meet our standard for inclusion in the analysis.
Government Operations, Frank Horton (R.-N.Y.), ranking
member, was left unclassified in light of his interpretable
but eccentric voting behavior (see Chapter 3).
    2. We use chairmanship style to characterize com-
mittee leadership here, on the assumption that the chair
exercises more influence than the ranking member. We omit
those committees that were unclassifiable on either the
cleavage or leadership dimension: Commerce in the Ninety-
second Congress and Post Office in the Ninety-third Congresses. Budget is included from the Ninety-fourth Congress onward.
    3. The six remaining cases are not altogether im-
plausible. Three (Post Office in the Ninety-second Congress and Rules and Agriculture in the Ninety-third) involve
unstructured cleavage and either extremity or bipartisan
leadership. Given voting fluidity, leaders may resort to

varying strategies to assemble a majority. Three cases
seem to reflect the behavior of particular leaders. As
noted, William Colmer, a southerner, differed ideologically
from the liberal Rules Committee Democrats, and Harley
Staggers became increasingly estranged from his Commerce
Committee colleagues after they had circumscribed the
chair's powers. In each instance, the leader voted his
convictions, even at the cost of being "out of touch" with
the committee majority.

4. Tables 5.1 through 5.5 are based on 45 cases; Post
Office in the Ninety-second and Ninety-third Congresses and
Commerce in the Ninety-second were not classified on one or
the other dimension, as described in the text. Budget
existed only in the Ninety-fourth Congress and thereafter.
These cases yield 34 Congress-to-Congress comparisons.

5. For a stimulating set of speculations about legislative change that suggests a greater likelihood of
significant shifts in congressional politics in the immediate future, see Dodd (1983).

6. The Court ruled, in effect, that the veto using
the concurrent resolution, which the president was not required to sign, was an improper way to legislate. The
technique, whether one House or one committee used it,
violated the "presentment clause" of the Constitution,
which mandates that legislation is valid only when presented
to and signed by the chief executive.

Appendix 1

The analysis is based on committee roll call votes made
available by provisions of the 1970 Legislative Reorganization Act. Nine House committees were chosen for analysis because they met our arbitrarily determined criteria that at
least ten roll calls from each Congress be available for analysis. A tenth, the House Budget Committee, was added even
though it did not come into existence until the Ninety-fourth
Congress. However, it too met the requirement demanded of
the other committees.

Once collected, the data were edited in three ways.
First, all procedural and miscellaneous roll call votes were
eliminated. This included votes to close committee meetings,
refer bills to subcommittee, raise points of order, postpone
action on legislation, reconsider votes, and specify floor
procedures. Second, the remaining pool of substantive roll
calls (dealing with amendments to bills or with decisions to
report legislation) was reduced further by eliminating all
unanimous or near-unanimous votes (those on which 10 percent
or fewer of the members took the minority position); one-sided
roll calls distort the bloc structure the cluster technique
identifies. Third, all members who participated in fewer
than 60 percent of a committee's roll call votes were excluded
from the analysis; widely varying numbers of votes distort
the correlations that define the voting clusters.

We identify the factional alignments within each committee, for each Congress, with cluster-bloc analysis. (For a
discussion of the technique and its use in roll call analysis,
see Anderson et al. 1966, chap. 4.) The procedure uses vote
correlations to build a first cluster of committee members
to the point where adding members would produce a heterogeneous cluster. Second and subsequent clusters are then built
until all individuals have been assigned or until the remaining members fail to meet the defined minimum correlation for
being added to an existing cluster or for beginning a new
cluster. The OSIRIS program MDC was used to compute the
Pearson product-moment correlation between each member's

committee voting and that of each other member. The resulting correlation matrix was used as input to the OSIRIS program CLUSTER. See OSIRIS III, vol. 1, pp. 465–71, 679–86,
and vol. 5, pp. 29–37.

To start a cluster, two variables (committee members)
must correlate (vote together) at a level equal to or greater
than a given minimum threshold (startmin). To enter a cluster, individuals must have an average correlation with the
variables already in the cluster that is equal to or exceeds
a specified minimum (endmin). To stay in the cluster, the individual's voting must correlate with those already in the
cluster, at a level equal to or greater than a specified minimum (staymin). The choice of cutoffs, or minimum thresholds,
is critical: cutoffs set too high will minimize clustering;
those set too low will create either a multiplicity of small,
virtually meaningless clusters or a single all-encompassing
bloc. Using these procedures, we obtained the clearest picture of committee factional structure when startmin = .50,
endmin = .35, and staymin = .30. These values mean that to
be in a cluster, members must have an average agreement of
.35 with all others in that cluster and an agreement of at
least .30 with each other member. The Banking and Rules Committees were exceptions to this rule. The thresholds for
these two committees were set at startmin = .40, endmin = .30,
and staymin = .30 because clusters failed to form at the
higher thresholds.

We have considerable confidence in the validity of the
committee voting structures these methods produce, not only
because they make sense intuitively but also because they
are for the most part statistically significant. Willetts
(1972; see also Garson 1976, pp. 212–13) has devised a test,
which uses both the number of cases and the levels of agreement between individuals, to assess the statistical significance of empirically defined cluster blocs. Applying his
technique and interpretive criteria (see his table 2, p. 574)
to our data reveals that 192 of the 216 clusters identified
are significant at the .10 level. The remaining 24 are significant at levels between .11 and .17 (that is, the likelihood of their being chance agreements does not exceed one in
eight), and most are small (N = 2) factions marginal to the
analysis. (A table of cutoff points, similar to the one
Willetts provides, is available upon request.)

Cluster-bloc analysis empirically defines voting blocs
from the propensity of legislators to vote together on issues

before their committees. It provides no clue, however, to
the reasons why the blocs develop. To specify further the
underlying nature of the factions the technique identifies,
we explore the partisan and ideological bases of the blocs.
We examine the following groups.

—Partisan blocs

    Republicans: all committee Republicans

    Democrats: all committee Democrats

    Southern Democrats: all Democrats from the 11 states
       of the old Confederacy, Kentucky, and Oklahoma

    Northern Democrats: all Democrats from the remaining
       37 states

—Ideological blocs

    Conservatives: all committee members whose Americans
       for Constitutional Action (ACA) ratings are above
       50 percent

    Liberals: all members with ACA scores of 50 percent
       and below

    Conservative Coalition: all Republican and southern
       Democratic members

We use average interagreement scores, reflecting agreement levels between each pair of committee members (see Anderson et al. 1966) to compare the committee chairperson
with the voting factions and with the party and ideological
groups within each committee, as well as to compare voting
clusters with each other. The vote correlation matrix used
to identify clusters contains additional information. Because each member's voting relationship with every other member is known, it is an easy matter to focus on particular
sets of associations in which we have some interest. Thus
we can compare the committee chairperson with all Democrats
(or any other group) simply by averaging the correlations
between the chair and each Democrat on the committee. This
average is the "(average) voting correlation" score. When
clusters are compared it is the "(average) intercluster correlation." The interagreement (IA) scores range from 1.0 (voting agreement between members of the criterion group on each
roll call on which they participated) to -1.0 (disagreement
with each member on each roll call).

To relate the leadership patterns to committee performance, we use the following measures:

—Partisan votes: the percentage of committee roll calls on
   which a majority of Democrats opposed a majority of
   Republicans
—Committee integration: the "proportion of times each committee member agrees with every other committee member"
   (Dyson and Soule 1970, pp. 633-35)
—Party integration: committee integration controlling for
   party
—Floor wins: the percentage of floor roll calls on which
   majorities of the reporting committee and the full House
   agree
—Chair wins: the percentage of committee roll calls on
   which the chairman is on the winning side.

The measure of floor wins (or floor success) includes votes
on amendments and final passage. If a majority of the committee and the full House agree, we assume that the former
are satisfied with the outcome. In fact, committee majorities oppose about three-fourths of all floor amendments, and
their position prevails on more than 80 percent of the floor
votes. Each of the three measures of committee performance
uses only those roll calls that meet the criteria for inclusion in the cluster-bloc analysis.

Appendix 2

TABLE 1

Agriculture, 92nd Congress

Representative	Party	State	Cluster (N = 011)					
			1	2	3	4	5	6
Abernathy, T.	D	Mississippi	.54					
De Lagarza, E.	D	Texas	.69					
Purcell, G.	D	Texas	.67					
Stubblefield, F.	D	Kentucky	.67					
Link, A.	D	North Dakota	.66					
Melcher, J.	D	Montana	.69					
Jones, E.	D	Tennessee	.66					
Burlison, B.	D	Maryland	.53					
Sisk, B.	D	California	.65					
Jones, W.	D	North Carolina	.65					
Poage, W.	D	Texas	.73					
Sebelius, K.	R	Kansas		.71				
Mayne, W.	R	Iowa		.61				
Wampler, W.	R	Virginia		.55				
Teague, C.	R	California		.62				
Abbitt, W.	D	Virginia			.61			
Price, R.	R	Texas			.71			
Mizell, W.	R	North Carolina			.65			
Zwach, J.	R	Minnesota				.50		
Denholm, F.	D	South Dakota				.51		
Alexander, B.	D	Arkansas				.63		
Mathis, D.	D	Georgia				.58		
Vigorito, J.	D	Pennsylvania					.69	
Matsunaga, S.	D	Hawaii					.69	

Name	Party	State		
Bergland, B.	D	Minnesota		.61
Foley, T.	D	Washington		.61
Belcher, P.	R	Oklahoma		
Goodling, G.	R	Pennsylvania		
Mathias, R.	R	California		
Miller, C.	R	Ohio		
Findley, P.	R	Illinois		
Kyl, J.	R	Iowa		
Rarick, J.	D	Louisiana*		
McMillan, J.	D	South Carolina*		
Baker, L.	R	Tennessee*		
Robinson, K.	R	Virginia*		
Dow, J.	D	New York*		

*Member participated in less than 60 percent of the votes.

Mean Cluster Scores

	1	2	3	4	5	6
ACA	52	80	94	50	16	07
Party identification (percent Democrat)	100	00	33	75	100	100
Conservative Coalition	54	82	88	53	27	19

Vote Correlation Between Leaders and Clusters

	1	2	3	4	5	6
Chairman	.73	-.20	.16	.13	.04	.61
Ranking Minority	-.25	.01	.01	-.05	-.10	-.02

Intercluster Correlation

	1	2	3	4	5
2	-.20				
3	.28	.04			
4	.13	.19	.08		
5	.18	.24	.10	-.13	
6	.37	.03	.00	-.14	.25

TABLE 2

Agriculture, 93rd Congress

Representative	Party	State	Cluster (N = 048)					
			1	2	3	4	5	6
Jones, W.	D	North Carolina	.44					
Gunter, B.	D	Florida	.44					
Bowen, D.	D	Mississippi	.51					
Mathis, D.	D	Georgia	.52					
Jones, E.	D	Tennessee	.50					
Madigan, E.	R	Illinois		.38				
Symms, S.	R	Idaho		.47				
Mathias, R.	R	California		.50				
Sebelius, K.	R	Kansas			.48			
Johnson, J.	R	Colorado			.45			
Young, E.	R	South Carolina			.55			
Alexander, B.	D	Arkansas				.43		
Brown, G.	D	California				.48		
Litton, J.	D	Missouri				.48		
Rose, C.	D	North Carolina				.45		
Denholm, F.	D	South Dakota					.52	
Foley, T.	D	Washington					.52	
Stubblefield, F.	D	Kentucky						.44
Rarick, J.	D	Louisiana						.52
Poage, W.	D	Texas						.52
Thone, C.	R	Nebraska						
Mizell, W.	R	North Carolina						
Baker, L.	R	Tennessee						
Findley, P.	R	Illinois						

Mayne, W.	R	Iowa
Price, R.	R	Texas
Zwach, J.	R	Minnesota
Melcher, J.	D	Montana
Matsunaga, S.	D	Hawaii
Bergland, R.	D	Minnesota
Teague, C.	R	California
Goodling, G.	R	Pennsylvania
Wampler, W.	R	Virginia
Sisk, B.	D	California
Vigorito, J.	D	Pennsylvania
De Lagarza, E.	D	Texas
Peyser, P.	R	New York*

*Member participated in less than 60 percent of the votes.

	Mean Cluster Scores					
	1	2	3	4	5	6
ACA	61	80	73	30	26	67
Party identification (percent Democrat)	100	00	00	100	100	100
Conservative Coalition	71	69	75	44	31	73

	Vote Correlation Between Leaders and Clusters					
	1	2	3	4	5	6
Chairman	.32	.03	.15	.22	.09	.51
Ranking Minority	-.22	.04	-.13	-.36	-.39	-.26
Wampler (Teague replaced by Wampler during 93rd Congress)	.02	.23	.25	.14	-.06	.13

	Intercluster Correlation				
	1	2	3	4	5
2	.14				
3	.10	-.37			
4	.35	-.08	.16		
5	.13	-.24	-.06	.18	
6	.33	-.05	.10	.27	.11

TABLE 3

Agriculture, 94th Congress

Representative	Party	State	Cluster (N = 075)				
			1	2	3	4	5
Baldus, A.	D	Wisconsin	.46				
Richmond, F.	D	Nevada	.47				
Bergland, B.	D	Minnesota	.58				
Melcher, J.	D	Montana	.45				
McHugh, M.	D	New York	.55				
Thone, C.	R	Nebraska		.51			
Grassley, C.	R	Iowa		.45			
Madigan, E.	R	Illinois		.51			
Johnson, J.	R	Colorado		.45			
Moore, W.	R	Louisiana		.47			
Fithian, F.	D	Indiana			.42		
Nolan, R.	D	Minnesota			.49		
Harkin, T.	D	Iowa			.50		
Poage, W.	D	Texas				.44	
Jones, W.	D	North Carolina				.48	
English, G.	D	Oklahoma				.38	
Jenrette, J.	D	South Carolina					.47
Mathis, D.	D	Georgia					.40
Litton, J.	D	Mississippi					.41
Breckinridge, J.	D	Kentucky					
Rose, C.	D	North Carolina					
Bowen, D.	D	Mississippi					
Brown, G.	D	California					
Krebs, J.	D	California					
Bedell, B.	D	Iowa					

Hightower, J.	D	Texas
Weaver, J.	D	Oregon
Jones, E.	D	Tennessee
Vigorito, J.	D	Pennsylvania
De Lagarza, E.	D	Texas
Foley, T.	D	Washington
Findley, P.	R	Illinois
Sebelius, K.	R	Kansas
Wampler, W.	R	Virginia
Symms, S.	R	Idaho
Peyser, P.	R	New York
Kelly, R.	R	Florida
Jeffords, J.	R	Vermont
Heckler, M.	R	Massachusetts
Hagedorn, T.	R	Minnesota
Thornton, R.	D	Arkansas*
D'Amours, N.	D	New Hampshire*

*Member participated in less than 60 percent of the votes.

	Mean Cluster Scores				
	1	2	3	4	5
ACA	13	79	19	82	54
Party identification (percent Democrat)	100	00	100	100	100
Conservative Coalition	20	81	24	86	56

	Vote Correlation Between Leaders and Clusters				
	1	2	3	4	5
Chairman	.26	-.27	.26	-.23	-.06
Ranking Minority	-.21	.27	-.07	.26	.01

	Intercluster Correlation			
	1	2	3	4
2	-.10			
3	.35	.00		
4	-.15	.23	-.15	
5	.17	.09	.10	-.23

TABLE 4

Agriculture, 95th Congress

Representative	Party	State	Cluster (N = 061)			
			1	2	3	4
Foley, T.	D	Washington	.48			
Jones, E.	D	Tennessee	.46			
Krebs, J.	D	California	.47			
Breckinridge, J.	D	Kentucky	.55			
Bowen, D.	D	Mississippi	.43			
Skelton, I.	D	Missouri	.51			
Thornton, P.	D	Arizona		.52		
Huckaby, T.	D	Louisiana		.39		
Whitley, C.	D	North Carolina		.41		
Rose, C.	D	North Carolina		.39		
Weaver, J.	D	Oregon			.43	
Hightower, J.	D	Texas			.36	
Glickman, D.	D	Kansas			.46	
Volkmer, H.	D	Mississippi			.40	
Akaka, D.	D	Hawaii				.43
Bedell, B.	D	Iowa				.37
Baldus, A.	D	Wisconsin				.40
Brown, G.	D	California				.44
Nolan, R.	D	Minnesota				
Richmond, F.	D	New York				
Harkin, T.	D	Iowa				
Jenrette, J.	D	South Carolina				
Fithian, F.	D	Indiana				
English, G.	D	Oklahoma				
McHugh, M.	D	New York				
Mathis, D.	D	Georgia				
Jones, W.	D	North Carolina				
De Lagarza, E.	D	Texas				

Poage, W.	D	Texas
Panetta, L.	D	California
Ammerman, J.	D	Pennsylvania
Wampler, W.	R	Virginia
Findley, P.	R	Illinois
Sebelius, K.	R	Kansas
Madigan, E.	R	Illinois
Johnson, J.	R	Colorado
Symms, S.	R	Idaho
Thone, C.	R	Nebraska
Marlenee, R.	R	Montana
Coleman, E.	R	Missouri
Moore, W.	R	Louisiana
Hagedorn, T.	R	Michigan
Grassley, C.	R	Iowa
Kelly, R.	R	Florida
Jeffords, J.	R	Vermont
Heckler, M.	R	Massachusetts
Risenhoover, T.	D	Oklahoma*

*Member participated in less than 60 percent of the votes.

	Mean Cluster Scores			
	1	2	3	4
ACA	43	45	38	09
Party identification (percent Democrat)	100	100	100	100
Conservative Coalition	53	63	49	17

	Vote Correlation Between Leaders and Clusters			
	1	2	3	4
Chairman	.48	.41	.39	.44
Ranking minority	-.08	.00	-.21	-.25

	Intercluster Correlation		
	1	2	3
2	.34		
3	.30	.27	
4	.30	.18	.24

TABLE 5

Agriculture, 96th Congress

Representative	Party	State	Cluster (N = 036)					
			1	2	3	4	5	6
Hopkins, L.	R	Kentucky	.45					
Hagedorn, T.	R	Minnesota	.55					
Grassley, C.	R	Iowa	.49					
Kelly, R.	R	Florida	.44					
Symms, S.	R	Idaho	.50					
Findley, P.	R	Illinois	.45					
Jones, E.	D	Tennessee		.45				
Jones, W.	D	North Carolina		.68				
Akaka, D.	D	Hawaii		.56				
Bedell, B.	D	Iowa		.50				
Rose, C.	D	North Carolina		.53				
Bowen, D.	D	Mississippi		.55				
Sebelius, K.	R	Kansas			.54			
Wampler, W.	R	Virginia			.51			
Johnson, J.	R	Colorado			.51			
Thomas, W.	R	California			.48			
Marlenee, R.	R	Montana			.37			
Harkin, T.	D	Iowa				.51		
Baldus, A.	D	Wisconsin				.52		
Glickman, D.	D	Kansas				.55		
Panetta, L.	D	California				.55		
Skelton, I.	D	Missouri					.49	
Whitley, C.	D	North Carolina					.47	
Anthony, B.	D	Arkansas					.39	
Hance, K.	D	Texas						.45
Stenholm, C.	D	Texas						.56
English, G.	D	Oklahoma						.47

Fithian, F.   D   Indiana
Huckaby, T.   D   Louisiana
Weaver, J.   D   Oregon
Nolan, R.   D   Minnesota
Richmond, F.   D   New York
Brown, G.   D   California
Mathis, D.   D   Georgia
De Lagarza, E. D   Texas
Foley, T.   D   Washington
Daschle, T.   D   South Carolina
Coelho, T.   D   California
Heckler, M.   R   Massachusetts
Madigan, E.   R   Illinois
Jeffords, J.   R   Vermont
Coleman, E.   R   Missouri

	Mean Cluster Scores					
	1	2	3	4	5	6
ACA	84	34	81	23	36	70
Party identification (percent Democrat)	00	100	00	100	100	100
Conservative Coalition	80	51	77	32	71	88

	Vote Correlation Between Leaders and Clusters					
	1	2	3	4	5	6
Chairman	-.38	.19	-.22	.12	.26	.02
Ranking minority	.44	-.18	.51	-.23	-.08	.05

	Intercluster Correlation				
	1	2	3	4	5
2	-.17				
3	.38	-.13			
4	-.30	.30	-.19		
5	.01	.23	-.05	-.01	
6	.02	.18	.12	.03	.05

TABLE 6

Armed Services, 92nd Congress

Representative	Party	State	Cluster (N = 034)					
			1	2	3	4	5	6
Fisher, O.	D	Texas	.54					
Price, M.	D	Illinois	.61					
Hunt, J.	R	New Jersey	.63					
Runnels, H.	D	New Mexico	.56					
Daniel, W.	D	Virginia	.51					
White, R.	D	Texas	.57					
Long, S.	D	Louisiana	.52					
Wilson, C.	D	California	.63					
Hagan, E.	D	Georgia		.50				
Montgomery, G.	D	Mississippi		.42				
Brinkley, J.	D	Georgia		.55				
Randall, W.	D	Missouri		.62				
Hall, D.	R	Missouri		.58				
Pirnie, A.	R	New York		.64				
Byrne, J.	D	Pennsylvania		.59				
Wilson, B.	R	California			.54			
Stratton, S.	D	New York			.37			
Lennon, A.	D	North Carolina			.43			
King, C.	R	New York			.46			
Mollohan, R.	D	West Virginia			.44			
Whitehurst, W.	R	Virginia			.43			
Clancy, D.	R	Ohio				.49		
Okonski, A.	R	Wisconsin				.51		
Arends, L.	R	Illinois				.56		
Hebert, E.	D	Louisiana				.44		
Bennett, C.	D	Florida					.58	
Spence, F.	R	South Carolina					.58	

Stafford, R.	R	Vermont	.51
Whalen, C.	R	Ohio	.51
Nichols, B.	D	Alabama	
Hicks, F.	D	Washington	
Leggett, R.	D	California	
Young, B.	R	Florida	
Harrington, M.	D	Massachusetts	
Aspin, L.	D	Wisconsin	
Gubser, C.	R	California	
Pike, O.	D	New York	
Ichord, R.	D	Missouri	
Nedzi, L.	D	Michigan	
Dickinson, W.	R	Alabama	
Bray, W.	R	Indiana	
Powell, W.	R	Ohio*	
Conover, W.	R	Pennsylvania*	

*Member participated in less than 60 percent of the votes.

Mean Cluster Scores

	1	2	3	4	5	6
ACA	70	71	68	73	82	05
Party identification (percent Democrat)	88	71	50	25	50	00
Conservative coalition	60	69	69	69	79	10

Vote Correlation Between Leaders and Clusters

	1	2	3	4	5	6
Chairman	.42	.25	.37	.44	.28	.16
Ranking minority	.08	.15	.11	.56	.06	.06

Intercluster Correlation

	1	2	3	4	5
2	.31				
3	.42	.32			
4	.13	.13	.15		
5	.24	.34	.20	.13	
6	-.04	-.02	-.08	.11	.17

197

TABLE 7

Armed Services, 93rd Congress

Representative	Party	State	Cluster (N = 025)			
			1	2	3	4
Bray, W.	R	Indiana	.66			
Hebert, E.	D	Louisiana	.72			
Fisher, O.	D	Texas	.69			
Price, M.	D	Illinois	.69			
Nichols, B.	D	Alabama	.72			
Spence, F.	R	South Carolina	.53			
Whitehurst, W.	R	Virginia	.56			
Bennett, C.	D	Florida	.69			
Davis, M.	D	South Carolina	.66			
Holt, M.	R	Maryland	.48			
Montgomery, G.	D	Mississippi	.60			
Daniel, W.	D	Virginia	.53			
Beard, R.	R	Tennessee	.51			
Brinkley, J.	D	Georgia		.39		
Armstrong, W.	R	Colorado		.54		
King, C.	R	New York		.51		
Treen, D.	R	Louisiana		.53		
Price, R.	R	Tennessee			.47	
Gubser, C.	R	California			.58	
Hunt, J.	R	New Jersey			.51	
Arends, L.	R	Illinois				.46
Wilson, B.	R	California				.49
Daniel, R.	R	Virginia				.42
Aspin, L.	D	Wisconsin				
Schroeder, P.	D	Colorado				
Mollohan, R.	D	West Virginia				
Mitchell, D.	R	New York				
Ichord, R.	D	Missouri				

Dickinson, W.	R	Alabama
Pike, O.	D	New York
Stratton, S.	D	New York
Hicks, F.	D	Washington
Wilson, C.	D	California
Leggett, R.	D	California
Powell, W.	R	Ohio*
Young, B.	R	Florida*
Randall, W.	D	Missouri*
Nedzi, L.	D	Michigan*
Murtha, J.	D	Pennsylvania*
Hillis, E.	R	Indiana*
Jones, J.	D	Oklahoma*
Dellums, R.	D	California*
Runnels, H.	D	New Mexico*
O'Brien, G.	R	Illinois*
White, R.	D	Texas*

*Member participated in less than 60 percent of the votes.

	Mean Cluster Scores			
	1	2	3	4
ACA	71	61	79	83
Party identification (percent Democrat)	61	25	00	00
Conservative coalition	76	78	76	82

	Vote Correlation Between Leaders and Clusters			
	1	2	3	4
Chairman	.72	.17	.53	.38
Ranking minority	.66	.29	.28	.25

	Intercluster Correlation		
	1	2	3
2	.20		
3	.38	.03	
4	.31	.04	.20

199

TABLE 8

Armed Services, 94th Congress

Representative	Party	State	Cluster (N = 022)					
			1	2	3	4	5	6
Price, M.	D	Illinois	.65					
Hebert, E.	D	Louisiana	.53					
Nichols, B.	D	Alabama	.56					
Daniel, R.	R	Virginia	.61					
Stratton, S.	D	New York	.56					
Kazen, A.	D	Texas	.46					
Brinkley, J.	D	Georgia		.61				
Hillis, E.	R	Indiana		.42				
White, R.	D	Texas		.54				
Wilson, B.	R	California			.56			
McDonald, L.	D	Georgia			.41			
Davis, M.	D	South Carolina			.48			
Montgomery, G.	D	Mississippi			.48			
Daniel, W.	D	Virginia				.61		
Mollohan, R.	D	West Virginia				.57		
Whitehurst, W.	R	Virginia				.55		
Bennett, C.	D	Florida				.58		
Holt, M.	R	Maryland				.51		
Ichord, R.	D	Mississippi				.55		
O'Brien, G.	R	Illinois					.65	
Schulze, R.	R	Pennsylvania					.65	
Dellums, R.	D	California						.44
Aspin, L.	D	Wisconsin						.55
Carr, B.	D	Michigan						.42
Downey, T.	D	New York						.48

200

Lloyd, J.   D   California
Schroeder, P.   D   Colorado
Beard, R.   R   Tennessee
Mitchell, D.   R   New York
Wilson, C.   D   California
Nedzi, L.   D   Michigan
Spence, F.   R   South Carolina
Leggett, R.   D   California
Hicks, F.   D   Washington
Dickinson, W.   R   Alabama
Treen, D.   R   Louisiana*
Hinshaw, A.   R   California*
Randall, W.   D   Missouri*
Won Pat, A.   D   Guam*
Runnels, H.   D   New Mexico*

*Member participated in less than 60 percent of the votes.

	Mean Cluster Scores					
	1	2	3	4	5	6
ACA	61	64	78	75	76	14
Party identification (percent Democrat)	83	68	75	67	00	100
Conservative coalition	62	77	80	78	80	13

	Vote Correlation Between Leaders and Clusters					
	1	2	3	4	5	6
Chairman	.65	.29	-.11	.02	.28	.10
Ranking minority	.09	.30	.56	.17	.36	.27

	Intercluster Correlation				
	1	2	3	4	5
2	.24				
3	-.07	.25			
4	.16	.19	.11		
5	.28	.29	.12	.40	
6	.06	-.15	.07	-.18	-.06

TABLE 9

Armed Services, 95th Congress

Representative	Party	State	Cluster (N = 028)				
			1	2	3	4	5
Whitehurst, W.	R	Virginia	.46				
Daniel, W.	D	Virginia	.52				
Brinkley, J.	D	Georgia	.47				
Holt, M.	R	Missouri	.55				
Beard, R.	R	Tennessee	.48				
Spence, F.	R	South Carolina	.53				
McDonald, L.	D	Georgia	.48				
Montgomery, G.	D	Mississippi	.52				
White, R.	D	Texas		.64			
Trible, P.	R	Virginia		.64			
Emery, D.	R	Maine			.49		
Mollohan, R.	D	West Virginia			.45		
Mitchell, D.	R	New York			.51		
Byron, G.	D	Maryland			.37		
Stump, B.	D	Arizona				.39	
Hillis, E.	R	Indiana				.49	
Daniel, R.	R	Virginia				.47	
Wilson, B.	R	California				.48	
Schroeder, P.	D	Colorado					.37
Downey, T.	D	New York					.46
Carr, B.	D	Michigan					.44
Lloyd, J.	D	California					
Davis, M.	D	South Carolina					
Badham, R.	R	California					
Price, M.	D	Illinois					
Stratton, S.	D	New York					
Dickinson, W.	R	Alabama					

Bennett, C.	D	Florida
Nichols, B.	D	Alabama
Ichord, R.	D	Maryland
Treen, D.	R	Louisiana
Nedzi, L.	D	Michigan
Leggett, R	D	California*
Wilson, C.	D	California*
Kazen, A.	D	Texas*
Dellums, R.	D	California*
Aspin, L.	D	Wisconsin*
Runnels, H.	D	New Mexico*
Breckinridge, J.	D	Kentucky*
Tonry, R.	D	Louisiana*
Whitley, C.	D	North Carolina*
Won Pat, A.	D	Guam*

*Member participated in less than 60 percent of the votes.

| | Mean Cluster Scores | | | | |
	1	2	3	4	5
ACA	73	65	54	56	20
Party identification (percent Democrat)	50	50	50	25	100
Conservative coalition	89	68	24	10	50

Vote Correlation Between Leaders and Clusters

	1	2	3	4	5
Chairman	.06	.20	-.04	.15	.28
Ranking Minority	.33	.16	.33	.48	-.28

Intercluster Correlation

	1	2	3	4
2	.33			
3	.16	.04		
4	.31	.22	.20	
5	-.26	-.32	-.14	-.30

TABLE 10

Armed Services, 96th Congress

Representative	Party	State	Cluster (N = 023)					
			1	2	3	4	5	6
Holt, M.	R	Maryland	.53					
Mitchell, D.	R	New York	.55					
Whitehurst, W.	R	Virginia	.61					
Bailey, D.	D	Pennsylvania	.42					
Daniel, R	R	Virginia	.62					
Stump, B.	D	Arizona		.50				
Spence, F.	R	South Carolina		.64				
Montgomery, G.	D	Mississippi		.55				
Stratton, S.	D	Nevada		.55				
Schroeder, P.	D	Colorado			.60			
Nedzi, L.	D	Michigan			.61			
Carr, B.	D	Michigan			.55			
Hillis, E.	R	Indiana				.50		
Leach, C.	D	Louisiana				.56		
Mavroules, N.	D	Massachusetts				.46		
White, R.	D	Texas				.51		
Brinkley, J.	D	Georgia				.38		
Price, M.	D	Illinois				.47		
Wyatt, J.	D	Texas					.59	
Emery, D.	R	Maine					.59	
Wilson, B.	R	California						.57
Davis, M.	D	South Carolina						.57
Daniel, W.	D	Virginia						
Aspin, L.	D	Wisconsin						
Beard, R.	R	Tennessee						
Mollohan, R.	D	West Virginia						
Nichols, B.	D	Alabama						
Wilson, C.	D	California						

Dickinson, W.   R   Alabama
Ichord, R.   D   Missouri
Bennett, C.   D   Florida
McDonald, L.   D   Georgia
Lloyd, J.   D   California
Won Pat, A.   D   Guam
Kazen, A.   D   Texas
Dougherty, C.   R   Pennsylvania
Byron, B.   D   Maryland
Trible, P.   R   Virginia
Courter, J.   R   New Jersey
Treen, D.   R   Louisiana*
Dellums, R.   D   California*
Runnels, H.   D   New Mexico*
Hutto, E.   D   Florida*
Evans, M.   D   Virginia*
Badham, R.   R   California*
Fazio, V.   D   California*
Hopkins, L.   R   Kentucky*

*Member participated in less than 60 percent of the votes.

	Mean Cluster Scores					
	1	2	3	4	5	6
ACA	74	73	22	47	66	51
Party identification (percent Democrat)	20	75	100	83	50	50
Conservative coalition	80	86	20	59	76	42

	Vote Correlation Between Leaders and Clusters					
	1	2	3	4	5	6
Chairman	.02	-.21	.20	.47	.22	.05
Ranking minority	.15	-.20	-.03	-.05	.14	.57

	Intercluster Correlation				
	1	2	3	4	5
2	.35				
3	-.31	-.29			
4	.17	.07	.16		
5	.02	.09	.31	.36	
6	.06	-.01	.12	.09	.07

TABLE 11

Banking, Finance, and Urban Affairs, 92nd Congress

Representative	Party	State	Cluster (N = 149)	
			1	2
Barrett, W.	D	Pennsylvania	.46	
Sullivan, L.	D	Maryland	.44	
Koch, E.	D	New York	.43	
Minish, J.	D	New Jersey	.36	
Johnson, A.	R	Pennsylvania		.42
McKinney, S.	R	Connecticut		.39
Williams, L.	R	Pennsylvania		.39
Brown, G.	R	Michigan		.42
Blackburn, B.	R	Georgia		.38
Wylie, C.	R	Ohio		
Rousselot, J.	R	California		
Frenzel, B.	R	Minnesota		
Archer, B.	R	Texas		
Stanton, W.	R	Ohio		
Widnall, W.	R	New Jersey		
Mitchell, P.	D	Maryland		
Chappell, B.	D	Florida		
Brasco, F.	D	New York		
Hanley, J.	D	New York		
Hanna, R.	D	California		
St. Germain, F.	D	Rhode Island		
Stephens, R.	D	Georgia		
Griffin, C.	D	Mississippi		
Rees, T.	D	California		
Annunzio, F.	D	Illinois		

Gettys, T.	D	South Carolina
Reuss, H.	D	Wisconsin
Moorhead, W.	D	Pennsylvania
Ashley, T.	D	Ohio
Patman, W.	D	Texas
Lent, N.	R	New York*
Crane, P.	R	Illinois*
Heckler, M.	R	Massachusetts*
Dwyer, F.	R	New Jersey*
Curlin, W.	D	Kentucky*
Cotter, W.	D	Connecticut*
Bevill, T.	D	Alabama*
Gonzalez, H.	D	Texas*

*Member participated in less than 60 percent of the votes.

Mean Cluster Scores

	1	2
ACA	16	73
Party identification (percent Democrat)	100	00
Conservative coalition	14	71

Vote Correlation Between Leaders and Clusters

	1	2
Chairman	.36	-.18
Ranking minority	-.11	.31

Intercluster Correlation

	1
2	-.20

TABLE 12

Banking, Finance, and Urban Affairs, 93rd Congress

Representative	Party	State	Cluster (N = 117)			
			1	2	3	4
Burgener, C.	R	California	.44			
Wylie, C.	R	Ohio	.39			
Stanton, W.	R	Ohio	.39			
Johnson, A.	R	Pennsylvania	.42			
Moakley, J.	D	Mississippi		.41		
Cotter, W.	D	Connecticut		.43		
Annunzio, F.	D	Illinois		.38		
St. Germain, F.	D	Rhode Island		.38		
Koch, E.	D	New York			.38	
Mitchell, P.	D	Maryland			.42	
Boggs, C.	D	Louisiana			.40	
Patman, W.	D	Texas			.43	
Heckler, M.	R	Massachusetts				.41
Rinaldo, M.	R	New Jersey				.41
Frenzel, B.	R	Minnesota				
McKinney, S.	R	Connecticut				
Rousselot, J.	R	California				
Williams, L.	R	Pennsylvania				
Brown, G.	R	Michigan				
Blackburn, B.	R	Georgia				
Barrett, W.	D	Pennsylvania				
Moorhead, W.	D	Pennsylvania				
Ashley, T.	D	Ohio				
Reuss, H.	D	Wisconsin				
Sullivan, L.	D	Missouri				
Widnall, W.	R	New Jersey				

Stark, F.	D	California
Young, A.	D	Georgia
Stephens, R.	D	Georgia
Minish, J.	D	New Jersey
Gonzalez, H.	D	Texas
Gettys, T.	D	South Carolina
Hanley, J.	D	New York
Rees, T.	D	California
Crane, P.	R	Illinois*
Fauntroy, W.	D	*	D.C.
Brasco, F.	D	New York*
Hanna, R.	D	California*
Conlan, J.	R	Arizona*
Roncallo, A.	R	New York*

*Member participated in less than 60 percent of the votes.

Mean Cluster Scores

	1	2	3	4
ACA	75	15	12	33
Party identification (percent Democrat)	00	100	100	00
Conservative coalition	75	20	20	27

Vote Correlation Between Leaders and Clusters

	1	2	3	4
Chairman	-.11	.24	.43	.13
Ranking minority	.19	-.01	.06	.10

Intercluster Correlation

	1	2	3
2	.11		
3	-.13	.23	
4	.13	.20	.15

209

TABLE 13

Banking, Finance, and Urban Affairs, 94th Congress

Representative	Party	State	Cluster (N = 080)					
			1	2	3	4	5	6
Reuss, H.	D	Wisconsin	.36					
Spellman, G.	D	Maryland	.48					
Blanchard, J.	D	Michigan	.42					
Boggs, C.	D	Louisiana	.48					
Hanley, J.	D	New York	.51					
Grassley, C.	R	Iowa		.44				
Kelly, R.	R	Florida		.49				
Hyde, H.	R	Illinois		.40				
Wylie, C.	R	Ohio		.36				
Neal, S.	D	North Carolina			.47			
Derrick, B.	D	South Carolina			.42			
Annunzio, F.	D	Illinois			.37			
Minish, J.	D	New Jersey				.45		
St. Germain, F.	D	Rhode Island				.41		
Patman, W.	D	Texas				.39		
Johnson, A.	R	Pennsylvania					.46	
Schulze, R.	R	Pennsylvania					.46	
Hubbard, C.	D	Kentucky						.43
Rees, T.	D	California						.43
Mitchell, P.	D	Maryland						
Patterson, J.	D	California						
Evans, D.	D	Indiana						
Hannaford, M.	D	California						
Hayes, P.	D	Indiana						
Tsongas, P.	D	Mississippi						
Lafalce, J.	D	New York						
Moorhead, W.	D	Pennsylvania						
McKinney, S.	R	Connecticut						
Gradison, W.	R	Ohio						

210

Rousselot, J.	R	California
Brown, G.	R	Michigan
Stanton, W.	R	Ohio
Fenwick, M.	R	New Jersey
Barrett, W.	D	Pennsylvania*
Gonzalez, H.	D	Texas*
Stephens, R.	D	Georgia
Ashley, T.	D	Ohio*
Sullivan, L.	D	Missouri*
Paul, R.	R	Texas*
Hansen, G.	R	Idaho*
Conlan, J.	R	Arizona*
Lundine, S.	D	New York*
D'Amours, N.	D	New Hampshire*
Allen, C.	D	Tennessee*
Aucoin, L.	D	Oregon*
Ford, H.	D	Tennessee*
Maguire, A.	D	New Jersey*
Fauntroy, W.	D	District of Columbia*

*Member participated in less than 60 percent of the votes.

	Mean Cluster Scores					
	1	2	3	4	5	6
ACA	12	86	42	23	77	36
Party identification (percent Democrat)	100	00	100	100	00	100
Conservative Coalition	22	84	50	13	78	49

	Vote Correlation Between Leaders and Clusters					
	1	2	3	4	5	6
Chairman	.36	-.19	.24	.15	-.11	.39
Ranking minority	-.21	.35	-.15	-.14	.46	.08

	Intercluster Correlation				
	1	2	3	4	5
2	-.10				
3	.33	-.15			
4	.25	-.10	.15		
5	-.08	.20	-.03	-.11	
6	.23	-.09	.20	-.02	.06

TABLE 14

Banking, Finance, and Urban Affairs, 95th Congress

Representative	Party	State	Cluster (N = 103)					
			1	2	3	4	5	6
Kelly, R.	R	Florida	.51					
Hansen, G.	R	Idaho	.40					
Rousselot, J.	R	California	.45					
Ashley, T.	D	Ohio		.49				
Spelman, G.	D	Maryland		.49				
Watkins, W.	D	Oklahoma			.41			
Barnard, D.	D	Georgia			.45			
Oakar, M.	D	Ohio			.38			
Fauntroy, W.	D	District of Columbia				.42		
Mitchell, P.	D	Maryland				.37		
Reuss, H.	D	Wisconsin				.36		
St. Germain, F.	D	Rhode Island					.43	
Hanley, J.	D	New York					.43	
Stanton, W.	R	Ohio						.37
Wylie, C.	R	Ohio						.38
Brown, G.	R	Michigan						.41
McKinney, S.	R	Connecticut						
Hyde, H.	R	Illinois						
Grassley, C.	R	Iowa						
Vento, B.	D	Minnesota						
Mattox, J.	D	Texas	E					
Cavanaugh, J.	D	Nebraska						
Pattison, E.	D	New York						
Hollenbeck, H.	R	New Jersey						
Caputo, B.	R	New York						
Evans, T.	R	Delaware						
Steers, N.	R	Maryland						
Leach, J.	R	Iowa						
Fenwick, M.	R	New Jersey						
Neal, S.	D	North Carolina						

Lafalce, J.	D	New York
Hubbard, C.	D	Kentucky
Blanchard, J.	D	Michigan
Patterson, J.	D	California
Aucoin, L.	D	Oregon
Derrick, B.	D	South Carolina
Tsongas, P.	D	Mississippi
Lundine, S.	D	New York
D'Amours, N.	D	New Hampshire
Evans, D.	D	Indiana
Hannaford, M.	D	California
Moorhead, W.	D	Pennsylvania
Annunzio, F.	D	Illinois
Minish, J.	D	New Jersey
Allen, C.	D	Tennessee*
Gonzalez, H.	D	Texas*
Green, W.	R	New York*
Garcia, R.	D	New York*
Badillo, H.	D	New York*

	Mean Cluster Scores					
	1	2	3	4	5	6
ACA	62	16	54	04	18	59
Party identification (percent Democrat)	00	100	100	100	100	00
Conservative Coalition	89	20	63	04	28	71

	Vote Correlation Between Leaders and Clusters					
	1	2	3	4	5	6
Chairman	-.24	.15	.04	.36	.42	-.05
Ranking minority	.22	.14	.21	-.18	-.12	.37

	Intercluster Correlation				
	1	2	3	4	5
2	-.10				
3	.06	.26			
4	-.18	.16	.04		
5	-.16	.20	.06	.29	
6	.26	.09	.17	-.15	-.06

TABLE 15

Banking, Finance, and Urban Affairs, 96th Congress

Representative	Party	State	Cluster (N = 053)					
			1	2	3	4	5	6
Green, W.	R	New York	.57					
Wylie, C.	R	Ohio	.65					
Stanton, W.	R	Ohio	.72					
Lowry, M.	D	Washington		.51				
Vento, B.	D	Minnesota		.64				
Reuss, H.	D	Wisconsin		.48				
St. Germain, F.	D	Rhode Island		.56				
Moorhead, W.	D	Pennsylvania		.42				
Oakar, M.	D	Ohio		.47				
Blanchard, J.	D	Michigan		.46				
Fauntroy, W.	D	District of Columbia		.56				
Annunzio, F.	D	Illinois		.58				
Paul, R.	R	Texas			.60			
Leach, J.	R	Iowa			.46			
Kelly, R.	R	Florida			.50			
Hyde, H.	R	Illinois			.52			
Hansen, G.	R	Idaho			.55			
Ritter, D.	R	Pennsylvania			.51			
Shumway, N.	R	California			.53			
Bethune, E.	R	Arizona			.52			
Mattox, J.	D	Texas				.49		
Garcia, R.	D	New York				.53		
Hanley, J.	D	New York				.41		
Mitchell, P.	D	Maryland					.49	
Hubbard, C.	D	Kentucky					.44	
Patterson, J.	D	California					.47	
Cavanaugh, J.	D	Nebraska						.43
Lundine, S.	D	New York						.46
D'Amours, N.	D	New Hampshire						.48

Evans, D.	D	Indiana
Aucoin, L.	D	Oregon
Spellman, G.	D	Maryland
Lafalce, J.	D	New York
Neal, S.	D	North Carolina
Minish, J.	D	New Jersey
Gonzalez, H.	D	Texas
Ashley, T.	D	Ohio
Watkins, W.	D	Oklahoma
Barnard, D.	D	Georgia
McKinney, S.	R	Connecticut
Evans, T.	R	Delaware
Campbell, C.	R	South Carolina
Hinson, J.	R	Mississippi
Porter, J.	R	Illinois*

*Member participated in less than 60 percent of the votes.

	Mean Cluster Scores					
	1	2	3	4	5	6
ACA	59	12	84	24	22	25
Party identification (percent Democrat)	00	100	00	100	100	100
Conservative coalition	55	15	80	28	34	29

	Vote Correlation Between Leaders and Clusters					
	1	2	3	4	5	6
Chairman	.02	.47	-.31	.24	.13	.36
Ranking minority	.72	-.09	.13	-.13	.02	-.13

	Intercluster Correlation				
	1	2	3	4	5
2	-.08				
3	.13	-.29			
4	-.13	.28	-.04		
5	-.02	.28	-.14	.16	
6	-.15	.30	-.14	.24	.09

TABLE 16

Education and Labor, 92nd Congress

Representative	Party	State	Cluster (N = 099)		
			1	2	3
Perkins, C.	D	Kentucky	.50		
Daniels, D.	D	New Jersey	.46		
Dent, J.	D	Pennsylvania	.54		
Thompson, F.	D	New Jersey	.46		
Badillo H.	D	New York	.48		
Grasso, E.	D	Connecticut	.48		
Chisholm, S.	D	New York	.60		
Clay, W.	D	Missouri	.55		
Burton, P.	D	California	.47		
Meeds, L.	D	Washington	.47		
Scheuer, J.	D	New York	.52		
Hawkins, A.	D	California	.59		
Brademas, J.	D	Indiana	.45		
Peyser, P.	R	New York		.42	
Kemp, J.	R	New York		.59	
Veysey, V.	R	California		.57	
Forsythe, E.	R	New Jersey		.58	
Ruth, E.	R	North Carolina		.49	
Hansen, O.	R	Idaho		.49	
Landgrebe, E.	R	Indiana		.50	
Steiger, W.	R	Wisconsin		.42	
Esch, M.	R	Michigan		.54	
Erlenborn, J.	R	Illinois		.59	
Quie, A.	R	Minnesota		.59	

O'Hara, J.	D	Michigan	.49
Ford, W.	D	Michigan	.46
Pucinski, R.	D	Illinois	.36
Green, E.	D	Oregon	
Mink, P.	D	Hawaii	
Gaydos, J.	D	Pennsylvania	
Biaggi, M.	D	New York	
Hicks, L.	D	Mississippi	
Mazzoli, R.	D	Kentucky	
Bell, A.	R	California	
Dellenback, J.	R	Oregon	
Ashbrook, J.	R	Ohio*	
Eshleman, E.	R	Pennsylvania*	
Reid, C.	R	Illinois*	

*Member participated in less than 60 percent of the votes.

Mean Cluster Scores

	1	2	3
ACA	11	68	14
Party identification (percent Democrat)	100	00	100
Conservative coalition	12	65	17

Vote Correlation Between Leaders and Clusters

	1	2	3
Chairman	.50	-.26	.32
Ranking minority	-.37	.59	-.35

Intercluster Correlation

	1	2
2	-.30	
3	.26	-.21

TABLE 17

Education and Labor, 93rd Congress

Representative	Party	State	Cluster (N = 064)			
			1	2	3	4
Huber, R.	R	Michigan	.50			
Sarasin, R.	R	Colorado	.55			
Towell, D.	R	Nevada	.62			
Kemp, J.	R	New York	.48			
Forsythe, E.	R	New Jersey	.50			
Hansen, O.	R	Idaho	.51			
Steiger, W.	R	Wisconsin	.40			
Eshleman, E.	R	Pennsylvania	.50			
Dellenback, J.	R	Oregon	.39			
Erlenborn, J.	R	Illinois	.66			
Thompson, F.	D	New Jersey		.58		
O'Hara, J.	D	Michigan		.55		
Brademas, J.	D	Indiana		.59		
Chisholm, S.	D	New York		.57		
Meeds, L.	D	Washington		.45		
Mink, P.	D	Hawaii		.63		
Ford, W.	D	Michigan		.51		
Hawkins, A.	D	California		.53		
Benitez, J.	D	Puerto Rico			.40	
Grasso, E.	D	Connecticut			.41	
Daniels, D.	D	New Jersey			.57	
Dent, J.	D	Pennsylvania			.54	
Perkins, C.	D	Kentucky			.52	

Quie, A.	R	Michigan	.52
Esch, M.	R	Minnesota	.52
Bell, A.	R	California	
Landgrebe, E.	R	Indiana	
Peyser, P.	R	New York	
Lehman, W.	D	Florida	
Andrews, I.	D	North Carolina	
Biaggi, M.	D	New York	
Badillo, H.	D	New York	
Mazzoli, R.	D	Kentucky	
Clay, W.	D	Missouri	
Gaydos, J.	D	Pennsylvania	
Burton, P.	D	California	
Ashbrook, J.	R	Ohio	

*Member participated in less than 60 percent of the votes.

Mean Cluster Scores

	1	2	3	4
ACA	52	10	14	49
Party identification (percent Democrat)	00	100	100	00
Conservative coalition	63	07	21	51

Vote Correlation Between Leaders and Clusters

	1	2	3	4
Chairman	.00	.33	.52	-.16
Ranking minority	.45	-.46	-.19	.53

Intercluster Correlation

	1	2	3
2	-.29		
3	-.05	.33	
4	.46	-.37	-.14

TABLE 18

Education and Labor, 94th Congress

Representative	Party	State	Cluster (N = 044)					
			1	2	3	4	5	6
Thompson, F.	D	New Jersey	.50					
Perkins, C.	D	Kentucky	.42					
Brademas, J.	D	Indiana	.53					
Daniels, D.	D	New Jersey	.54					
Dent, J.	D	Pennsylvania	.52					
Zefferetti, L.	D	New York	.55					
Blouin, M.	D	Iowa	.46					
Benitez, J.	D	Puerto Rico	.49					
Lehman, W.	D	Florida	.53					
Burton, P.	D	California	.52					
Ford, W.	D	Michigan	.53					
Eshleman, E.	R	Pennsylvania		.54				
Erlenborn, J.	R	Illinois		.63				
Ashbrook, J.	R	Ohio		.52				
Quie, A.	R	Minnesota		.38				
Hall, T.	D	Illinois			.44			
Hawkins, A.	D	California			.51			
Meeds, L.	D	Washington			.50			
Beard, E.	D	Rhode Island			.41			
O'Hara, J.	D	Michigan			.40			
Bell, A.	R	California				.37		
Jeffords, J.	R	Vermont				.51		
Sarasin, R.	R	Connecticut				.50		
Simon, P.	D	Illinois					.63	
Mink, P.	D	Hawaii					.63	
Gaydos, J.	D	Pennsylvania						.50

Chisholm, S.	D	New York
Mottl, R.	D	Ohio
Esch, M.	R	Michigan
Buchanan, J.	R	Alabama
Pressler, L.	R	South Carolina
Smith, V.	R	Nebraska
Goodling, W.	R	Pennsylvania
Clay, W.	D	Maryland
Cornell, R.	D	Wisconsin
Biaggi, M.	D	New York
Risenhoover, T.	D	Oklahoma*
Andrews, I.	D	North Carolina*
Peyser, P.	R	New York*
Miller, G.	D	California*

*Member participated in less than 60 percent of the votes.

Mean Cluster Scores

	1	2	3	4	5	6
ACA	11	71	13	59	07	32
Party identification (percent Democrat)	100	00	100	00	100	100
Conservative coalition	17	73	16	52	11	23

Vote Correlation Between Leaders and Clusters

	1	2	3	4	5	6
Chairman	.43	-.13	.36	-.30	.32	.16
Ranking minority	-.35	.39	-.51	.40	-.38	-.40

Intercluster Correlation

	1	2	3	4	5
2	-.21				
3	.41	-.38			
4	-.12	.25	-.19		
5	.27	-.20	.38	-.14	
6	.29	-.25	.30	-.14	.26

TABLE 19

Education and Labor, 95th Congress

Representative	Party	State	Cluster (N = 079)			
			1	2	3	4
Weiss, T.	D	New York	.58			
Lefante, J.	D	New Jersey	.51			
Myers, M.	D	Pennsylvania	.51			
Zeferetti, L.	D	New York	.65			
Beard, E.	D	Rhode Island	.53			
Biaggi, M.	D	New York	.50			
Burton, P.	D	California	.52			
Corrada, B.	D	Puerto Rico	.53			
Ashbrook, J.	R	Ohio		.52		
Quie, A.	R	Minnesota		.50		
Sarasin, R.	R	Colorado		.39		
Erlenborn, J.	R	Illinois		.51		
Pettis, S.	R	California		.47		
Shuster, E.	R	Pennsylvania		.45		
Pressler, L.	R	South Carolina		.38		
Kildee, D.	D	Michigan			.51	
Clay, W.	D	Missouri			.41	
Miller, G.	D	California			.46	
Thompson, F.	D	New Jersey			.54	
Perkins, C.	D	Kentucky			.42	
Ford, W.	D	Michigan			.55	
Brademas, J.	D	Indiana				.42
Dent, J.	D	Pennsylvania				.50
Gaydos, J.	D	Pennsylvania				.44

Simon, P.	D	Illinois
Cornell, R.	D	Wisconsin
Blouin, M.	D	Iowa
Mottl, R.	D	Ohio
Murphy, A.	D	Pennsylvania
Heftel, C.	D	Hawaii
Hawkins, A.	D	California
Jeffords, J.	R	Vermont
Buchanan, J.	R	Alabama
Goodling, W.	R	Pennsylvania
Edwards, M.	R	Oklahoma
Pursell, C.	R	Michigan
Andrews, I.	D	North Carolina*

*Member participated in less than 60 percent of the votes.

Mean Cluster Scores

	1	2	3	4
ACA	10	72	09	16
Party identification (percent Democrat)	100	00	100	100
Conservative coalition	18	68	12	24

Vote Correlation Between Leaders and Clusters

	1	2	3	4
Chairman	.31	-.31	.42	.32
Ranking minority	-.53	.50	-.30	-.32

Intercluster Correlation

	1	2	3
2	-.38		
3	.38	-.31	
4	.32	-.27	.37

TABLE 20

Education and Labor, 96th Congress

Representative	Party	State	Cluster (N = 036)					
			1	2	3	4	5	6
Thompson, F.	D	New Jersey	.56					
Perkins, C.	D	Kentucky	.60					
Burton, P.	D	California	.49					
Stack, E.	D	Florida	.57					
Kildee, D.	D	Michigan	.47					
Corrada, B.	D	Puerto Rico	.52					
Weiss, T.	D	New York	.51					
Simon, P.	D	Illinois	.49					
Kogovsek, R.	D	Colorado	.57					
Erlenborn, J.	R	Illinois		.70				
Ashbrook, J.	R	Ohio		.51				
Edwards, M.	R	Oklahoma		.62				
Goodling, W.	R	Pennsylvania		.47				
Hinson, J.	R	Mississippi		.66				
Crane, D.	R	Illinois		.57				
Tauke, T.	R	Iowa		.55				
Kramer, K.	R	Colorado		.63				
Murphy, A.	D	Pennsylvania			.80			
Peyser, P.	D	New York			.80			
Ratchford, W.	D	Connecticut				.52		
Myers, M.	D	Pennsylvania				.49		
Biaggi, M.	D	New York				.53		
Brademas, J.	D	Indiana				.53		
Buchanan, J.	R	Alabama				.35		

Bailey, D.	D	Pennsylvania	.52
Ford, W.	D	Michigan	.41
Beard, E.	D	Rhode Island	.56
Miller, G.	D	California	.48
Clay, W.	D	Mississippi	.43
Hawkins, A.	D	California	.52
Gaydos, J.	D	Pennsylvania	
Andrews, I.	D	North Carolina	
Williams, P.	D	Montana	
Jeffords, J.	R	Vermont	
Coleman, E.	R	Missouri	
Erdahl, A.	R	Minnesota	
Petri, T.	R	Wisconsin	
Musto, R.	D	Pennsylvania*	

*Member participated in less than 60 percent of the votes.

Mean Cluster Scores

	1	2	3	4	5	6
ACA	13	79	26	22	20	10
Party identification (percent Democrat)	89	00	100	80	100	100
Conservative coalition	16	78	36	26	37	05

Vote Correlation Between Leaders and Clusters

	1	2	3	4	5	6
Chairman	.60	-.38	.35	.44	.36	.37
Ranking minority	-.32	.51	-.10	-.13	-.08	-.49

Intercluster Correlation

	1	2	3	4	5
2	-.36				
3	.35	-.23			
4	.33	-.15	.19		
5	.28	-.25	.12	.06	
6	.37	-.38	.29	.12	.18

TABLE 21

Government Operations, 92nd Congress

Representative	Party	State	Cluster (N = 013)					
			1	2	3	4	5	6
Holifield, C.	D	California	.74					
Garmatz, E.	D	Maryland	.74					
Monagan, J.	D	Connecticut	.74					
Thone, C.	R	Nebraska	.61					
Goldwater, B.	R	California	.63					
Brown, G.	R	Michigan	.77					
Buchanan, J.	R	Alabama	.81					
Brown, C.	R	Ohio	.77					
Wydler, J.	R	New York	.58					
Erlenborn, J.	R	Illinois	.81					
Horton, F.	R	New York	.74					
Dwyer, F.	R	New Jersey	.74					
Abzug, B.	D	New York		.51				
Randall, W.	D	Missouri		.65				
Gallager, C.	D	New Jersey		.69				
Alexander, B.	D	Arizona		.52				
Wright, J.	D	Texas		.56				
Moss, J.	D	California		.66				
Fountain, L.	D	North Carolina		.65				
St. Germain, F.	D	Rhode Island			.72			
Conyers, J.	D	Michigan			.62			
Moorhead, W.	D	Pennsylvania			.79			
MacDonald, T.	D	Mississippi			.72			
Reuss, H.	D	Wisconsin			.72			
Fascell, D.	D	Florida			.79			
McCloskey, P.	R	California			.55			
Gude, G.	R	Maryland			.36			

Robinson, K.	R	Virginia	
Powell, W.	R	Ohio	.96
Rosenthal, B.	D	New York	.96
Culver, J.	D	Iowa	.82
Hicks, F.	D	Washington	.82
Collins, G.	D	Illinois	.54
Brooks, J.	D	Texas	.65
Jones, R.	D	Alabama	.60
Fuqua, D.	D	Florida	
Vander, J.	R	Michigan*	
Reid, O.	R	New York*	
Mallary, R.	R	Vermont*	
Heinz, J.	R	Pennsylvania*	
Steiger, S.	R	Arizona*	

*Member participated in less than 60 percent of the votes.

Mean Cluster Scores

	1	2	3	4	5	6
ACA	58	38	13	94	09	21
Party identification (percent Democrat)	25	100	75	00	100	100
Conservative coalition	57	39	14	93	04	30

Vote Correlation Between Leaders and Clusters

	1	2	3	4	5	6
Chairman	.74	.12	.31	.14	-.46	.27
Ranking minority	.74	.12	.31	.14	-.46	.27

Intercluster Correlation

	1	2	3	4	5
2	-.07				
3	.08	-.20			
4	.35	-.50	.21		
5	-.68	.33	.11	-.68	
6	-.04	.32	.40	-.10	.33

TABLE 22

Government Operations, 93rd Congress

Representative	Party	State	Cluster (N = 018)					
			1	2	3	4	5	6
Holifield, C.	D	California	.46					
Jones, R.	D	Alabama	.54					
Ryan, L.	D	California	.68					
Donohue, H.	D	Mississippi	.62					
Culver, J.	D	Iowa	.70					
St. Germain, F.	D	Rhode Island	.60					
Steelman, A.	R	Texas	.51					
Mallary, R.	R	Vermont	.50					
Gude, G.	R	Maryland		.69				
Wright, J.	D	Texas		.61				
Rosenthal, B.	D	New York		.48				
Moorhead, W.	D	Pennsylvania		.79				
MacDonald, T.	D	Mississippi		.77				
Conyers, J.	D	Michigan		.78				
Moss, J.	D	California		.68				
Brooks, J.	D	Texas		.74				
Brown, C.	R	Ohio			.70			
Erlenborn, J.	R	Illinois			.46			
Regula, R.	R	Ohio			.46			
Thone, C.	R	Nebraska			.50			
Brown, G.	R	Michigan			.51			
Buchanan, J.	R	Alabama			.47			
Wydler, J.	R	New York				.51		
Horton, F.	R	New York				.48		
McCloskey, P.	R	California				.53		
Pritchard, J.	R	Washington				.59		
Hanrahan, R.	R	Illinois				.54		
Fascell, D.	D	Florida					.54	

Hicks, F.	D	Washington	.52
Abzug, B.	D	New York	.48
Stanton, J.	D	Ohio	.60
Randall, W.	D	Missouri	.63
Fuqua, D.	D	Florida	.45
Alexander, B.	D	Arkansas	.50
Fountain, L.	D	North Carolina	.48
Reuss, H.	D	Wisconsin	
Vander, J.	R	Michigan	
Collins, C.	D	Illinois	
Steiger, S.	R	Arizona	
Hinshaw, A.	R	California	
Parris, S.	R	Virginia	
Burton, J.	D	California*	

*Member participated in less than 60 percent of the votes.

	Mean Cluster Scores					
	1	2	3	4	5	6
ACA	27	15	67	46	20	57
Party identification (percent Democrat)	75	88	00	00	100	100
Conservative coalition	33	21	63	51	26	70

	Vote Correlation Between Leaders and Clusters					
	1	2	3	4	5	6
Chairman	.46	.13	.13	.37	.11	.20
Ranking minority	.43	.06	.33	.48	-.02	.14

	Intercluster Correlation			
	1	2	3	4	5
2	.21				
3	-.11	-.42			
4	.20	.16	.21		
5	.09	.44	-.28	.05	
6	.08	.12	.08	.00	-.08

TABLE 23

Government Operations, 94th Congress

Representative	Party	State	Cluster (N = 016)					
			1	2	3	4	5	6
Moorhead, W.	D	Pennsylvania	.65					
Fascell, D.	D	Florida	.67					
Moss, J.	D	California	.73					
Mezvinsky, E.	D	Iowa	.55					
Harrington, M.	D	Mississippi	.64					
Burton, J.	D	California	.73					
Abzug, B.	D	New York	.64					
Conyers, J.	D	Michigan	.74					
Hicks, F.	D	Washington	.66					
Wright, J.	D	Texas	.60					
Rosenthal, B.	D	New York	.55					
Maguire, A.	D	New Jersey	.65					
Wydler, J.	R	New York		.64				
Erlenborn, J.	R	Illinois		.81				
Thone, C.	R	Nebraska		.80				
Brown, G.	R	Michigan		.77				
Steiger, S.	R	Arizona		.74				
McCloskey, P.	R	California		.70				
Brown, C.	R	Ohio		.81				
Gradison, W.	R	Ohio		.81				
Kasten, R.	R	Wisconsin		.80				
Forsythe, E.	R	New Jersey		.62				
Ryan, L.	D	California		.54				
Drinan, R.	D	Mississippi			.50			
Fuqua, D.	D	Florida			.51			
Steelman, A.	R	Texas			.63			
Levitas, E.	D	Georgia			.60			
Horton, F.	R	New York				.59		

Pritchard, J.	R	Washington	.68
Gude, G.	R	Maryland	.57
Aspin, L.	D	Wisconsin	.56
Stanton, J.	D	Ohio	.51
St. Germain, F.	D	Rhode Island	.40
Jordan, B.	D	Texas	.50
Randall, W.	D	Missouri	.55
Moffett, T.	D	Connecticut	.60
Evans, D.	D	Indiana	
Fountain, L.	D	North Carolina	
Brooks, J.	D	Texas	
English, G.	D	Oklahoma	
Preyer, R.	D	North Carolina	
MacDonald, T.	D	Mississippi*	
Collins, C.	D	Illinois*	

*Member participated in less than 60 percent of the votes.

Mean Cluster Scores

	1	2	3	4	5	6
ACA	10	66	46	33	27	26
Party identification (percent Democrat)	100	09	75	00	100	100
Conservative Coalition	15	64	48	42	13	31

Vote Correlation Between Leaders and Clusters

	1	2	3	4	5	6
Chairman	.49	-.49	-.10	-.27	-.14	-.20
Ranking minority	-.49	.58	-.22	.59	.29	-.10

Intercluster Correlation

	1	2	3	4	5
2	-.61				
3	.05	.12			
4	-.28	.46	-.04		
5	.00	.04	-.21	.12	
6	.43	-.29	.03	.02	.07

TABLE 24

Government Operations, 95th Congress

Representative	Party	State	Cluster (N = 038)					
			1	2	3	4	5	6
Moss, J.	D	California	.58					
Maguire, A.	D	New Jersey	.56					
Collins, C.	D	Illinois	.41					
Stangeland, A.	R	Minnesota		.57				
Quayle, J.	R	Indiana		.52				
McCloskey, P.	R	California		.39				
Wydler, J.	R	New York		.50				
Harrington, M.	D	Mississippi			.48			
Preyer, R.	D	North Carolina			.52			
Moffett, T.	D	Connecticut			.55			
Moorhead, W.	D	Pennsylvania			.54			
Brooks, J.	D	Texas			.50			
Drinan, R.	D	Mississippi				.53		
St. Germain, F.	D	Rhode Island				.58		
Weiss, T.	D	New York				.48		
Blouin, M.	D	Iowa					.36	
Fithian, F.	D	Indiana					.47	
Hightower, J.	D	Texas					.49	
Conyers, J.	D	Michigan						.46
Jordan, B.	D	Texas						.37
Rosenthal, B.	D	New York						.48
Fascell, D.	D	Florida						
Fountain, L.	D	North Carolina						
Levitas, E.	D	Georgia						
English, G.	D	Oklahoma						
Evans, D.	D	Indiana						
Waxman, H.	D	California						
Ryan, L.	D	California						

232

Fuqua, D.	D	Florida
Burton, J.	D	California
Jenrette, J.	D	South Carolina
Kostmayer, P.	D.	Pennsylvania
Erlenborn, J.	R	Illinois
Horton, F.	R	New York
Brown, C.	R	Ohio
Brown, G.	R	Michigan
Walker, R.	R	Pennsylvania
Corcoran, T.	R	Illinois
Thone, C.	R	Nebraska
Aspin, L.	D	Wisconsin*
Kasten, R.	R	Wisconsin*
Pritchard, J.	R	Washington*
Cunningham, J.	R	Washington*
Kindness, T.	R	Ohio*

*Member participated in less than 60 percent of the votes.

	Mean Cluster Scores					
	1	2	3	4	5	6
ACA	09	72	15	05	38	04
Party identification (percent Democrat)	100	00	100	100	100	100
Conservative Coalition	08	68	24	10	50	09

	Vote Correlation Between Leaders and Clusters					
	1	2	3	4	5	6
Chairman	.06	-.31	.50	.22	.27	.04
Ranking minority	.05	-.47	.27	.25	.07	.00

	Intercluster Correlation				
	1	2	3	4	5
2	-.04				
3	.22	-.17			
4	.17	-.15	.27		
5	.02	-.10	.33	.14	
6	.21	.00	.15	.23	.06

TABLE 25

Government Operations, 96th Congress

Representative	Party	State	Cluster (N = 031)					
			1	2	3	4	5	6
St. Germain, F.	D	Rhode Island	.55					
Moorhead, W.	D	Pennsylvania	.44					
Weiss, T.	D	New York	.51					
Waxman, H.	D	California	.54					
Aspin, L.	D	Wisconsin	.49					
Maguire, A.	D	New Jersey	.58					
Drinan, R.	D	Mississippi	.50					
Preyer, R.	D	North Carolina	.42					
Collins, C.	D	Illinois	.44					
Matsui, R.	D	California	.54					
Burton, J.	D	California		.43				
Conyers, J.	D	Michigan		.48				
Moffett, T.	D	Connecticut		.53				
Evans, D.	D	Indiana		.51				
Kostmayer, P.	D	Pennsylvania		.58				
Fithian, F.	D	Indiana			.56			
Brooks, J.	D	Texas			.66			
Horton, F.	R	New York			.65			
Brown, C.	R	Ohio				.63		
Butler, C.	R	Virginia				.44		
Stangeland, A.	R	Michigan				.53		
Walker, R.	R	Pennsylvania				.56		
Kindness, T.	R	Ohio					.66	
Snowe, O.	R	Maine					.66	

Synar, M.	D	Oklahoma	.47
Deckard, H.	R	Indiana	.41
English, G.	D	Oklahoma	.56
Levitas, E.	D	Georgia	
Fuqua, D.	D	Florida	
Fountain, L.	D	North Carolina	
Fascell, D.	D	Florida	
Rosenthal, B.	D	New York	
Atkinson, E.	D	Pennsylvania	
McCloskey, P.	R	California	
Wydler, J.	R	New York	
Erlenborn, J.	R	Illinois	
Grisham, W.	R	California	
Jeffries, J.	R	Kansas	
Williams, L.	R	Ohio	

	Mean Cluster Scores					
	1	2	3	4	5	6
ACA	16	26	31	86	82	60
Party identification (percent Democrat)	100	100	67	00	00	67
Conservative Coalition	13	22	47	83	80	71

	Vote Correlation Between Leaders and Clusters					
	1	2	3	4	5	6
Chairman	.32	.46	.66	-.47	-.29	.26
Ranking minority	.40	.41	.65	-.45	-.45	.10

	Intercluster Correlation				
	1	2	3	4	5
2	.29				
3	.29	.39			
4	-.33	-.22	-.35		
5	-.27	-.33	-.26	.21	
6	-.15	.02	.24	-.04	.23

TABLE 26

Interstate, Commerce, 92nd Congress

Representative	Party	State	Cluster (N = 025)					
			1	2	3	4	5	6
Harvey, J.	R	Michigan	.62					
Broyhill, J.	R	North Carolina	.61					
Nelson, A.	R	Minnesota	.54					
Shoup, R.	R	Montana	.57					
McCollister, J.	R	Nebraska	.70					
Collins, J.	R	Texas	.71					
Hastings, J.	R	New York	.47					
Brown, C.	R	Ohio		.46				
Carter, T.	R	Kentucky		.51				
Thompson, F.	R	Georgia		.56				
Schmitz, J.	R	California		.60				
Keith, H.	R	Mississippi		.67				
Tiernan, R.	D	Rhode Island			.63			
Metcalfe, R.	D	Illinois			.55			
Symington, J.	D	Maryland			.55			
Adams, B.	D	Washington			.58			
Eckhardt, B.	D	Texas				.59		
Carney, C.	D	Ohio				.52		
Roy, W.	D	Kansas				.49		
Van, D.	D	California				.62		
Rogers, P.	D	Florida				.53		
Moss, J.	D	California				.70		
Dingell, J.	D	Michigan					.53	
MacDonald, T.	D	Mississippi					.48	
Rooney, F.	D	Pennsylvania					.56	
Pickle, J.	D	Texas					.60	
Jarman, J.	D	Oklahoma						.50
Springer, W.	R	Illinois						.54
Skubitz, J.	R	Kansas						.48

Frey, L.	R	Florida
Ware, J.	R	Pennsylvania
Satterfield, D.	D	Virginia
Kyros, P.	D	Maine
Podell, B.	D	New York
Preyer, R.	D	North Carolina
Byron, G.	D	Maryland
Stuckey, B.	D	Georgia*
Murphy, J.	D	New York*
Staggers, H.	D	West Virginia*
Blanton, R.	D	Tennessee*
Kuykendall, O.	R	Tennessee*
Devine, S.	R	Ohio*
Helstoski, H.	D	New Jersey*

*Member participated in less than 60 percent of the votes.

| | Mean Cluster Scores | | | | | |
	1	2	3	4	5	6
ACA	79	77	08	24	30	78
Party identification (percent Democrat)	00	00	100	100	100	33
Conservative Coalition	80	75	09	24	33	72

| | Vote Correlation Between Leaders and Clusters | | | | | |
	1	2	3	4	5	6
Chairman (participated in less than 60 percent of the votes)						
Ranking minority	-.33	.35	.12	-.16	-.06	.53

| | Intercluster Correlation | | | | |
	1	2	3	4	5
2	.22				
3	.03	-.15			
4	-.49	-.13	.23		
5	-.18	.17	.13	.29	
6	.14	.29	.15	-.10	-.08

TABLE 27

Interstate, Commerce, 93rd Congress

Representative	Party	State	Cluster (N = 051)		
			1	2	3
Moss, J.	D	California	.43		
Eckhardt, B.	D	Texas	.64		
Adams, B.	D	Washington	.53		
Devine, S.	R	Ohio		.41	
Lent, N.	R	New York		.44	
Ware, J.	R	Pennsylvania		.40	
Frey, L.	R	Florida		.46	
Hastings, J.	R	New York		.45	
Staggers, H.	D	West Virginia			.50
Rogers, P.	D	Florida			.43
Dingell, J.	D	Michigan			.43
Pickle, J.	D	Texas			
Van Deerlin, L.	D	California			
Jarman, J	D	Oklahoma			
Nelson, A.	R	Minnesota			
Carter, T.	R	Kentucky			
Broyhill, J.	R	North Carolina			
Breckinridge, J.	D	Kentucky			
Roy, W.	D	Kansas			
Byron, G.	D	Maryland			
Metcalfe, R.	D	Illinois			
Kyros, P.	D	Maine			
Satterfield, D.	D	Virginia			
Murphy, J.	D	New York			
Preyer, R.	D	North Carolina			
Carney, C.	D	Ohio			
Symington, J.	D	Missouri			
Young, S.	R	Illinois			

Heinz, J.   R   Pennsylvania
Goldwater, B.   R   California
Shoup, R.   R   Montana
Skubitz, J.   R   Kansas
Kuykendall, D.   R   Tennessee
Brown, C.   R   Ohio
Collins, J.   R   Texas
McCollister, J.   R   Nebraska
Rooney, F.   D   Pennsylvania*
MacDonald, T.   D   Mississippi*
Madigan, E.   R   Illinios*
Luken, T.   D   Ohio*
Hudnut, W.   R   Indiana*
Harvey, J.   R   Michigan*
Helstoski, H.   D   New Jersey*
Podell, B.   D   New York*
Stuckey, B.   D   Georgia*

*Member participated in less than 60 percent of the votes.

	Mean Cluster Scores		
	1	2	3
ACA	13	76	33
Party identification (percent Democrat)	100	00	100
Conservative coalition	09	76	43

	Vote Correlation Between Leaders and Clusters		
	1	2	3
Chairman	.38	-.14	.50
Ranking minority	.01	.41	-.20

	Intercluster Correlation	
	1	2
2	-.14	
3	.29	-.05

TABLE 28

Interstate, Commerce, 94th Congress

Representative	Party	State	Cluster (N = 105)			
			1	2	3	4
Moorhead, C.	R	California	.47			
Madigan, E.	R	Illinois	.41			
McCollister, J.	R	Nebraska	.54			
Collins, J.	R	Texas	.46			
Skubitz, J.	R	Kansas	.42			
Brown, C.	R	Ohio	.57			
Carter, T.	R	Kentucky	.41			
Broyhill, J.	R	North Carolina	.47			
Devine, S.	R	Ohio	.45			
Maguire, A.	D	New Jersey		.51		
Moffett, T.	D	Connecticut		.55		
Florio, J.	D	New Jersey		.49		
Moss, J.	D	California		.60		
Dingell, J.	D	Michigan		.45		
Brodhead, W.	D	Michigan		.59		
Sharp, P.	D	Indiana		.55		
Waxman, H.	D	California		.44		
Ottinger, R.	D	New York		.58		
Scheuer, J.	D	New York		.52		
Metcalfe, R.	D	Illinois		.54		
Eckhardt, B.	D	Texas		.53		
Adams, B.	D	Washington		.51		
Rogers, P.	D	Florida			.48	
Rooney, F.	D	Pennsylvania			.38	
Staggers, H.	D	West Virginia			.45	
Van Deerlin, L.	D	California				.38
Symington, J.	D	Missouri				.50
Preyer, R.	D	North Carolina				.44
Wirth, T.	D	Colorado				.42

Hefner, W.	D	North Carolina
Krueger, R.	D	Texas
Carney, C.	D	Ohio
Satterfield, D.	D	Virginia
Murphy, J.	D	New York
Santini, J.	D	Nevada
Frey, L.	R	Florida
Heinz, J.	R	Pennsylvania
Lent, N.	R	New York
Moore, W.	R	Louisiana*
Rinaldo, M.	R	New Jersey*
Hastings, J.	R	New York*
Russo, M.	D	Illinois*
Byron, G.	D	Maryland*
Stuckey, B.	D	Georgia*
MacDonald, T.	D	Mississippi*

*Member participated in less than 60 percent of the votes.

Mean Cluster Scores			
1	2	3	4
ACA	84	07	29	20
Party identification (percent Democrat)	00	100	100	100
Conservative coalition	83	12	38	32

Vote Correlation Between Leaders and Clusters

	1	2	3	4
Chairman	-.25	.27	.45	.25
Ranking minority	.45	-.27	-.26	-.21

Intercluster Correlation

	1	2	3
2	-.26		
3	-.23	.29	
4	-.23	.41	.27

TABLE 29

Interstate, Commerce, 95th Congress

Representative	Party	State	Cluster (N = 065)			
			1	2	3	4
Stockman, D.	R	Michigan	.54			
Moore, W.	R	Louisiana	.52			
Moorhead, C.	R	California	.58			
Madigan, E.	R	Illinois	.51			
Lent, N.	R	New York	.53			
Frey, L.	R	Florida	.51			
Collins, J.	R	Texas	.58			
Carter, T.	R	Kentucky	.35			
Gammage, R.	D	Texas		.68		
Krueger, R.	D	Texas		.63		
Satterfield, D.	D	Virginia		.67		
Murphy, J.	D	New York			.53	
Carney, C.	D	Ohio			.50	
Florio, J.	D	New Jersey			.57	
Maguire, A.	D	New Jersey			.43	
Moffett, T.	D	Connecticut			.52	
Van Deerlin, L.	D	California			.42	
Markey, E.	D	Massachusetts			.49	
Broyhill, J.	R	North Carolina				.46
Devine, S.	R	Ohio				.49
Skubitz, J.	R	Kansas				.37
Mikulski, B.	D	Maryland				
Gore, A.	D	Tennessee				
Luken, T.	D	Ohio				
Walgren, D.	D	Pennsylvania				
Marks, M.	R	Pennsylvania				

Rooney, F.	D	Pennsylvania
Rogers, P.	D	Florida
Dingell, J.	D	Michigan
Moss, J.	D	California
Staggers, H.	D	West Virginia
Santini, J.	D	Nevada
Russo, M.	D	Illinois
Sharp, P.	D	Indiana
Wirth, T.	D	Colorado
Metcalfe, R.	D	Illinois
Waxman, H.	D	California
Ottinger, R.	D	New York
Preyer, R.	D	North Carolina
Eckhardt, B.	D	Texas
Rinaldo, M.	R	New Jersey*
Scheuer, J.	D	New York*

*Member participated in less than 60 percent of the votes.

Mean Cluster Scores

	1	2	3	4
ACA	64	67	15	84
Party identification (percent Democrat)	00	100	100	00
Conservative coalition	78	69	16	82

Vote Correlation Between Leaders and Clusters

	1	2	3	4
Chairman	-.19	-.12	.17	-.25
Ranking minority	-.44	.24	.10	.49

Intercluster Correlation

	1	2	3
2	.27		
3	.03	.15	
4	.39	.31	.13

TABLE 30

Interstate, Commerce, 96th Congress

Representative	Party	State	Cluster (N = 099)				
			1	2	3	4	5
Eckhardt, B.	D	Texas	.46				
Walgren, D.	D	Pennsylvania	.54				
Markey, E.	D	Mississippi	.46				
Maguire, A.	D	New York	.44				
Moffett, T.	D	Connecticut	.52				
Florio, J.	D	New Jersey	.49				
Waxman, H.	D	California	.51				
Ottinger, R.	D	New York	.54				
Scheuer, J.	D	New York	.47				
Leland, M.	D	Texas	.46				
Carter, T.	R	Kentucky		.43			
Broyhill, J.	R	North Carolina		.50			
Devine, S.	R	Ohio		.50			
Corcoran, T.	R	Illinois		.43			
Moorhead, C.	R	California		.40			
Lent, N.	R	New York		.49			
Collins, J.	R	Texas		.48			
Satterfield, D.	D	Virginia		.40			
Stockman, D.	R	Michigan			.47		
Brown, C.	R	Ohio			.49		
Shelby, R.	D	Alabama			.40		
Gramm, P.	D	Texas			.47		
Loeffler, T.	R	Texas			.49		
Lee, G.	R	New York			.48		
Sharp, P.	D	Indiana				.49	
Wirth, T.	D	Colorado				.54	
Mikulski, B.	D	Maryland				.45	

Name	Party	State					5
Preyer, R.	D	North Carolina					.53
Van Deerlin, L.	D	California					.53
Murphy, J.	D	New York					
Dingell, J.	D	Michigan					
Staggers, H.	D	West Virginia					
Mottl, R.	D	Ohio					
Gore, A.	D	Tennessee					
Santini, J.	D	Nevada					
Luken, T.	D	Ohio					
Dannemeyer, W.	R	California					
Swift, A.	D	Washington					
Rinaldo, M.	R	New Jersey					
Marks, M.	R	Pennsylvania					
Madigan, E.	R	Illinois*					
Russo, M.	D	Illinois*					
Matsui, R.	D	California*					

*Member participated in less than 60 percent of the votes.

	Mean Cluster Scores				
	1	2	3	4	5
ACA	11	87	81	23	18
Party identification (percent Democrat)	100	13	33	100	100
Conservative Coalition	10	86	85	29	31

	Vote Correlation Between Leaders and Clusters				
	1	2	3	4	5
Chairman	.13	-.19	-.17	.15	.30
Ranking minority	.06	.50	.42	.05	.17

	Intercluster Correlation			
	1	2	3	4
2	-.01			
3	-.03	.39		
4	.40	.00	.04	
5	.35	.07	.11	.32

TABLE 31

Post Office, 92nd Congress

Representative	Party	State	Cluster (N = 023)		
			1	2	3
Hanley, J.	D	New York	.62		
Daniels, D.	D	New Jersey	.62		
Dulski, T.	D	New York	.51		
Ford, W.	D	Michigan	.51		
Waldie, J.	D	California	.40		
Chappell, B.	D	Florida		.40	
Brasco, F.	D	Nevada		.52	
Nix, R.	D	Pennsylvania		.50	
Henderson, D.	D	North Carolina		.52	
Rousselot, J.	R	California			.59
Derwinski, E.	R	Illinois			.59
Johnson, A.	R	Pennsylvania			
Hogan, L.	R	Maryland			
Scott, W.	R	Virginia			
Hillis, E.	R	Indiana			
Mills, W.	R	Maryland			
Purcell, G.	D	Texas			
Gross, H.	R	Iowa			
White, R.	D	Texas			
Hamilton, L.	D	Indiana			

Udall, M.	D	Arizona
Wilson, C.	D	California
Andrews, E.	D	Alabama*
Mallary, R.	R	Vermont*
Young, B.	R	Florida*
Powell, W.	R	Ohio*
McClure, J.	R	Idaho*
Corbett, R.	R	Pennsylvlania*
Bevill, T.	D	Alabama*

*Member participated in less than 60 percent of the votes.

Mean Cluster Scores

	1	2	3
ACA	21	47	93
Party identification (percent Democrat)	100	100	00
Conservative coalition	21	51	64

Vote Correlation Between Leaders and Clusters

	1	2	3
Chairman	.51	.39	-.04
Ranking minority	-.13	.14	.01

Intercluster Correlation

	1	2
2	.30	
3	.00	-.06

TABLE 32

Post Office, 93rd Congress

Representative	Party	State	Cluster (N = 019)			
			1	2	3	4
Waldie, J.	D	California	.45			
Wilson, C.	D	California	.52			
Hanley, J.	D	New York	.71			
Daniels, D.	D	New Jersey	.67			
Dulski, T.	D	New York	.59			
Moakley, J.	D	Mississippi	.57			
Clay, W.	D	Missouri	.68			
Brasco, F.	D	New York	.60			
Ford, W.	D	Michigan	.63			
Hogan, L.	R	Maryland		.61		
Johnson, A.	R	Pennsylvania		.64		
Henderson, D.	D	North Carolina		.48		
Rousselot, J.	R	California			.69	
Bafalis, L.	R	Florida			.69	
White, R.	D	Texas				.66
Schroeder, P.	D	Colorado				.53
Udall, M.	D	Arizona				.54
Gross, H.	R	Iowa				
Lehman, W.	D	Florida				
Mallary, R.	R	Vermont				

Hillis, E.	R	Indiana
Derwinski, E.	R	Illinois
Taylor, G.	R	Missouri*
Collins, J.	R	Texas*
Traxler, R.	D	Michigan*
Hinshaw, A.	R	California*
Mills, W.	R	Maryland*
Powell, W.	R	Ohio*
Nix, R.	D	Pennsylvania*

*Member participated in less than 60 percent of the votes.

Mean Cluster Scores

	1	2	3	4
ACA	16	66	92	27
Party identification (Democrat)	100	33	00	100
Conservative coalition	16	80	82	31

Vote Correlation Between Leaders and Clusters

	1	2	3	4
Chairman	-.59	.41	-.20	.21
Ranking minority	-.21	-.12	.30	-.27

Intercluster Correlation

	1	2	3
2	.28		
3	-.06	-.28	
4	.11	.15	-.34

TABLE 33

Post Office, 94th Congress

Representative	Party	State	Cluster (N = 016)			
			1	2	3	4
Gilman, B.	R	New York	.50			
Taylor, G.	R	Missouri	.59			
Collins, J.	R	Texas	.67			
Rousselot, J.	R	California	.67			
Derwinski, E.	R	Illinois	.67			
Lott, T.	R	Missouri	.55			
Mineta, N.	D	California		.57		
Harris, H.	D	Virginia		.59		
Lehman, W.	D	Florida		.59		
Wilson, C.	D	California		.65		
Hanley, J.	D	New York		.56		
White, R.	D	Texas			.63	
Jenrette, J.	D	South Carolina			.63	
Solarz, S.	D	New York				.46
Clay, W.	D	Missouri				.43
Nix, R.	D	Pennsylvania				.51
Daniels, D.	D	New Jersey				
Henderson, D.	D	North Carolina				
Schroeder, P.	D	Colorado				
Spellman, G.	D	Maryland				

Brodhead, W.	D	Michigan
Simon, P.	D	Illinois
Johnson, A.	R	Pennsylvania
Udall, M.	D	Arizona*
Neal, S.	D	North Carolina*
Ford, W.	D	Michigan*
Beard, R.	R	Tennessee*
Hinshaw, A.	R	California*

*Member participated in less than 60 percent of the votes.

Mean Cluster Scores

	1	2	3	4
ACA	80	12	57	02
Party identification (percent Democrat)	00	100	100	100
Conservative coalition	80	18	68	08

Vote Correlation Between Leaders and Clusters

	1	2	3	4
Chairman	.14	-.06	-.13	-.01
Ranking minority	.67	-.47	.20	.10

Intercluster Correlation

	1	2	3
2	-.47		
3	.03	.25	
4	-.15	.18	.19

TABLE 34

Post Office, 95th Congress

Representative	Party	State	Cluster (N = 059)		
			1	2	3
Udall, M.	D	Arizona	.57		
Nix, R.	D	Pennsylvania	.50		
Ryan, L.	D	California	.49		
Metcalfe, R.	D	Illinois	.50		
Myers, M.	D	Pennsylvania	.62		
Solarz, S.	D	Nebraska	.53		
Clay, W.	D	Missouri	.53		
Spellman, G.	D	Maryland		.58	
Harris, H.	D	Virginia		.59	
Wilson, C.	D	California		.46	
Corcoran, T.	R	Illinois			.50
Leach, J.	R	Iowa			.51
Lott, T.	R	Maryland			.39
Hanley, J.	D	New York			
Ford, W.	D	Michigan			
White, R.	D	Texas			
Heftel, C.	D	Hawaii			
Lehman, W.	D	Florida			

252

Schroeder, P.	D	Colorado
Garcia, R.	D	New York
Derwinski, E.	R	Illinois
Gilman, B.	R	New York
Taylor, G.	R	Missouri
Collins, J.	R	Texas
Rousselot, J.	R	California
Howard, J.	D	New Jersey*

*Member participated in less than 60 percent of the votes.

Mean Cluster Scores

	1	2	3
ACA	08	20	79
Party identification (percent Democrat)	100	100	00
Conservative coalition	12	23	82

Vote Correlation Between Leaders and Clusters

	1	2	3
Chairman	.50	-.01	-.15
Ranking minority	.05	-.17	.24

Intercluster Correlation

	1	2
2	.28	
3	-.15	-.14

TABLE 35

Post Office, 96th Congress

Representative	Party	State	Cluster (N = 012)				
			1	2	3	4	5
Dannemeyer, W.	R	California	.49				
Pashayan, C.	R	California	.65				
Courter, J.	R	New Jersey	.67				
Corcoran, T.	R	Illinois	.68				
Leach, J.	R	Iowa	.57				
Ferraro, G.	D	New York		.78			
Garcia, R.	D	New York		.76			
Harris, H.	D	Virginia		.76			
Spellman, G.	D	Maryland		.81			
Udall, M.	D	Arizona		.73			
Schroeder, R.	D	Colorado		.73			
Ford, W.	D	Michigan		.71			
Wilson, C.	D	California			.55		
Clay, W.	D	Missouri			.71		
Leland, M.	D	Texas			.66		
Albosta, D.	D	Michigan				.82	
Hanley, J.	D	New York				.82	
Derwinski, E.	R	Illinois					.63
Taylor, G.	R	Missouri					.63

254

Crane, D.   R   Illinois
Stenholm, C.   D   Texas
Cavanaugh, J.   D   Nebraska*
Gilman, B.   R   New York*
Oakar, M.   D   Ohio*
Yatron, G.   D   Pennsylvania*

*Member participated in less than 60 percent of the votes.

Mean Cluster Scores

	1	2	3	4	5
ACA	82	14	11	23	84
Party identification (percent Democrat)	00	100	100	100	00
Conservative coalition	80	18	11	45	80

Vote Correlation Between Leaders and Clusters

	1	2	3	4	5
Chairman	-.52	.27	.25	.82	-.09
Ranking Minority	.34	-.42	-.34	-.04	.63

Intercluster Correlation

	1	2	3	4
2	-.43			
3	-.14	.44		
4	-.49	.32	.25	
5	.25	-.36	-.26	.02

TABLE 36

Rules, 92nd Congress

Representative	Party	State	Cluster (N = 021) 1	2	3	4
Latta, D.	R	Ohio	.63			
Quillen, J.	R	Tennessee	.62			
Martin, D.	R	Nebraska	.51			
Smith, A.	R	California	.69			
Matsunaga, S.	D	Hawaii		.59		
Madden, R.	D	Indiana		.53		
O'Neill, T.	D	Mississippi		.63		
Sisk, B.	D	California			.35	
Delaney, J.	D	New York			.41	
Pepper, C.	D	Florida			.45	
Anderson, W.	D	Tennessee				.50
Colmer, W.	D	Missouri				.50
Bolling, R.	D	Missouri				
Young, J.	D	Texas				
Anderson, J.	R	Illinois				

	Mean Cluster Scores 1	2	3	4
ACA	90	10	36	59
Party identification (percent Democrat)	00	100	100	100
Conservative coalition	80	14	44	52

	Vote Correlation Between Leaders and Clusters 1	2	3	4
Chairman	.35	−.22	.28	.50
Ranking minority	.69	−.47	−.00	.07

	Intercluster Correlation 1	2	3
2	−.50		
3	−.04	.20	
4	.13	.00	.31

TABLE 37

Rules, 93rd Congress

Representative	Party	State	Cluster (N = 086) 1	Cluster (N = 086) 2
Latta, D.	R	Ohio	.49	
Quillen, J.	R	Tennessee	.49	
Madden, R.	D	Indiana		.44
Pepper, C.	D	Florida		.37
Bolling, R.	D	Missouri		.41
Sisk, B.	D	California		
Young, J.	D	Texas		
Delaney, J.	D	New York		
Anderson, J.	R	Illinois		
Martin, D.	R	Nebraska		
McSpadden, C.	D	Oklahoma		
Long, G.	D	Louisiana		
Murphy, M.	D	Illinois		
Matsunaga, S.	D	Hawaii		
Clawson, D.	R	California		

	Mean Cluster Scores 1	Mean Cluster Scores 2
ACA	80	10
Party identification (percent Democrat)	00	100
Conservative coalition	83	20

	Vote Correlation Between Leaders and Clusters 1	Vote Correlation Between Leaders and Clusters 2
Chairman	-.48	.44
Ranking minority	.22	-.27

	Intercluster Correlation 1
2	-.35

TABLE 38

Rules, 94th Congress

Representative	Party	State	Cluster (N = 099) 1	Cluster (N = 099) 2
Bolling, R.	D	Missouri	.57	
Pepper, C.	D	Florida	.53	
Madden, R.	D	Indiana	.61	
Young, A.	D	Georgia	.47	
Moakley, J.	D	Mississippi	.60	
Quillen, J.	R	Tennessee		.42
Latta, D.	R	Ohio		.41
Lott, T.	R	Missouri		.45
Clawson, D.	R	California		
Anderson, J.	R	Illinois		
Long, G.	D	Louisiana		
Murphy, M.	D	Illinois		
Matsunaga, S.	D	Hawaii		
Young, J.	D	Texas		
Sisk, B.	D	California		
Delaney, J.	D	New York		

	Mean Cluster Scores 1	Mean Cluster Scores 2
ACA	09	89
Party identification (percent Democrat)	100	00
Conservative coalition	13	89

	Vote Correlation Between Leaders and Clusters 1	Vote Correlation Between Leaders and Clusters 2
Chairman	.61	-.54
Ranking minority	-.38	.42

	Intercluster Correlation 1
2	-.41

258

TABLE 39

Rules, 95th Congress

Representative	Party	State	Cluster (N = 065) 1	2	3
Bolling, R.	D	Missouri	.43		
Long, G.	D	Louisiana	.38		
Delaney, J.	D	New York	.44		
Meeds, L.	D	Washington	.55		
Moakley, J.	D	Mississippi	.52		
Murphy, M.	D	Illinois		.57	
Pepper, C.	D	Florida		.41	
Young, J.	D	Texas		.47	
Quillen, J.	R	Tennessee			.50
Latta, D.	R	Ohio			.52
Lott, T.	R	Missouri			.40
Clawson, D.	R	California			
Anderson, J.	R	Illinois			
Dodd, C.	D	Connecticut			
Chisholm, S.	D	New York			
Sisk, B.	D	California			
Bauman, R.	R	Maryland*			

*Member participated in less than 60 percent of the votes.

	Mean Cluster Scores 1	2	3
ACA	11	22	85
Party identification (percent Democrat)	100	100	00
Conservative coalition	22	32	87

	Vote Correlation Between Leaders and Clusters 1	2	3
Chairman	.44	.36	-.57
Ranking minority	-.30	-.28	.50

	Intercluster Correlation 1	2
2	.35	
3	-.34	-.24

TABLE 40

Rules, 96th Congress

Representative	Party	State	Cluster (N = 070)		
			1	2	3
Long, G.	D	Louisiana	.44		
Beilenson, A.	D	California	.41		
Derrick, B.	D	South Carolina	.35		
Zeferetti, L.	D	New York		.44	
Moakley, J.	D	Mississippi		.44	
Frost, M.	D	Texas			.42
Bolling, R.	D	Missouri			.42
Bauman, R.	R	Maryland			
Lott, T.	R	Mississippi			
Latta, D.	R	Ohio			
Quillen, J.	R	Tennessee			
Dodd, C.	D	Connecticut			
Chisholm	D	New York			
Murphy, M.	D	Illinois			
Pepper, C.	D	Florida			
Anderson, J.	R	Illinois*			
Taylor, G.	R	Missouri*			

*Member participated in less than 60 percent of the votes.

	Mean Cluster Scores		
	1	2	3
ACA	25	12	21
Party identification (percent Democrat)	00	100	100
Conservative coalition	30	25	28

	Vote Correlation Between Leaders and Clusters		
	1	2	3
Chairman	.30	.18	.42
Ranking minority	-.20	-.32	-.14

	Intercluster Correlation	
	1	2
2	.17	
3	.29	.23

TABLE 41

Ways and Means, 92nd Congress

Representative	Party	State	Cluster (N = 032) 1	2	3	4
Landrum, P.	D	Georgia	.65			
Pettis, J.	R	California	.66			
Chamberlain, C.	R	Michigan	.72			
Conable, B.	R	New York	.62			
Broyhill, J.	R	Virginia	.59			
Collier, H.	R	Illinois	.66			
Schneebeli, H.	R	Pennsylvania	.68			
Betts, J.	R	Ohio	.77			
Byrnes, J.	R	Wisconsin	.58			
Brotzman, D.	R	Colorado	.72			
Duncan, J.	R	Tennessee	.62			
Carey, H.	D	New York		.64		
Green, W.	D	Pennsylvania		.59		
Fulton, R.	D	Tennessee		.52		
Rostenkowski, D.	D	Illinois		.63		
Burke, J.	D	Mississippi		.51		
Burleson, O.	D	Texas			.78	
Waggoner, J.	D	Louisiana			.78	
Corman, J.	D	California				.79
Vanik, C.	D	Ohio				.79
Gibbons, S.	D	Florida				
Griffiths, M.	D	Michigan				
Ullman, A.	D	Oregon				
Watts, J.	D	Kentucky				
Mills, W.	D	Arkansas				
Karth, J.	D	Minnesota*				

*Member participated in less than 60 percent of the votes.

	Mean Cluster Scores 1	2	3	4
ACA	80	12	84	11
Party identification (percent Democrat)	09	100	100	100
Conservative coalition	77	14	89	10

	Vote Correlation Between Leaders and Clusters 1	2	3	4
Chairman	.44	.30	.05	−.07
Ranking minority	.58	−.18	.43	−.35

	Intercluster Correlation 1	2	3
2	−.05		
3	.40	−.47	
4	−.43	.45	−.66

TABLE 42

Ways and Means, 93rd Congress

Representative	Party	State		Cluster (N = 075)	
			1	2	3
Landrum, P.	D	Georgia	.49		
Pettis, J.	R	California	.55		
Chamberlain, C.	R	Michigan	.63		
Broyhill, J.	R	Virginia	.59		
Waggonner, J.	D	Louisiana	.57		
Burleson, O.	D	Texas	.55		
Archer, B.	R	Texas	.67		
Clancy, D.	R	Ohio	.57		
Fulton, R.	D	Tennessee		.46	
Green, W.	D	Pennsylvania		.54	
Vanik, C.	D	Ohio		.57	
Rustenkowski, D.	D	Illinois		.42	
Burke, J.	D	Mississippi		.50	
Griffiths, M.	D	Michigan			.47
Corman, J.	D	California			.53
Gibbons, S.	D	Florida			.44
Carey, H.	D	New York			
Karth, J.	D	Minnesota			

262

Conable, B.   R   New York
Collier, H.   R   Illinois
Schneebeli, H.   R   Pennsylvania
Brotzman, D.   R   Colorado
Duncan, J.   R   Tennessee
Ullman, A.   D   Oregon
Mills, W.   D   Arkansas

Mean Cluster Scores

	1	2	3
ACA	82	13	20
Party identification (percent Democrat)	38	100	100
Conservative coalition	82	19	24

Vote Correlation Between Leaders and Clusters

	1	2	3
Chairman	-.04	.21	.12
Ranking minority	.30	-.36	-.05

Intercluster Correlation

	1	2
2	-.38	
3	-.27	.21

263

TABLE 43

Ways and Means, 94th Congress

Representative	Party	State	Cluster (N = 235)			
			1	2	3	4
Bafalis, L.	R	Florida	.45			
Martin, J.	R	North Carolina	.45			
Crane, P.	R	Illinois	.53			
Archer, B.	R	Texas	.58			
Clancy, D.	R	Ohio	.51			
Fisher, J.	D	Virginia		.50		
Vanik, C.	D	Ohio		.46		
Keys, M.	D	Kansas		.46		
Mikva, A.	D	Illinois		.51		
Stark, F.	D	California		.47		
Rangel, C.	D	New York		.40		
Vander, V.	D	Michigan		.48		
Pike, O.	D	New York		.39		
Karth, J.	D	Minnesota		.54		
Green, W.	D	Pennsylvania		.40		
Corman, J.	D	California		.49		
Waggonner, J.	D	Louisiana			.45	
Burleson, O.	D	Texas			.48	
Landrum, P.	D	Georgia			.49	
Schneebeli, H.	R	Pennsylvania				.44
Conable, B.	R	New York				.50
Frenzel, B.	R	Minnesota				.43
Ketchum, W.	R	California				
Duncan, J.	R	Tennessee				

Steiger, W.	R	Wisconsin
Vander, J.	R	Michigan
Rostenkowski, D.	D	Illinois
Burke, J.	D	Mississippi
Ullman, A.	D	Oregon
Gibbons, S.	D	Florida
Pickle, J.	D	Texas
Helstoski, H.	D	New Jersey
Cotter, W.	D	Connecticut
Jacobs, A.	D	Indiana
Jones, J.	D	Oklahoma
Mills, W.	D	Arkansas*
Ford, H.	D	Tennessee*
Fulton, R.	D	Tennessee*
Pettis, J.	R	California*

*Member participated in less than 60 percent of the votes.

Mean Cluster Scores			
1	2	3	4
93	09	85	70
00	100	100	00
88	12	83	68

ACA
Party identification (percent Democrat)
Conservative coalition

Vote Correlation Between Leaders and Clusters			
1	2	3	4
-.30	.39	-.03	-.03
.27	-.22	.22	.44

Chairman
Ranking minority

	Intercluster Correlation		
	1	2	3
2	-.33		
3	.26	-.22	
4	.25	-.17	.16

265

TABLE 44

Ways and Means, 95th Congress

Representative	Party	State	Cluster (N = 161)					
			1	2	3	4	5	6
Gradison, W.	R	Ohio	.37					
Bafalis, L.	R	Florida	.38					
Martin, J.	R	North Carolina	.40					
Crane, P.	R	Illinois	.46					
Vander, J.	R	Michigan	.48					
Archer, B.	R	Texas	.48					
Duncan, J.	R	Tennessee	.42					
Brodhead, W.	D	Michigan		.45				
Mikva, A.	D	Illinois		.39				
Stark, F.	D	California		.49				
Rangel, C.	D	New York		.40				
Jacobs, A.	D	Indiana			.56			
Keys, M.	D	Kansas			.56			
Waggonner, J.	D	Louisiana				.56		
Burleson, O.	D	Texas				.56		
Corman, J.	D	California					.40	
Rostenkowski, D.	D	Illinois					.45	
Ullman, A.	D	Oregon					.42	
Fisher, J.	D	Virginia					.35	
Steiger, W.	R	Wisconsin						.51
Conable, B.	R	New York						.52
Frenzel, B.	R	Minnesota						.52
Schulze, R.	R	Pennsylvania						
Ketchum, W.	R	California						
Lederer, R.	D	Pennsylvania						

Tucker, J.	D	Arkansas
Gephardt, R.	D	Maryland
Jenkins, E.	D	Georgia
Holland, K.	D	South Carolina
Ford, H.	D	Tennessee
Gibbons, S.	D	Florida
Pickle, J.	D	Texas
Pike, O.	D	New York
Cotter, W.	D	Connecticut
Jones, J.	D	Oklahoma
Burke, J.	D	Mississippi
Vanik, C.	D	Ohio
Rousselot, J.	R	California*

*Member participated in less than 60 percent of the votes.

Mean Cluster Scores

	1	2	3	4	5	6
ACA	84	07	28	80	13	71
Party identification (percent Democrat)	00	100	100	100	100	00
Conservative Coalition	85	04	37	91	22	65

Vote Correlation Between Leaders and Clusters

	1	2	3	4	5	6
Chairman	-.11	.16	.11	-.01	.42	-.04
Ranking minority	.34	-.18	-.13	.23	-.03	.52

Intercluster Correlation

	1	2	3	4	5
2	-.23				
3	-.14	.24			
4	.20	-.31	-.16		
5	-.12	-.24	.17	-.09	
6	.32	-.18	-.17	.15	-.09

TABLE 45

Ways and Means, 96th Congress

Representative	Party	State	Cluster (N = 112)		
			1	2	3
Moore, W.	R	Louisiana	.48		
Rousselot, J.	R	California	.37		
Gradison, W.	R	Ohio	.45		
Schulze, R.	R	Pennsylvania	.45		
Bafalis, L.	R	Florida	.51		
Martin, J.	R	North Carolina	.43		
Frenzel, B.	R	Minnesota	.38		
Crane, P.	R	Illinois	.48		
Archer, B.	R	Texas	.49		
Duncan, J.	R	Tennessee	.48		
Shannon, J.	D	Mississippi		.50	
Corman, J.	D	California		.47	
Vanik, C.	D	Ohio		.48	
Lederer, R.	D	Pennsylvania		.47	
Brodhead, W.	D	Michigan		.54	
Ford, H.	D	Tennessee		.56	
Fisher, J.	D	Virginia		.45	
Stark, F.	D	California		.46	
Rangel, C.	D	New York		.51	
Guarini, F.	D	New Jersey			.44
Heftel, C.	D	Hawaii			.36
Downey, T.	D	New York			.39
Rostenkowski, D.	D	Illinois			.45
	D	Oregon			

268

Pickle, J.	D	Texas
Gibbons, S.	D	Florida
Fowler, W.	D	Georgia
Jenkins, E.	D	Georgia
Gephardt, R.	D	Missouri
Cotter, W.	D	Connecticut
Jones, J.	D	Oklahoma
Jacobs, A.	D	Indiana
Holland, K.	D	South Carolina
Conable, B.	R	New York
Vander, J.	R	Michigan
Mikva, A.	D	Illinois*
Russo, M.	D	Illinois*

*Member participated in less than 60 percent of the votes.

Mean Cluster Scores

	1	2	3
ACA	86	10	16
Party identification (percent Democrat)	00	100	100
Conservative coalition	85	11	27

Vote Correlation Between Leaders and Clusters

	1	2	3
Chairman	-.22	.42	.33
Ranking minority	.40	-.31	-.23

Intercluster Correlation

	1	2
2	-.35	
3	-.22	.34

TABLE 46

Budget, 94th Congress

Representative	Party	State	1	Cluster (N = 020)		4
				2	3	
Clawson, D.	R	California	.84			
Broyhill, J.	R	North Carolina	.71			
Schneebeli, H.	R	Pennsylvania	.84			
Cederberg, E.	R	Michigan	.85			
Latta, D.	R	Ohio	.84			
Landrum, P.	D	Georgia	.50			
Holt, M.	R	Maryland	.79			
Conable, B.	R	New York	.77			
Shriver, G.	R	Kansas	.80			
Mitchell, P.	D	Maryland		.75		
Leggett, R.	D	California		.53		
Stokes, L.	D	Ohio		.53		
Mink, P.	D	Hawaii		.66		
Adams, B.	D	Washington		.59		
Wright, J.	D	Texas		.67		
O'Neill, T.	D	Mississippi		.68		
O'Hara, J.	D	Michigan		.57		
Smith, N.	D	Iowa			.48	
Giaimo, R.	D	Connecticut			.60	
Holtzman, E.	D	New York			.52	

Runnels, H.	D	New Mexico	.59
Burleson, O.	D	Texas	.59
Gibbons, S.	D	Florida	
Derrick, B.	D	South Carolina	
Ashley, T.	D	Ohio	
Hastings, J.	R	Nevada*	

*Member participated in less than 60 percent of the votes.

Mean Cluster Scores

	1	2	3	4
ACA	84	12	12	88
Party identification (percent Democrat)	11	100	100	100
Conservative coalition	80	18	19	88

Vote Correlation Between Leaders and Clusters

	1	2	3	4
Chairman	-.60	.59	.42	-.37
Ranking minority	.84	-.69	-.22	.35

Intercluster Correlation

	1	2	3
2	-.61		
3	-.17	.38	
4	.32	-.26	.08

TABLE 47

Budget, 95th Congress

			Cluster (N = 067)	
Representative	Party	State	1	2
Holtzman, E.	D	New York	.62	
Mitchell, P.	D	Maryland	.69	
Leggett, R.	D	California	.53	
Giaimo, R.	D	Connecticut	.55	
Mineta, N.	D	California	.68	
Simon, P.	D	Illinois	.70	
Lehman, W.	D	Florida	.59	
Obey, D.	D	Wisconsin	.59	
Fraser, D.	D	Minnesota	.55	
Broyhill, J.	R	North Carolina		.58
Latta, D.	R	Ohio		.64
Duncan, J.	R	Tennessee		.55
Holt, M.	R	Maryland		.63
Conable, B.	R	New York		.56
Regula, R.	R	Ohio		.52
Burgener, C.	R	California		.61
Rousselot, J.	R	California		
Mattox, J.	D	Texas		

Pike, O.   D   New York
Derrick, B.   D   South Carolina
Fisher, J.   D   Virginia
Stokes, L.   D   Ohio
Ashley, T.   D   Ohio
Wright, J.   D   Texas
Burleson, O.   D   Texas*

*Member participated in less than 60 percent of the votes.

Mean Cluster Scores

	1	2
ACA	11	81
Party identification (percent Democrat)	100	00
Conservative coalition	12	85

Vote Correlation Between Leaders and Clusters

	1	2
Chairman	.55	-.38
Ranking minority	-.64	.64

Intercluster Correlation

	1
2	-.53

TABLE 48

Budget, 96th Congress

Representative	Party	State	Cluster (N = 073)			
			1	2	3	4
Regula, R.	R	Ohio	.61			
Holt, M.	R	Maryland	.74			
Conable, B.	R	New York	.76			
Broyhill, J.	R	North Carolina	.74			
Latta, D.	R	Ohio	.73			
Rudd, E.	R	Arizona	.76			
Frenzel, B.	R	Minnesota	.68			
Shuster, E.	R	Pennsylvania	.75			
Brodhead, W.	D	Michigan		.44		
Solarz, S.	D	New York		.54		
Mineta, N.	D	California		.50		
Wright, J.	D	Texas		.56		
Giaimo, R.	D	Connecticut		.50		
Ashley, T.	D	Ohio		.58		
Stokes, L.	D	Ohio			.66	
Obey, D.	D	Wisconsin			.50	
Holtzman, E.	D	New York			.59	
Simon, P.	D	Illinois			.57	
Gray, W.	D	Pennsylvania			.60	

Nelson, B.	D	Florida	.42
Gephardt, R.	D	Missouri	.44
Jones, J.	D	Oklahoma	.49
Mattox, J.	D	Texas	
Panetta, L.	D	California	
Wirth, T.	D	Colorado	

Mean Cluster Scores

	1	2	3	4
ACA	83	14	10	40
Party identification (percent Democrat)	00	100	100	100
Conservative coalition	81	17	06	57

Vote Correlation Between Leaders and Clusters

	1	2	3	4
Chairman	-.10	.50	.13	.23
Ranking minority	.73	-.33	-.65	.20

Intercluster Correlation

	1	2	3
2	-.32		
3	-.60	.33	
4	.19	.05	-.15

Appendix 3

TABLE 1

Interagreement Scores: Committee Chairpersons with Committee Groups

Committee and Congress/Ch.	Committee Groups							
	Dem	Rep	Lib	Con	CC	N Dem	R Min	N
Agriculture								
92 Poage	-.52	-.08	.44	.16	.20	.44	-.21	11
93 Poage	.21	.05	.10	.16	.16	.06	-.29a	48
94 Foley	.11	-.17	.22	-.19	-.13	.25	-.19	75
95 Foley	.33	-.18	.26	.06	.08	.31	-.10	61
96 Foley	.18	-.28	.17	-.16	-.10	.21	-.28	36
Armed Services								
92 Hebert	.28	.27	.23	.30	.29	.24	.72	34
93 Hebert	.39	.42	.24	.49	.50	.18	.48	25
94 Price	.09	.23	-.04	.23	.22	-.01	.06	22
95 Price	.13	.07	.13	.09	.07	.17	-.04	28
96 Price	.11	.06	.09	.10	.12	.06	-.06	23
Banking								
92 Patman	.15	-.14	.15	-.10	.10	.18	-.04	149
93 Patman	.28	-.04	.25	-.05	.03	.31	-.13	117
94 Reuss	.25	-.09	.22	-.06	.01	.25	-.16	80
95 Reuss	.18	-.09	.17	-.07	-.05	.21	-.06	103
96 Reuss	.30	-.21	.31	-.17	-.12	.35	.02	53

(continued)

Table 1, continued

Committee and Congress/Ch.	Committee Groups							
	Dem	Rep	Lib	Con	CC	N Dem	R Min	N
Budget								
94 Adams	.29	-.63	.52	-.48	-.39	.43	-.70	20
95 Giaimo	.45	-.37	.45	-.37	-.09	.49	-.55	67
96 Giaimo	.26	-.10	.25	-.06	.01	.28	-.11	73
Education and Labor								
92 Perkins	.42	-.24	.31	-.18	-.20	.43	-.38	99
93 Perkins	.35	.01	.27	-.06	.07	.35	-.12	64
94 Perkins	.36	-.19	.31	-.12	-.14	.36	-.25	44
95 Perkins	.33	-.26	.24	-.27	-.26	.33	-.31	79
96 Perkins	.44	-.28	.39	-.30	-.18	.43	-.23	36
Government Operations								
92 Holifield	.24	.52	.32	.41	.38	.30	1.00	13
93 Holifield	.20	.19	.21	.18	.19	.22	.75	18
94 Brooks	.26	-.46	.22	-.31	-.23	.31	-.40	16
95 Brooks	.18	-.19	.17	-.10	-.03	.18	.32	38
96 Brooks	.33	-.11	.33	-.07	.01	.37	.75	31
Commerce								
92 Staggersb								
93 Staggers	.15	-.11	.14	-.07	-.03	.14	-.20	51
94 Staggers	.24	-.22	.26	-.19	-.10	.26	-.26	105
95 Staggers	.14	-.19	.14	-.18	-.11	.18	-.28	65
96 Staggers	.11	-.16	.14	-.16	-.09	.12	-.29	99

280

Post Office								
92 Dulski	.34	.12	.34	.19	.19	.34	.10	23
93 Dulski	.45	-.18	.37	-.04	-.06	.52	-.47	19
94 Henderson	-.01	.09	.03	.01	.03	.02	.02	16
95 Nix	.26	-.19	.20	-.14	-.07	.27	-.06	59
96 Hanley	.29	-.37	.32	-.33	-.23	.35	-.19	12
Rules								
92 Colmer	.03	.28	.02	.22	.22	-.02	.32	21
93 Madden	.31	-.34	.21	-.40	.07	.33	-.25	86
94 Madden	.34	-.45	.30	-.53	-.08	.31	-.52	99
95 Delaney	.32	-.40	.24	-.57	-.13	.32	-.52	65
96 Bolling	.22	-.20	.22	-.20	.07	.15	-.17	70
Ways and Means								
92 Mills	.21	.44	.22	.38	.34	.25	.43	32
93 Mills	.15	-.01	.20	-.02	.01	.20	-.05	75
94 Ullman	.28	-.19	.36	-.11	.07	.35	-.00	235
95 Ullman	.21	-.08	.25	-.04	.03	.25	.05	161
96 Ullman	.32	-.19	.32	-.12	-.00	.33	-.06	112

aTeague (Texas) was replaced as ranking minority member by Wampler (Virginia) during the Ninety-third Congress. Poage/Wampler correlation = .24.

bStaggers participated in less than 60 percent of the roll call votes.

TABLE 2

Interagreement Scores: Committee Ranking Minority with Committee Groups

Committee and Congress/ Ranking Minority	Committee Groups							N
	Dem	Rep	Lib	Con	CC	N Dem	Chmn	
Agriculture								
92 Belcher	-.16	.12	-.11	-.01	-.02	-.11	-.21	11
93 Wampler[a]	.04	.17	.01	.15	.13	-.01	.24	48
94 Wampler	-.04	.16	-.12	.18	.13	-.14	-.19	75
95 Wampler	-.12	.20	-.19	.15	.10	-.22	-.10	61
96 Wampler	-.10	.40	-.10	.26	.19	-.15	-.28	36
Teague[a]	-.13	-.04	-.24	-.09	-.13	-.20	-.29	
Armed Services								
92 Arends	.10	.12	.10	.11	.12	.08	.48	34
93 Bray	.37	.36	.24	.43	.46	.17	.72	25
94 Wilson	.15	.27	.12	.23	.27	.07	.06	22
95 Wilson	.09	.35	.02	.31	.30	-.01	-.04	28
96 Wilson	.05	.12	.07	.07	.08	.05	-.06	23
Banking and Currency								
92 Widnall	.06	.24	.03	.25	.23	.01	-.04	149
93 Widnall	.06	.17	.06	.18	.14	.06	-.13	117
94 Johnson	-.14	.27	-.13	.29	.17	-.17	-.16	80
95 Stanton	.04	.17	.02	.21	.14	.03	-.06	103
96 Stanton	-.07	.24	-.04	.16	.60	-.08	.02	53

Budget								
94 Latta	-.33	.90	-.56	.61	.52	-.47	-.70	20
95 Latta	-.47	.61	-.47	.61	.25	-.58	-.55	67
96 Latta	-.28	.73	-.32	.67	.50	-.42	-.11	73
Education and Labor								
92 Quie	-.31	.56	-.17	.47	.45	-.32	-.38	99
93 Quie	-.32	.40	-.13	.44	.28	-.36	-.12	64
94 Quie	-.36	.34	-.29	.24	.22	-.36	-.25	44
95 Quie	-.32	.42	-.26	.46	.36	-.32	-.31	79
96 Ashbrook	-.22	.43	-.17	.42	.32	-.23	-.23	36
Government Operations								
92 Dwyer	.28	.48	.32	.41	.35	.35	1.00	13
93 Horton	.14	.34	.18	.32	.26	.16	.75	18
94 Horton	-.23	.54	-.21	.37	.26	-.27	-.40	16
95 Horton	.11	-.31	.11	-.19	-.10	.11	.32	38
96 Horton	.36	-.19	.36	-.12	-.01	.40	.75	31
Interstate and Foreign Commerce								
92 Springer	-.03	.32	-.05	.24	.22	-.04	.20	25
93 Devine	.01	.25	.01	.21	.16	.04	-.20	51
94 Devine	-.19	.43	-.20	.36	.24	-.22	-.26	105
95 Devine	.03	.43	.03	.40	.29	.02	-.28	65
96 Devine	.12	.44	.08	.43	.34	.11	-.29	99

(continued)

Table 2, continued

Committee and Congress/ Ranking Minority	Committee Groups							
	Dem	Rep	Lib	Con	CC	N Dem	Chmn	N
Post Office								
92 Gross	-.04	.13	-.13	.14	.14	-.13	.10	23
93 Gross	-.21	.19	-.14	.06	.08	-.22	-.47	19
94 Derwinski	-.21	.62	-.25	.48	.29	-.26	.02	16
95 Derwinski	-.06	.12	-.06	.20	.03	-.03	-.06	59
96 Derwinski	-.34	.35	-.33	.26	.12	-.32	-.19	12
Rules								
92 Smith	-.21	.61	-.30	.35	.27	-.31	.32	21
93 Martin	-.24	.14	-.19	.22	-.05	-.24	-.25	86
94 Quillen	-.18	.32	-.15	.37	.09	-.19	-.52	99
95 Quillen	-.24	.37	-.17	.50	.12	-.25	-.52	65
96 Quillen	-.19	.15	-.19	.15	-.00	-.24	-.17	70
Ways and Means								
92 Byrnes	.00	.58	-.12	.55	.42	-.19	.43	32
93 Schneebeli	-.12	.34	-.20	.30	.23	-.25	-.05	75
94 Schneebeli	-.08	.32	-.17	.26	.24	-.16	-.00	235
95 Conable	-.02	.36	-.07	.30	.22	-.08	.05	161
96 Conable	-.14	.39	-.15	.33	.23	-.22	-.06	112

[a]Teague (Texas) was replaced as ranking minority member by Wampler (Virginia) during the Ninety-third Congress.

Bibliography

Anderson, L. H., M. W. Watts, Jr., and A. R. Wilcox. 1966. _Legislative Roll Call Analysis_. Evanston, Ill.: Northwestern University Press.

Barton, W. V. 1976. "Coalition-Building in the U.S. House of Representatives: Agricultural Legislation in 1973." In _Cases in Public Policy-Making_, edited by J. E. Anderson. New York: Praeger.

Bass, B. M. (Ed.). 1981. _Stogdill's Handbook of Leadership: A Survey of Theory and Research_. New York: Free Press.

Berg, J. 1978. "The Effects of Seniority Reform on Three House Committees." In _Legislative Reform: The Policy Impact_, edited by L. N. Rieselbach. Lexington, Mass.: Lexington Books.

Brady, D. W., and C. S. Bullock III. 1981. "Coalition Politics in the House of Representatives." In _Congress Reconsidered_, 2nd ed., edited by L. C. Dodd and B. I. Oppenheimer. Washington, D.C.: Congressional Quarterly Press.

_____. 1980. "Is There a Conservative Coalition in the House?" _Journal of Politics_ 42: 549–59.

Brady, D., J. Cooper, and P. A. Hurley. 1979. "The Decline of Party in the U.S. House of Representatives, 1887–1968." _Legislative Studies Quarterly_ 4: 381–407.

Bullock, C. S. III. 1979. "House Committee Assignments." In _The Congressional System: Notes and Readings_, 2nd ed., edited by L. N. Rieselbach. North Scituate, Mass.: Duxbury Press.

_____. 1976. "Motivations for U.S. Congressional Commit-
tee Preferences: Freshmen of the 92nd Congress." Legislative Studies Quarterly 1: 201–12.

Burn, J. M. 1978. Leadership. New York: Harper & Row.

Clausen, A. R. 1973. How Congressmen Decide: A Policy Focus.
New York: St. Martin's Press.

Clausen, A. R., and C. E. Van Horn. 1977. "The Congressional Response to a Decade of Change, 1963–1972."
Journal of Politics 39: 624:66.

Clubb, J. M., and S. A. Traugott. 1977. "Partisan Cleavage
and Cohesion in the House of Representatives, 1861–1974."
Journal of Interdisciplinary History 7: 375–401.

Cohen, R. E. 1983. "House Task Force May Propose Radical
Changes to Toughen the Budget Process." National Journal
15: 1740–42.

Congressional Directory. Annual Editions. Washington, D.C.:
Government Printing Office.

Congressional Quarterly. 1977. Congress and the Nation,
Vol. 4. Washington, D.C.: Congressional Quarterly Press.

Cook, T. E. 1980. "Policy Considerations and Committee
Assignments: The House Armed Services and Interior Com-
mittees." Paper presented to the Everett McKinley Dirksen
Congressional Research Center, Sam Rayburn Library Con-
ference, Understanding Congressional Leadership: The
State of the Art.

Cook, T. E., and L. Ragsdale. 1982. "Connecting the Styles
from Washington to Home: Constituency Perceptions of
the Representatives in Congress." Paper presented to the
Annual Meeting of the Midwest Political Science Association.

Cooper, J. 1970. Origins of the Standing Committees and
the Development of the Modern House. Houston: Rice
University Studies.

Cooper, J., and W. West. 1981. "The Congressional Career
    in the 1970s." In Congress Reconsidered, 2nd ed., edited
    by L. C. Dodd and B. I. Oppenheimer. Washington, D.C.:
    Congressional Quarterly Press.

Davidson, R. H. 1981. "Subcommittee Government: New Chan-
    nels for Policy." In The New Senate, edited by T. E.
    Mann and N. J. Ornstein. Washington, D.C.: American
    Enterprise Institute.

Davidson, R. H., D. M. Kovenock, and M. K. O'Leary. 1966.
    Congress in Crisis: Politics and Congressional Reform.
    Belmont, Calif.: Wadsworth.

Davidson, R. H., and W. J. Oleszek. 1981. Congress and Its
    Members. Washington, D.C.: Congressional Quarterly
    Press.

_____. 1977. Congress Against Itself. Bloomington, Ind.:
    Indiana University Press.

Deering, C. J. 1982. "Subcommittee Government in the U.S.
    House: An Analysis of Bill Management." Legislative
    Studies Quarterly 7: 533-46.

Dexter, L. A. 1969. "Congressmen and the Making of Mili-
    tary Policy." In New Perspectives on the House of Rep-
    resentatives, 2nd ed., edited by R. L. Peabody and N. W.
    Polsby. Chicago: Rand McNally.

Dodd, L. C. 1983. "The Calculus of Legislative Change."
    Paper presented to the Annual Meeting of the Midwest
    Political Science Association.

Dodd, L. C., and B. I. Oppenheimer. 1981. "The House in
    Transition." In Congress Reconsidered, 2nd ed., edited
    by L. C. Dodd and B. I. Oppenheimer. Washington, D.C.:
    Congressional Quarterly Press.

Dodd, L. C., and R. L. Schott. 1979. Congress and the Ad-
    ministrative State. New York: Wiley.

Dodd, L. C., and T. Sullivan. 1981. "Majority Party Leadership and Partisan Vote Gathering: The House Democratic Whip System." In Understanding Congressional Leadership, edited by F. H. Mackaman. Washington, D.C.: Congressional Quarterly Press.

Dyson, J. W., and J. W. Soule. 1970. "Congressional Committee Behavior on Roll Call Votes: The U.S. House of Representatives, 1955-1964." Midwest Journal of Political Science 14: 626-47.

Ellwood, J. W., and J. A. Thurber. 1977. "The New Congressional Budget Process: The Hows and Whys of House-Senate Differences." In Congress Reconsidered, edited by L. C. Dodd and B. I. Oppenheimer. New York: Praeger.

Eulau, H., and V. McCluggage. 1982. "Legislative Committees: A Critical Inventory of Research Over Three Decades." Paper presented to the National Science Foundation Conference on Legislative Research, Iowa City, Iowa.

Farnsworth, D. N. 1961. The Senate Committee on Foreign Relations: A Study of the Decision-Making Process. Urbana: University of Illinois Press.

Fenno, R. F., Jr. 1978. Home Style: Representatives in the Districts. Boston: Little, Brown.

_____. 1973. Congressmen in Committees. Boston: Little, Brown.

_____. 1966. The Power of the Purse: Appropriations Politics in Congress. Boston: Little, Brown.

Fessler, P. 1983. "Rostenkowski Seeks More Influential Role." Congressional Quarterly Weekly Report 41: 192-98.

Fleisher, R., and J. R. Bond. 1983. "Beyond Committee Control: Committee and Party Leader Influence on Floor Amendments in Congress." American Politics Quarterly 11: 131-61.

Frantzich, S. E. 1978. "Opting Out: Retirement from the House of Representatives, 1966–1974." American Politics Quarterly 6: 251–73.

Froman, L. A., Jr., and R. B. Ripley. 1965. "Conditions for Party Leadership: The Case of the House Democrats." American Political Science Review 59: 52–63.

Garson, G. D. 1976. Political Science Methods. Boston: Holbrook Press.

Giaimo, R. N. 1982. "The Congressional Budget Process." In The United States Congress: Proceedings of the Thomas P. O'Neill, Jr. Symposium, edited by D. Hale. Boston: Boston College.

Gibb, C. A. 1968. "Leadership: Psychological Aspects." In International Encyclopedia of Social Sciences, Vol. 9, pp. 91–101. New York: Macmillan.

Goodman, W. 1968. The Committee: The Extraordinary Career of the House Committee on Un-American Activities. New York: Farrar, Straus & Giroux.

Goodwin, G., Jr. 1970. The Little Legislatures: Committees of Congress. Amherst, Mass.: University of Massachusetts Press.

Green, H. P., and A. Rosenthal. 1963. Government of the Atom: The Integration of Powers. New York: Atherton Press.

Hammond, S. W., and L. I. Langbein. 1981. "The Impact of Complexity and Reform on Congressional Committee Output." Mimeographed.

Harris, J. P. 1964. Congressional Control of Administration. Washington, D.C.: Brookings Institution.

Havemann, J. 1978. Congress and the Budget. Bloomington, Inc.: Indiana University Press.

Hibbing, J. R. 1982a. "Voluntary Retirement from the U.S. House: The Costs of Congressional Service." Legislative Studies Quarterly 7: 57-74.

_____. 1982b. "Voluntary Retirement from the U.S. House of Representatives: Who Quits?" American Journal of Political Science 26: 467-84.

Hinckley, B. 1983. Stability and Change in Congress, 3rd ed. New York: Harper & Row.

_____. 1981. Congressional Elections. Washington, D.C.: Congressional Quarterly Press.

_____. 1976. "Seniority 1975: Old Theories Confront New Facts." British Journal of Political Science 6: 383-99.

Horn, S. 1970. Unused Power: The Work of the Senate Committee on Appropriations. Washington, D.C.: Brookings Institution.

Huntington, S. P. 1973. "Congressional Responses to the Twentieth Century." In The Congress and America's Future, 2nd ed., edited by D. B. Truman. Englewood Cliffs, N.J.: Prentice-Hall.

Ippolito, D. S. 1981. Congressional Spending. Ithaca, N.Y.: Cornell University Press.

Jewell, M. E., and C. Chu. 1974. "Membership Movement and Committee Attractiveness in the U.S. House of Representatives, 1963-1971." American Journal of Political Science 18: 433-41.

Jewell, M. E., and S. C. Patterson. 1977. The Legislative Process in the United States, 3rd ed. New York: Random House.

Jones, C. O. 1981. "House Leadership in an Age of Reform." In Understanding Congressional Leadership, edited by F. H. Mackaman. Washington, D. C.: Congressional Quarterly Press.

_____. 1977. "How Reform Changes Congress." In Legisla-
tive Reform and Public Policy, edited by S. Welch and
J. G. Peters. New York: Praeger.

_____. 1961. "Representation in Congress: The Case of
the House Agriculture Committee." American Political
Science Review 55: 358-67.

Kingdon, J. W. 1981. Congressmen's Voting Decisions, 2nd
ed. New York: Harper & Row.

Lees, J. C. 1979. "Committees in the United States Con-
gress." In Committees in Legislatures: A Comparative
Perspective, edited by J. D. Lees and M. Shaw. Durham,
N. C.: Duke University Press.

_____. 1967. The Committee System of the U.S. Congress.
London: Routledge & Kegan Paul.

LeLoup, L. T. 1979. "Process vs. Policy: The House
Budget Committee." Legislative Studies Quarterly 4:
227-54.

McConachie, L. 1898. Congressional Committees. New York:
Crowell.

MacRae, D., Jr. 1958. Dimensions of Congressional Voting.
Berkeley: University of California Press.

_____. 1956. "Roll Call Votes and Leadership." Public
Opinion Quarterly 20: 543-58.

Manley, J. S. 1973. "The Conservative Coalition in Congress."
American Behavioral Scientist 17: 223-47.

_____. 1970. The Politics of Finance. Boston: Little,
Brown.

Mann, T. E., and N. J. Ornstein (Eds.). 1981. The New
Senate. Washington, D. C. American Enterprise Institute.

Matsunaga, S. M., and P. Chen. 1976. Rulemakers of the House. Urbana: University of Illinois Press.

Matthews, D. R., and J. A. Stimson. 1975. Yeas and Nays: Normal Decision-Making in the U.S. House of Representatives. New York: Wiley.

Mayhew, D. R. 1974. Congress: The Electoral Connection. New Haven, Conn.: Yale University Press.

Morrow, W. L. 1969. Congressional Committees. New York: Scribners.

Murphy, J. T. 1974. "Political Parties and the Porkbarrel: Party Conflict and Cooperation in House Public Works Committee Decision-Making." American Political Science Review 68: 169-85.

Ogul, M. 1976. Congress Oversees the Bureaucracy: Studies in Legislative Supervision. Pittsburgh: University of Pittsburgh Press.

Oppenheimer, B. I. 1981. "The Changing Relationship Between House Leadership and the Committee on Rules." In Understanding Congressional Leadership, edited by F. H. Mackaman. Washington, D.C.: Congressional Quarterly Press.

_____. 1980. "Policy Effects of House Reform: Decentralization and the Capacity to Resolve Energy Issues." Legislative Studies Quarterly 5: 5-30.

_____. 1977. "The Rules Committee: New Arm of the Leadership in a Decentralized House." In Congress Reconsidered, edited by L. C. Dodd and B. I. Oppenheimer. New York: Praeger.

Ornstein, N. J. (Ed.). 1975. Congress in Change: Evolution and Reform. New York: Praeger.

_____. (Ed.). 1974. Changing Congress: The Committee System. Annals 411: entire issue.

Ornstein, N. J., and D. W. Rohde. 1977. "Shifting Forces, Changing Rules, and Political Outcomes: The Impact of Congressional Change on Four House Committees." In New Perspectives on the House of Representatives, 3rd ed., edited by R. L. Peabody and N. W. Polsby. Chicago: Rand McNally.

OSIRIS III. 1974. Vols. 1 and 5. Ann Arbor: University of Michigan.

Owens, J. E. 1980. "Do Bankers Control the Banking Committee? Industry Influence in the House Banking and Currency Committee." Paper presented to the Political Studies Association (Great Britain).

———. 1979. "Defining Party in a Congressional Committee: A Roll Call Analysis of Decision-Making in the House Banking and Currency Committee." Paper presented to the American Politics Group of the Political Studies Association (Great Britain).

Parker, G. R. 1979. "The Selection of Committee Leaders in the House of Representatives." American Politics Quarterly 7: 71–93.

Parker, G. R., and S. L. Parker. 1979. "Factions in Committees: The U.S. House of Representatives." American Political Science Review 73: 85–102.

Patterson, S. C. 1978. "The Semi-Sovereign Congress." In The New American Political System, edited by A. King. Washington, D.C.: American Enterprise Institute.

———. 1963. "Legislative Leadership and Political Ideology." Public Opinion Quarterly 27: 399–410.

Peabody, R. L. 1982. "Leadership in Legislatures: Evolution, Selection, Functions and Influence." Paper presented to the National Science Foundation Conference on Legislative Research, Iowa City, Iowa.

———. 1976. Leadership in Congress: Stability, Succession, and Change. Boston: Little, Brown.

_____. 1963. "The Enlarged Rules Committee." In New Per-
spectives on the House of Representatives, edited by
R. L. Peabody and N. W. Polsby. Chicago: Rand McNally.

Peters, J. G. 1978. "The U.S. House Agriculture Committee:
Continuity and Change in U.S. Farm Policy." Paper pre-
sented to the Annual Meeting of the Midwest Political
Science Association.

Polsby, N. W. 1968. "The Institutionalization of the House
of Representatives." American Political Science Review
62: 144-68.

Price, D. E. 1981. "Congressional Committees in the Policy
Process." In Congress Reconsidered, 2nd ed., edited by
L. C. Dodd and B. I. Oppenheimer. Washington, D.C.:
Congressional Quarterly Press.

_____. 1979. Policymaking in Congressional Committees:
The Impact of "Environmental" Factors. Tucson: Institute of Government Research, University of Arizona.

_____. 1978. "The Impact of Reform: The House Commerce
Subcommittee on Oversight and Investigations." In Legis-
lative Reform: The Policy Impact, edited by L. N.
Rieselbach. Lexington, Mass.: Lexington Books.

_____. 1972. Who Makes the Laws? Creativity and Power in
Senate Committees. Cambridge, Mass.: Schenkman.

Ray, B. A. 1982. "Committee Attractiveness in the U.S.
House, 1963-1981." American Journal of Political Science
26: 609-13.

_____. 1980. "The Responsiveness of the U.S. Congressional
Armed Services Committees to Their Parent Bodies."
Legislative Studies Quarterly 5: 501-15.

Rieselbach, L. N. 1983. "Legislative Reform." In The Policy Studies Field: Its Basic Literature, edited by S. S.
Nagel. Greenwich, Conn.: JAI Press.

_____. 1982. "Assessing Congressional Change, or What Hath Reform Wrought (or Wreaked)?" In The United States Congress: Proceedings of the Thomas P. O'Neill, Jr. Symposium, edited by D. Hale. Boston: Boston College.

_____. 1978. Legislative Reform: The Policy Impact. Lexington, Mass.: Lexington Books.

_____. 1977. Congressional Reform in the Seventies. Morristown, N.J.: General Learning Press.

Ripley, R. B. 1978. Congress: Process and Policy. New York: Norton.

Robinson, J. A. 1963. The House Rules Committee. Indianapolis, Ind.: Bobbs-Merrill.

Rohde, D. W., and K. A. Shepsle. 1978. "Thinking About Legislative Reform." In Legislative Reform: The Policy Impact, edited by L. N. Rieselbach. Lexington, Mass.: Lexington Books.

Rudder, C. E. 1978. "The Policy Impact of Reform of the Committee on Ways and Means." In Legislative Reform: The Policy Impact, edited by L. N. Rieselbach. Lexington, Mass.: Lexington Books.

_____. 1977. "Committee Reform and the Revenue Process." In Congress Reconsidered, edited by L. C. Dodd and B. I. Oppenheimer. New York: Praeger.

Salamon, L. B., and associates. 1975. The Money Committees. New York: Grossman.

Schick, A. 1980. Congress and Money: Budgeting, Spending and Taxing. Washington, D.C.: Urban Institute.

Schneider, J. E. 1979. Ideological Coalitions in Congress. Greenwich, Conn.: Greenwood Press.

Scicchitano, M. J. 1981. "Legislative Goals and Information Use." American Politics Quarterly 9: 103-10.

Shaffer, W. R. 1980. Party and Ideology in the United States Congress. Lanham, Md.: University Press of America.

Shepsle, K. A. 1978. The Giant Jigsaw Puzzle: Democratic Committee Assignment in the Modern House. Chicago: University of Chicago Press.

Sinclair, B. D. 1981a. "Majority Party Leadership Strategies for Coping with the New House." Legislative Studies Quarterly 6: 391–414.

_____. 1981b. "The Speaker's Task Force in the Post-Reform House of Representatives." American Political Science Review 75: 397–410.

Sinclair, B. D., and C. J. Deering. 1983. "Changing Motives for Committee Preferences of New Members of the U.S. House." Legislative Studies Quarterly 8: 271–281.

Stanga, J. E., and D. N. Farnsworth. 1978. "Seniority and Democratic Reforms in the House of Representatives." In Legislative Reform: The Policy Impact, edited by L. N. Rieselbach. Lexington, Mass.: Lexington Books.

Sundquist, J. L. 1981. The Decline and Resurgence of Congress. Washington, D.C.: Brookings Institution.

Truman, D. B. 1959. The Congressional Party. New York: Wiley.

Turner, J., and E. V. Schneier. 1970. Party and Constituency: Pressures on Congress. Baltimore: Johns Hopkins University Press.

Unekis, J. K. 1978. "From Committee to Floor: Consistency in Congressional Voting." Journal of Politics 40: 761–69.

Vogler, D. J. 1981. "Ad Hoc Committees in the House of Representatives and Purposive Models of Legislative Behavior." Polity 14: 89–109.

Welch, S., and J. G. Peters (Eds.). 1977. Legislative Reform and Public Policy. New York: Praeger.

Willetts, P. 1972. "Cluster-bloc Analysis and Statistical Inference." American Political Science Review 66: 569-82.

Wilson, W. 1885. Congressional Government. Cleveland: World.

Index

About the Authors

LEROY N. RIESELBACH is Professor of Political Science at Indiana University. Among his works on Congress are The Roots of Isolationism (1966), Congressional Politics (1973), and Congressional Reform in the Seventies (1977). He has also published articles in The American Political Science Review, the American Journal of Political Science, Legislative Studies Quarterly, and other journals.

JOSEPH K. UNEKIS is Assistant Professor of Political Science at Kansas State University. He received his Ph.D. in political science from Indiana University in 1977. Interested in Congress, his articles on the subject have appeared in The Journal of Politics, Congress and the Presidency, Congressional Studies, and Legislative Studies Quarterly.